ENLISTED SOLDIER'S GUIDE

ENLISTED SOLDIER'S GUIDE

3rd Edition

Revised by

Frank Cox

STACKPOLE
BOOKS

Published by
STACKPOLE BOOKS
5067 Ritter Road
Mechanicsburg, PA 17055

3rd edition

Cover photo courtesy Soldiers *magazine*
Cover design by Caroline Miller
All photos courtesy of the U.S. Army

Printed in the U.S.A.

Library of Congress Cataloging-in-Publication Data

Cox, Frank, 1954–
    Enlisted soldier's guide. — 3rd ed. / revised by Frank Cox.
        p.   cm.
    Updated ed. of: Enlisted soldier's guide / Dennis D. Perez. 2nd ed.
© 1990.
    Includes bibliographical references and index.
    ISBN 0-8117-2540-5
    1. United States.   Army—Handbooks, manuals, etc.   I. Perez,
Dennis D.   Enlisted soldier's guide.   II. Title.
U113.C69   1993
345′.00973 — dc20   92-45037
                                                                              CIP

Contents

Preface

As *Enlisted Soldier's Guide, 3rd edition*, was going to press, the Army was more than halfway through a wrenching five-year force reduction and realignment, widely known as "the drawdown." In the last several years, thousands of enlisted soldiers have voluntarily or involuntarily separated with valuable cash incentives and other benefits. Substandard soldiers continue to be separated involuntarily with reduced benefits or nothing.

Solid enlisted performers who want to be retained in the Army after the fog clears in 1995 or later must stay in their "lane," according to Sergeant Major of the Army Richard A. Kidd. That is, today's junior enlisted soldiers must strive to become leaders who will ensure that tomorrow's soldiers are physically and mentally fit, technically and tactically skilled, and ready to fight, win, and survive.

Enlisted Soldier's Guide is a career compass; through three editions, it has aimed at educating, advising, and informing soldiers about key aspects of military service. Today, the guide is valuable because enlisted service standards are at an all-time high. The following get much attention in command circles:

- Soldiers who fail two consecutive Army Physical Fitness Tests are barred from reenlisting or are separated from service.

- Overweight soldiers who report to NCO Education System schools such as the Primary Leadership Development Course (PLDC) are denied enrollment. Soldiers enrolled but then eliminated for misconduct or lack of self-discipline are barred or separated. Soldiers must graduate from PLDC to be eligible for promotion to sergeant.
- First-term soldiers may no longer reenlist for retraining (except for sergeants or soldiers with GT scores of 110 or higher). The retention control point (mandatory separation point) is eight years for specialists and corporals, and for *promotable* specialists and corporals.
- All first-time drug abusers with three or more years' service, and all second-time abusers, are separated. Alcohol and Drug Abuse Prevention and Control Program failures are also separated.

These and other strict standards are being applauded, followed, and enforced by NCOs, warrant officers, and commissioned officers because the Army of the 1990s must be healthy, vigilant, and able to respond quickly and decisively to any threats in an unstable world.

Department of the Army Pamphlet 600-32, *Leader Development for the Total Army*, states that we have "the best-prepared, highest-quality force in our nation's history." *Enlisted Soldier's Guide*, a commercial byproduct of Army life, is dedicated to ensuring that junior enlisted men and women have a single-source reference to help them become successful members of the force.

Acknowledgments

Volumes could be filled thanking everyone responsible for making *Enlisted Soldier's Guide, 3rd edition*, possible. Instead, I offer my appreciation to each individual who has helped produce the myriad public resources I relied on for information.

I include the following: Army Training and Doctrine Command and U.S. Army Sergeants Major Academy members responsible for NCO Education System documents; Association of the United States Army officials who produce AUSA Institute of Land Warfare literature; countless unsung Army officials involved in the production of official regulations, field manuals, pamphlets, circulars, common tables of allowance, and the Chain Teaching Program; Civilian Health and Medical Program of the Uniformed Services officials for their medical program advice; Defense Finance and Accounting Service members who produce military pay tables; Noncommissioned Officers Association officials; Judge Advocate Generals Corps officials who produce legal guides for soldiers; and Army Continuing Education System officials, so many of whom are expertly involved in helping enlisted people earn college degrees. If I may drop one name, it is Kelly Cox, my loving wife, who has raised pressure-free encouragement to an art form.

Frank Cox

1

Army Traditions

Traditions are tied directly to Army history, dating to 14 June 1775, when the Army began to take shape in Pennsylvania, Maryland, and Virginia. In 1776, the Continental Congress established the Board of War and Ordnance, which later became the War Office, which became the Department of War, which was created by George Washington on 7 August 1789 to add the Army charter to the Constitution. Soldiers are the defenders of the Constitution, and Army traditions, customs, and courtesies are based on this role.

In a chapter entry entitled "The Profession of Arms," Field Manual 100-1, *The Army* states, "The men and women serving in today's Army are members of a proud profession long in history and rich in heritage and tradition. . . . Taking pride as we demonstrate loyalty, duty, selfless service, and integrity—the professional Army ethic—is essential to building unit esprit and to maintaining an effective fighting force."

Soldiers perpetuate Army traditions when they demonstrate the professional Army ethic and when they show commitment, competence, candor, and mental and physical courage. They also uphold Army traditions by being model citizens, by respecting one another, and by showing symbols of national unity such as the U.S. flag.

New soldiers march in a first-termers' parade

Military Courtesy

Military courtesy is the respect shown to superiors by subordinates and the mutual respect demonstrated between senior and subordinate personnel. It is basic to military discipline and founded upon respect for and loyalty to authority. Military courtesy has an effect on every aspect of military life.

The Salute

The most common military courtesy is the salute. While many forms of salutes are authorized, depending upon the arms you may be carrying and the situation involved, the most common salute is the hand salute. A sharp, crisp salute shows pride in recognizing the comrade in arms; conversely, a sloppy or halfhearted salute shows a lack of pride and is a poor reflection upon the soldier rendering it.

The hand salute is required whenever you recognize an officer. Exceptions are made when the situation so requires—in public transportation (such as buses and planes) or in public places (such as theaters), or when the salute would be impractical (at work, when driving a vehicle, or when actively engaged in athletics). Even though saluting an officer is not re-

When the garrison cap, cold weather cap, or beret is worn, the hand salute is to the forehead — except when wearing glasses, when the tip of the fingers should touch the corner of the frame. When the utility cap, camouflage cap, or helmet is worn, the salute is to the visor.

quired by military regulation when both soldier and officer are in civilian clothes, the soldier who renders this courtesy is following long-standing military tradition.

Every soldier should learn the following guidelines:

- If running, slow to a walk before saluting.
- Always hold your salute until it is returned by the officer.
- Never salute while holding an object in your right hand.
- Render the greeting of the day in a firm, crisp voice. A confident "Good morning, sir" demonstrates pride in yourself.
- In formation, salute only on the command "Present arms." Keep in mind that if you are in charge of a fatigue detail or formation, you are responsible for rendering the courtesies for the group.

The salute itself should be made in one movement, raising the right arm so that the upper arm is horizontal and bending the elbow so that the tip of the forefinger touches the forehead slightly to the right of the right eyebrow. The fingers and thumb should be extended, with the fingers "joined" or touching one another. Neither the palm nor the back of the hand should be visible from a front view.

If you wear eyeglasses, the fingertip of your right hand should touch the point on the glasses where the front frame joins the temple or earpiece. When you are wearing a utility cap, a service cap, or a helmet, your fingertip should touch the visor of the headgear.

On some occasions you should salute the officer twice. Specifically, if you salute an officer, and the officer stays in your general vicinity but does not converse directly with you, all military courtesies have been fulfilled. When the officer spends a few moments talking with you, however, you should salute a second time at the end of the conversation. This custom can be considered a preliminary greeting followed by a farewell.

When a vehicle passes carrying an officer that you recognize, you should render a salute. Likewise, if an official vehicle passes displaying vehicle plates or flags that depict the rank of the passenger, you should salute.

The salute is also used to show respect to the American flag, when the flag passes or during the retreat ceremony. (See *Courtesy to the Flag* and *The Retreat Ceremony* in this chapter for details.)

The best advice on saluting is to render the salute whenever any doubt exists as to whether the salute is actually required. Rendering the salute is a matter of pride.

Other Courtesies to Officers

A number of customs and courtesies for showing respect to senior-ranking servicemembers have evolved over the years. Most are based on the notion that the position on the right is the place of honor. The origins of this custom lie in ancient days when men fought with swords. Since most men were right-handed, the left side became the defensive side, to be protected by the subordinate.

Today this courtesy is rendered by the junior soldier who walks on the left-hand side of a ranking officer. The same is true for riding in vehicles — the subordinate sits to the left of the superior.

There are similar customs for entering a vehicle or small boat. The occupants enter by rank, with the highest ranking entering last and exiting first.

An officer entering a room is also shown special courtesy. The first soldier to recognize the officer calls the other personnel in the room to attention, but the soldier does not salute. A salute is rendered indoors only when the soldier is reporting. Soldiers should remain at attention until the officer gives an "at ease" command. Do not call the room to attention if the entering officer is junior in grade to an officer already in the room. Coming to attention in the work environment is required at the start of the day when the commander or senior person first enters the building. It is not required thereafter. If at all practical, however, when an officer not commonly working directly with a soldier is in the work environment and addresses the soldier directly, the soldier should stand.

Outside of the work environment, standing at attention is always expected of the soldier when he or she is talking with an officer. Frequently the officer will instruct the soldier to stand at ease. When the conversation is completed, the soldier should return to attention, salute, and voice an appropriate acknowledgment of the conversation, such as, "Yes, sir," or "Good afternoon, sir."

One final recommendation on rendering courtesies to officers: you should regard "requests," "desires," or "wishes" expressed by a commanding officer as orders. Frequently, the wording is softened as a courtesy to the subordinate, but the intent is the same as an order.

Courtesy to the Flag

Honoring the nation's flag is an integral part of military customs and courtesies. The hand salute is rendered to show respect when the flag passes in front of a soldier in uniform. You should initiate the salute when

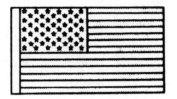

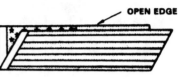

FOLD THE LOWER STRIPED SECTION OF THE FLAG OVER THE BLUE FIELD.

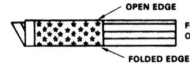

FOLD THE FOLDED EDGE OVER TO MEET THE OPEN EDGE.

START A TRIANGULAR FOLD BY BRINGING THE STRIPED CORNER OF THE FOLDED EDGE TO THE OPEN EDGE.

FOLD THE OUTER POINT INWARD PARALLEL WITH THE OPEN EDGE TO FORM A SECOND TRIANGLE.

CONTINUE FOLDING UNTIL THE ENTIRE LENGTH OF THE FLAG IS FOLDED INTO A TRIANGLE WITH ONLY THE BLUE FIELD AND MARGIN SHOWING.

TUCK THE REMAINING MARGIN INTO THE POCKET FORMED BY THE FOLDS AT THE BLUE FIELD EDGE OF THE FLAG.

THE PROPERLY FOLDED FLAG SHOULD RESEMBLE A COCKED HAT.

The U.S. flag should always be folded properly

the flag is approaching and is within six paces, and then you should hold the salute until the flag has passed six paces. If you are walking past a stationary flag, the same six-pace rule applies. In addition, you should turn your head in the direction of the flag. Soldiers marching in formation render salute only on command. If you are indoors when the flag passes, do not render the hand salute.

A soldier in civilian clothes still honors the flag with a salute, but it is modified to a "civilian salute" with the right hand placed over the heart. If headgear is worn with civilian clothing by a male soldier, the headgear is removed with the right hand and held over the heart; a female soldier in civilian clothing wearing headgear does not remove the headgear but still places her right hand over her heart.

The national flag should never be dipped low as a means of salute or greeting. The only exception is made for military vessels under specific international courtesies. Organizational flags, including the U.S. Army flag, are dipped lower than the national flag during the playing of the national anthem, "To the Color," or a foreign national anthem.

Out of respect for the flag, you should never use it as part of a costume, on a float, or on a vehicle, unless it is displayed on a staff. No lettering of any kind should ever be added to the flag. When a flag is damaged, soiled, or weathered, it should be burned or disposed of in a dignified manner. No portion of the flag should ever be allowed to touch the ground; if it does, the flag is considered soiled. The proper way of folding the flag should be followed exactly (see illustration).

Four common sizes exist for the national flag. The garrison flag, flown on special occasions and holidays, measures 20 x 38 feet. The post flag, flown for general use, is 10 x 19 feet. The storm flag, used in inclement weather, is 5 x 9.5 feet. The last size is that of the grave decorating flag, which measures 7 x 11 inches.

In addition to the national flag, we can speak of the national color, the national standard, and the national ensign. The national color, carried by dismount units, is a 3 x 4 foot flag trimmed on three sides by a golden yellow fringe measuring 2.5 inches in width. The national standard is identical to the national color, except that it is carried by a mechanized, motorized, or mounted unit; only the name is different. The national ensign is a naval term designating a flag of any size used to indicate the nationality of ship personnel. The term *flag* does not technically refer to colors, standards, or ensigns. Other terms associated with flags are also a part of military tradition. The *hoist* is the width, the *fly* is the length, and the *truck* is the ball at the top of the flagstaff.

Another means of showing respect to the flag is the Pledge of Allegiance, first adopted by Congress in 1942. The tradition surrounding the pledge specifies that it should be said while standing at attention, with the right hand over the heart. The Pledge of Allegiance is normally not recited in military formations or in military ceremonies.

Military customs and traditions govern the raising and lowering of the flag, as well. Reveille is the daily military ceremony honoring the flag at the beginning of the day. Retreat is the counterpart when the flag is lowered at the end of the day. Reveille is a bugle call, often recorded and played over a public address system on military installations today. The flag is hoisted quickly to the top of the flagpole, beginning on the first note of reveille. Retreat ceremonies, full of traditions, are discussed in the following section.

The flag is sometimes flown at half-staff as a salute to the honored dead. Memorial Day, the last Monday in May, is one occasion when the flag is flown at half-staff from reveille to 1200 hours. A 21-gun salute is then fired before the flag is raised to the top of the staff until retreat. Whenever the flag is to be flown at half-staff, it should first be hoisted to the top of the staff and then lowered to the midpoint. Likewise, before lowering the flag, it should be again hoisted the full height of the staff and then lowered and properly folded.

Full details on flag courtesies can be found in AR 840-10.

Customs

The customs of the service make up the unwritten "common law" of the Army. These customs are rich in tradition, and every soldier should know and observe them.

The Retreat Ceremony

The purpose of the retreat ceremony is to honor the national flag at the end of the day. Often the evening gun is fired at the time of retreat so that soldiers throughout the installation will be aware of the ceremony even if they are outside the range of the bugle. The evening gun is also used to mark the end of the work day.

Retreat is not necessarily observed at the same time at each installation. The post commander sets the time of the sounding of both reveille and retreat.

During the retreat ceremony, the evening gun is fired at the last note of retreat. At that time a band, a bugler, or recorded music plays the national anthem or sounds "To the Color." Soldiers will begin lowering the flag on the first note of the national anthem or "To the Color" at a rate that will ensure that the lowering is completed with the last note of music. Then, following strict customs, the flag will be folded and stored until reveille the next morning.

Special respect is rendered to the flag and to the national anthem during retreat by soldiers all across the installation, not merely by those participating directly in the ceremony. Under no circumstances should a soldier run into a building to avoid rendering this courtesy to the flag.

During the playing of the national anthem, soldiers in uniform should stand at attention, facing the flag if visible, or the music if the flag is not visible. A salute should be rendered on the first note and held until the final note. The same courtesy applies to "To the Color." When indoors, the salute is omitted. Soldiers in civilian clothing render the "civilian salute" in the same manner as to the flag. Women never remove headgear.

All vehicular traffic should stop during the retreat ceremony. For cars and motorcycles, the driver and passengers should get out of the vehicle and show proper respect. For other vehicles, such as buses or armored vehicles, the ranking soldier should get out and render the appropriate salute. All other passengers should sit quietly at attention inside the vehicle. Commanding officers of tanks or armored cars can salute from the vehicle.

The same respect should be rendered to the national anthems of friendly nations when they are played during official occasions.

Bugle Calls

In addition to reveille and retreat, several other bugle calls play important roles in military tradition. In general, bugle calls can be divided into four categories: Alarm, Formation, Service (which includes reveille and retreat), and Warning.

First call is the first bugle of the day. Considered a warning call, it alerts you that reveille is about to take place and that you will be late if you're not ready within the next few minutes.

The last bugle call of the day is *Taps,* a service call dating back to Civil War days. Taps is traditionally used at military funerals, as well, giving the final bugle call for the fallen soldier.

"To the Color" is the alternate music used during the retreat ceremony. It signals that the flag is being lowered. You should render the salute during "To the Color" much as you would during the national anthem. Both are meant to honor the flag.

Tattoo is usually played near 2100 hours and has traditionally been the call for lights out in 15 minutes.

Unit Customs

Individual units foster pride and esprit de corps by observing a variety of customs that set them apart from the rest of the Army. Since it is a matter of personal honor for a soldier to know in which battles his or her unit took part, soldiers joining a new unit should learn its history. A quick check with the post library is often the best way to start.

Units perpetuate their history through their organizational properties, mottoes, and insignia. A unit's organizational properties include flags and standards (including battle honors and campaign streamers) and other physical representations of its heritage. Many units claim regimental silver with a unique history as part of their organizational property. For example, the 23d Infantry's silver bowl was made from the metal of 5,610 Combat Infantryman's Badges earned by the 23d's infantrymen during the first 18 months of combat in Korea. Perhaps the most famous regimental silver property is the 31st Infantry's "Shanghai Bowl," which was presented to the regiment by the citizens of Shanghai after the Boxer Rebellion.

Unit mottoes provide another link with the past. The 14th Infantry's motto, "The Rock of Chickamauga," recalls the regiment's service at the Battle of Chickamauga. The 7th Cavalry's motto and song, "Garry Owen," was brought to the regiment in the 1860s by Irish immigrants. The song was played to sound the charge into battle at the Washita in 1868 and at the Little Bighorn in 1876.

Many units have acquired nicknames as a result of past service. The 31st Infantry is known as the "Polar Bears" as a result of duty in northern Russia after the end of World War I. The 28th Infantry's "Lions of Cantigny" recalls the regiment's service at the first American offensive battle in World War I.

Unit insignia also embody unit traditions. For example, shoulder sleeve insignia, first authorized during World War I, were originally conceived to foster esprit de corps and heighten the individual soldier's identification with his unit. The 81st Infantry Division was the first division to develop a sleeve insignia, that of a black wildcat on a circular patch. The idea was so well received by the headquarters of the American Expeditionary Forces that General Pershing directed the other divisions in the American Expeditionary Force to develop their own distinctive cloth patches.

Songs and Cadences

The Army Song

Another tradition that literally brings soldiers to their feet is the Army Song. When you hear it being sung or being played, the appropriate action is to stand at attention. The melody is that of the "Caisson Song," composed in the early 1900s by then Lt. Edmund L. Gruber, who later was promoted to brigadier general. But the words for "The Army Goes Rolling Along" were selected much later. The eight-year process began in 1948 with a nationwide contest to create an official Army song. Within four years the Army had also enlisted the aid of several music composers, publishers, and recording studios. Their joint efforts produced the new lyrics, set to the music of the old "Caisson Song." "The Army Goes Rolling Along" became the official Army song when it was dedicated on Veterans Day, 11 November 1956, at Army installations throughout the world.

THE ARMY GOES ROLLING ALONG

Verse:

March along, sing our song
   With the army of the free.
Count the brave, count the true
   Who have fought to victory.
We're the Army and proud of our name!
We're the Army and proudly proclaim:

1st Chorus:

First to fight for the right
   And to build the nation's might,
And THE ARMY GOES ROLLING ALONG.
Proud of all we have done,
   Fighting till the battle's won,
And THE ARMY GOES ROLLING ALONG.

Refrain:

Then it's hi! hi! hey!
   The Army's on its way,
Count off the cadence loud and strong:
For where'er we go, you will always know
That THE ARMY GOES ROLLING ALONG.

2nd Chorus:

Valley Forge, Custer's ranks,
   San Juan Hill and Patton's tanks,
And the Army went rolling along.
Minutemen from the start,
   Always fighting from the heart,
And the Army keeps rolling along.

Refrain:

Then it's hi! hi! hey!
   The Army's on its way,
Count off the cadence loud and strong:
For where'er we go, you will always know
That THE ARMY GOES ROLLING ALONG.

3d Chorus: Men in rags, men who froze,
                       Still that Army met its foes,
                And the Army went rolling along.
                Faith in God, then we're right
                       And we'll fight with all our might
                As the Army keeps rolling along.

Refrain: Then it's hi! hi! hey!
                       The Army's on its way,
                Count off the cadence loud and strong:
                       (two! three!)
                For where'er we go, you will always know
                That THE ARMY GOES ROLLING ALONG!
                       (Keep it rolling!)
                And THE ARMY GOES ROLLING ALONG!

Marching Cadences

Cadence calling is an old tradition that recalls the days when drummers, usually young boys not old enough to carry weapons into battle, would beat out the speed of the march to keep the line of soldiers in step. Since World War II, cadence calling has evolved into a series of creative verses, called or sung by the soldier in charge of a moving formation. Soldiers often modify cadences or create entirely new ones to enhance unit morale and esprit. All soldiers should know several different cadences to call in case they need to lead a formation.

CAPTAIN JACK

Hey, hey, Captain Jack,
Meet me down by the railroad track.
With my weapon in my hand,
I'm going to be a fighting man.

Hey, hey, Captain Jack,
Meet me down by the railroad track.
With my knife in my hand,
I'm going to be a cutting man.

Hey, hey, Captain Jack,
Meet me down by the railroad track.
With a bottle in my hand,
I'm going to be a drinking man.

Hey, hey, Captain Jack,
Meet me down by the railroad track.
With a suitcase in my hand,
I'm going to be a traveling man.

Hey, hey, Captain Jack,
Meet me down by the railroad track.
With my lady, holding hands,
I'm going to be a loving man.

HONEY BABY

You get a line and I'll get a pole,
Honey, Honey.
You get a line and I'll get a pole,
Baby, Baby.
You get a line and I'll get a pole,
and we'll go down to the fishing hole.
Honey, oh Baby, be mine.
Go with your left, your right, your left.
Go with your left, your right, your left.

I knew a girl who lived on a hill,
Honey, Honey.
I knew a girl who lived on a hill,
Baby, Baby.
I knew a girl who lived on a hill,
She said she loves me and she always will.
Honey, oh Baby, be mine.
Go with your left, your right, your left.
Go with your left, your right, your left.

I knew a girl who lived on a creek,
Honey, Honey.
I knew a girl who lived on a creek,
Baby, Baby.
I knew a girl who lived on a creek,
She was pretty and she kissed so sweet.
Honey, oh Baby, be mine.
Go with your left, your right, your left.
Go with your left, your right, your left.

Running Cadences

OLD LADY

Saw an old lady
Walking down the street.
Had a pack on her back
And boots on her feet.

Said "Hey, old lady,
Where ya' goin' to?"
She said, "The U.S. Army
Airborne School."

Said "Airborne, Airborne,
Haven't you heard?
You gotta jump
From a big iron bird."

Said "Hey, old lady,
Don't you know,
Airborne School's for
The brave and the bold?"

Said the old lady
With a mean old grin,
"If I'm not ready,
Then I won't get in."

"I may look old
And I may look frail,
But it's airborne school,
And I won't fail."

UP IN THE MORNING

Up in the morning
  'fore the break of day.
I don't like this
  NO WAY!

Eat my breakfast
  too soon.
Hungry as a bear
  'fore noon.

Went to the mess sergeant
  on my knees.
Said, "Mess sergeant, mess sergeant,
  feed me please."

The mess sergeant said
  with a mean, old grin,
"If you want to soldier
  you gotta' be thin."

No more whiskey,
  no more wine.
Gotta keep doing
  that double time.

2

Training

If a soldier is untrained and you send him into battle, it's murder. It's worse because the soldier has faith in you, that what you've taught him will help him to survive and win. It's criminal if you haven't. This carries all the way through the ranks. Treat every moment and everything you do like it will be the one lesson that will save your soldiers' lives and enable them to be successful in combat. You've got to be tough. Do the hard things correctly.

Captain Tim Stoy
Fort Knox, Kentucky

The officer quoted above was speaking to soldiers of the 194th Armored Brigade's 4th Battalion, 15th Infantry. His comments were made during a combined arms live-fire exercise, or CALFEX, conducted during a virtual blizzard in February 1988.

An article published later in *Soldiers* magazine described his audience, which filled a musty Army GP medium tent: "Damp, mud-covered soldiers sat on gray steel folding chairs or stood in the back. A battery-powered fluorescent lamp dimly lit the scene. Near the middle front of the tent, a too-hot potbelly stove tempted the tired infantrymen, tankers, and combat engineers to sleep. None did. Instead, they leaned forward or sat up straight in their chairs and tuned into the 'Old Man' of Charlie Company."

The soldiers listened to their commander because they had just trained very hard and they wanted to know where the boss thought the unit stood professionally. He gave them a B, which they knew meant more training.

Tough, realistic training is one of the six Army Fundamental Imperatives. Trained, intelligent soldiers filled the ranks of Army units when Captain Stoy made his remarks — just as thousands did who served in the hostile jungles of Panama in 1989, and as hundreds of thousands did on the deadly sands of Southwest Asia in 1991.

Similarly, success during disaster relief operations like those conducted in 1992 in Florida and Louisiana after Hurricane Andrew ravaged parts of those states is the result of properly trained soldiers. The Army prides itself on quality enlisted men and women who are products of an unparalleled training system — the Enlisted Personnel Management System. It is the foundation of enlisted training. The system produces winners.

Enlisted Personnel Management System

While on active duty, your opportunity for military training is extensive. The Enlisted Training System (ETS) is a subsystem of the Enlisted Personnel Management System (EPMS), an integrated program combining classification, evaluations, promotions, assignments, and training.

The ETS is characterized by five skill levels that represent progressively higher levels of performance capability, experience, and grade. Five levels of training have been established to support these skill levels and are administered in two distinct but closely related phases of the ETS — Initial Entry Training (IET) and the Noncommissioned Officer Education System (NCOES).

IET equips the soldier with the foundation of professional and technical knowledge needed to perform at the first duty station; combined with subsequent individual training in the unit, the soldier qualifies at skill level one. The next four skill levels are taught through NCOES.

Career Management Fields

From initial entry through duty as a command sergeant major, all enlisted soldiers are grouped into career management fields (CMFs) so

Enlisted Training System

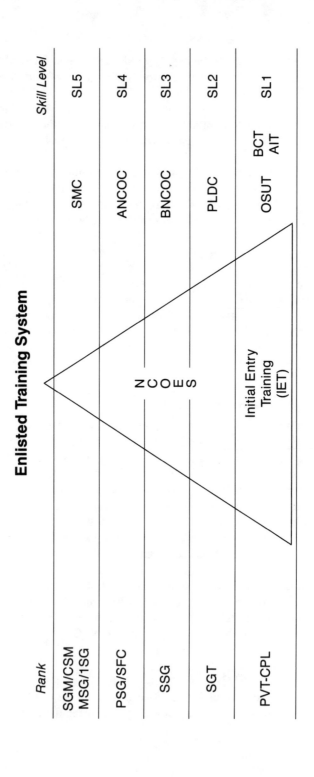

Rank			Skill Level
SGM/CSM MSG/1SG		SMC	SL5
PSG/SFC		ANCOC	SL4
SSG		BNCOC	SL3
SGT		PLDC	SL2
PVT-CPL		OSUT	BCT AIT	SL1

NCOES

Initial Entry Training (IET)

that opportunities for progress and training can be managed through EPMS.

Each CMF is a grouping of related military occupational specialties (MOSs). MOSs are grouped so that soldiers in one specialty have the abilities and aptitudes appropriate for training and assignments in most of the other specialties within that CMF. Progression and promotions are facilitated by training. Each soldier has a logical career path mapped out for him or her, identifying appropriate schooling, assignments, and opportunities for specialization and advancement.

As soldiers climb the promotion ladder within a CMF, new recruits fill in the lower rungs of the ladder, preparing themselves for upward mobility as well. The Army has established career paths for each CMF so that soldiers can be adequately counseled on the training and education they will need. The grouping of related MOSs provides enough flexibility that a soldier can move laterally within a CMF as well.

Within each CMF, the EPMS has identified the skills necessary for successfully functioning at each rank. Soldiers looking toward promotions need to be constantly preparing themselves for the next higher skill level. Skill level one identifies those skills, proficiencies, and abilities typically needed to perform efficiently up through the rank of specialist. Skill level two relates to sergeant; skill level three to staff sergeant; skill level four to platoon sergeant; and skill level five to master sergeant through command sergeant major. It should be noted that due to the grouping of MOSs into CMFs, the skills necessary for skill level two in one CMF will not necessarily be the same skills required at that level in a different CMF.

The EPMS has established 33 CMFs for enlisted soldiers.

CMF 11   Infantry
CMF 12   Combat Engineering
CMF 13   Field Artillery
CMF 16   Air Defense Artillery
CMF 18   Special Forces
CMF 19   Armor
CMF 23   Air Defense System Maintenance
CMF 25   Visual Information
CMF 27   Land Combat and Air Defense System Direct and General
          Support Maintenance
CMF 29   Signal Maintenance
CMF 31   Signal Operations
CMF 33   Electronic Warfare/Intercept Systems Maintenance
CMF 35   Electronic Maintenance and Calibration

CMF 46   Public Affairs
CMF 51   General Engineering
CMF 54   Chemical
CMF 55   Ammunition
CMF 63   Mechanical Maintenance
CMF 67   Aircraft Maintenance
CMF 71   Administration
CMF 74   Automatic Data Processing
CMF 76   Supply and Services
CMF 77   Petroleum and Water
CMF 79   Recruitment and Reenlistment
CMF 81   Topographic Engineering
CMF 88   Transportation
CMF 91   Medical
CMF 93   Aviation Operations
CMF 94   Food Service
CMF 95   Military Police
CMF 96   Military Intelligence
CMF 97   Band
CMF 98   Signals Intelligence (SIGINT)/Electronic Warfare (EW)
          Operations

The 33 CMFs are organized into three branches: combat arms, combat support, and combat service support. The ETS recognizes the distinction necessary among branches, but leadership training is required to some degree in all three branches.

Initial Entry Training (IET)

Every soldier in the Army has gone through Initial Entry Training (IET), whether or not he or she was aware of the label applied to the training received. There are two phases of IET: Basic Training (BT) and Advanced Individual Training (AIT), which is MOS training.

Generally, soldiers entering the combat arms branch or the military police MOS receive One-Station Unit Training (OSUT); they remain in the same unit for their BT and MOS training. Soldiers entering the combat support or combat service support branches generally must change duty assignments for their AIT, due primarily to the highly technical nature of many of the MOSs in these branches.

The primary functions of IET are to prepare recruits for military life and to provide soldiers with basic military combat skills and skill level one technical training.

Soldiers practice decontamination procedures at Fort McClellan, Alabama

The drill sergeant is the key figure in preparing a recruit for the rigors of Army life. It is the responsibility of the drill sergeant to teach the new soldier about the Army and to help him or her appreciate how individuals can contribute to the military structure. The drill sergeant must develop self-confidence, self-respect, and self-discipline in young soldiers so they can take full advantage of available opportunities. Equally important, the drill sergeant must ensure that the new soldier is strong and physically fit.

Since the main business of the Army is national defense, it is essential that each soldier be proficient in the basics of combat, regardless of the branch in which he or she will serve. Skills such as marksmanship, NBC (nuclear, biological, and chemical) defense, and small-unit teamwork are emphasized.

To reinforce the training initiated in Basic Training, all soldiers are given additional training in basic skills during the AIT phase of IET. Field training exercises frequently are used to combine the specialized MOS training the soldier must receive with the basic soldier skills that need to be reinforced. AIT narrows the perspective of IET, though, highlighting the specific skills soldiers will need to perform in their particular MOS at skill level one.

Upon completion of IET, soldiers go to their units with skills sufficient to effectively contribute to the team. The training, however, is by no means complete. Field units are responsible for providing continuing on-the-job training to round out the soldier's initial training and to enhance the first-termer's potential.

Unit and Individual Training

Upon assignment to a unit, the new soldier continues to refine the individual soldier skills learned in BT and AIT. The Individual Training and Evaluation Program (ITEP) provides a formal structure for the soldier's ongoing training. The ITEP focuses on three main areas — Common Task Training, the Self Development Test, and the Commander's Evaluation.

Common Task Training (CTT) emphasizes the combat survival skills that all soldiers must practice in order to maintain an acceptable level of proficiency. Tasks such as map reading, communications procedures, and proper response to a nuclear, biological, and chemical environment must be constantly reinforced through performance-oriented, hands-on training. Each year, soldiers must pass a battery of common skills tests that evaluates the soldier's ability to perform these basic skills.

The SDT was fielded throughout the active Army in fiscal year 1991, and in the Reserve and the National Guard in FY 1992. Skill level one soldiers do not take the SDT; they are assessed for technical competence through an annual Commander's Evaluation.

Junior enlisted soldiers should quickly prepare for the SDT, however, because in a few short years they can advance to the junior NCO ranks. Then they are expected to excel on the test (score 80 percent or higher) if they want to be considered for promotion to more senior NCO ranks.

The SDT must be taken by all sergeants through sergeants first class — annually by active NCOs, every two years by Reserve and Guard NCOs. The SDT is designed to motivate soldiers to remain current on MOS requirements; it assists in preparing soldiers for future assignments and helps make NCOs more versatile.

The SDT contains MOS technical questions and military leadership and training management questions. Sixty percent of the questions relate to MOS and come from the Soldiers Manual and supporting references. The rest are split evenly between questions about leadership and training. Leadership questions are taken from FM 22-100, *Military Leadership*; FM 22-101, *Leadership Counseling*; and FM 22-102, *Soldier Team Develop-*

ment. Training management questions come from FM 25-101, *Battle Focused Training.*

Preparing for the two-hour, multiple-choice SDT is an individual responsibility. No unit training time is devoted to preparation. In 1994, test results will be used by promotion, assignment, and school attendance boards under the auspices of the Enlisted Personnel Management System.

The Commander's Evaluation (CE) is a hands-on test administered by each command. It is designed to help unit leaders determine the level of proficiency each soldier has achieved in relationship to the standards outlined in the soldier's job book, the appropriate soldier's manual, and the unit's Army Training and Evaluation Program (ARTEP) requirements.

Although the focus of each soldier's training is on developing individual soldier skills, unit leaders are responsible for ensuring that the unit is trained to perform collective tasks. At the unit level, the Army Training and Evaluation Program is the planning process that assists commanders in identifying the appropriate training standards that each type of unit should reach. In this process, each commander evaluates his or her unit's wartime mission and assesses which tasks require emphasis in the unit's training plans. The commander then uses the ARTEP manuals to develop a unit training strategy by which he or she can develop, execute, and evaluate unit training.

Noncommissioned Officer Education System (NCOES)

The second phase of the Enlisted Training System is the Noncommissioned Officer Education System (NCOES), which has a single goal as its objective—to train NCOs to be trainers and leaders for the soldiers who work under their supervision. Training in NCOES is designed to prepare soldiers to perform duty at the next higher skill level and combines leadership study with technical training.

NCOES provides an extensive network of courses at all levels of the NCO corps and is not limited to a single school or location. It is conducted in service schools and NCO academies (NCOA), both within CONUS and overseas.

Four levels of training within NCOES are the Primary Leadership Development Course (PLDC), the Basic NCO Course (BNCOC), Advanced NCO Course (ANCOC), and the U.S. Army Sergeants Major Academy (USASMA). Each level focuses on a specific grade or experience level.

The Primary Leadership Development Course (PLDC) is a non-MOS-specific leadership course that concentrates on how to lead and train and emphasizes the duties, responsibilities, and authority of the NCO.

This four-week course is conducted at NCOAs and is open to soldiers in all MOSs who have not previously attended a primary-level leadership course.

The Basic NCO Course (BNCOC), conducted at NCOAs, is designed to produce hard-hitting squad and section leaders who can lead and train soldiers in combat. The length of the course varies according to MOS. Graduation from BNCOC is required for consideration for promotion to staff sergeant.

Advanced NCO Courses (ANCOC) stress MOS-related tasks, with emphasis on technical and common leader combat skills required to train and lead other soldiers at the platoon or comparable level. Courses are presented at NCOAs and vary in length according to the requirements of the particular MOS. Beginning in October 1993, ANCOC will be required for consideration for promotion to sergeant first class. Until then, AN-COC is required for consideration for promotion to master sergeant.

The U.S. Army Sergeants Major Academy (USASMA) is the capstone of NCO training, regardless of the branch in which a soldier serves. USASMA prepares master sergeants and first sergeants for troop and staff assignments throughout the Army and the Department of Defense. Beginning in October 1993, graduation from the U.S. Army Sergeants Major Course at the USASMA must precede promotion to sergeant major. When the change occurs, master sergeants and first sergeants selected for promotion to sergeant major will not be promoted until the Sergeants Major Course is successfully completed.

Academic Evaluation Form

All soldiers who attend mandatory NCO Education System schools, including the Primary Leadership Development Course (PLDC), are evaluated by course instructors on DA Form 1059, the *Service School Academic Evaluation Report*. The form is forwarded for posting to soldiers' official records. Once entered on the official record, the report is available for review by members of Army promotion and selection boards.

Block 13, Performance Summary, is completed to indicate a soldier's overall performance. Notice that the Exceeded Course Standards block is limited to the top 20 percent of a class. Block 14 is used to rate soldiers in the specific areas listed. Block 15 indicates whether a soldier should be selected for higher-level military education and training. Block 16 is completed by the service school instructor and routinely includes specific information about a soldier's academic performance, physical fitness, and leadership ability.

Soldiers assigned to a water purification unit in Germany test fresh water during a training exercise

Junior soldiers who have not attended PLDC should pay special attention to the areas that are evaluated in block 14. Soldiers who remain physically fit and strive to develop written and oral communications skills and leadership skills, and who make a strong effort to support group work and do effective research, will have an advantage when attending PLDC.

Other Military Training Opportunities

Military educational opportunities are not limited to NCOES courses. The Army provides myriad special programs designed to fit the needs of each soldier.

During basic training, soldiers whose native language is not English are tested and evaluated on their English comprehension. For those soldiers having difficulty with their second language (English), self-paced instruction is available through Army Education Centers (AEC). English as a Second Language (ESL) courses are presented to the basic trainee. In addition, refresher and sustaining courses are available at most installations worldwide. Once at the permanent duty station, the ESL graduate requests further training through his unit commander. The primary consideration is the soldier's willingness to learn and to use English skills to enhance his productivity and efficiency.

The Army Apprenticeship Program is a unique educational opportunity provided by the Army through the Department of Labor. Under the program, a soldier's on-the-job training and experience are documented. Once the servicemember has completed 6,000 to 8,000 hours of training and/or experience (approximately three to four years), he or she can apply to the Bureau of Apprenticeship and Training of the Department of Labor for a Certificate of Completion at the Journeyworker level in the particular trade or vocation in which he or she has been serving. The certificate earned through the Army program is identical to one earned through civilian sources. Although this program doesn't guarantee you a job if you return to the civilian community, it will make you eligible for vocations requiring the certification. Basically, it gives you a competitive advantage. Equally important, the apprenticeship program encourages soldiers to strive for excellence within their military career fields.

Ambitious soldiers striving to excel in their military performance can improve their promotion potential through military education. Many soldiers compete for the space allocations in NCOES; not all soldiers can be selected at a given time. Soldiers can become more competitive by enrolling in military correspondence courses. The first sergeant or training NCO can provide further information on these courses.

MOS Related Instruction courses are also available through the Army education center on each post. Any soldier may enroll in these programs, which are designed to improve skills and enhance advancement potential.

The Basic Skills Education Program (BSEP) is yet another avenue toward personal and military development. BSEP courses are organized in two skill levels, each covering functional job-related skills, such as reading, math, and verbal communications. Entry into BSEP must be approved by the soldier's commander. Operated through the Army education center, BSEP's aim is to bring the soldier's abilities up to the skill level one and skill level two standards acceptable in NCOES. With sufficient motivation and hard work, a soldier can overcome most deficiencies.

Similar to BSEP, the Advanced Skills Education Program (ASEP) enhances the career potential of selected NCOs. With the commander's recommendation, an NCO can enroll in ASEP for the purpose of reinforcing managerial, supervisory, and communication skills, all inherent to performing successfully at skill levels three, four, and five.

Leadership Performance Indicators

Soldiers striving to become NCOs must indicate skill and knowledge in the following areas: communications, supervision, teaching and counseling, soldier-team development, technical and tactical proficiency, decision making, planning, use of available automated systems (computer literacy), and professional ethics.

Communications
Skills

- Issue clear and concise oral orders to small groups.
- Write performance counseling statements.
- Provide input on personnel actions affecting subordinates.
- Participate in after-action reviews.

Knowledge

- Listening and watching principles (FM 22-101).
- Reading grade level 10 (AR 621-5 and AR 25-30).
- Writing grade level 10 (Test of Adult Basic Education).

Supervision
Skills

- Enforce Army standards of appearance and conduct.
- Control and account for subordinates.
- Lead and evaluate individual training.
- Lead small groups in performance of collective tasks.
- Supervise maintenance of equipment, living areas, and workplace.
- Enforce safety policies.
- Enforce equal opportunity and sexual harassment policies.

Knowledge

- Duty, responsibility, and authority (TC 22-6).
- Wear and appearance of the uniform (AR 670-1).
- Drill and ceremonies (FM 22-5).
- Unit standing operating procedures.
- Army training system and responsibilities of trainers (FM 25-100 and FM 25-101).
- Equipment operation (TM-10 series).
- Unit supply procedures (AR 735 series).

- Army Safety Program (AR 385 series).
- Equal opportunity and sexual harassment policy (AR 600-20).

Teaching and Counseling
Skills

- Teach subordinates individual tasks for Common Task Training.
- Teach subordinates MOS skill level one tasks.
- Teach subordinates common leader combat skills.
- Teach subordinates performance-oriented training.
- Coach subordinates in proper execution of tasks.
- Evaluate tasks to standards.
- Provide feedback through performance counseling and after-action reviews.

Knowledge

- Common Tasks skill level one (STP 21-1-SMCT).
- Tasks, conditions, and standards for individual tasks (Soldier's Manual).
- Common leader combat skills (chain of command).
- Army training systems and responsibilities of trainers (FM 25-100 and FM 25-101).
- Performance counseling of individuals (FM 22-101).
- After-action review techniques (FM 25-101).
- Individual Training Evaluation Program (AR 350-37).

Soldier-Team Development
Skills

- Develop small-group cohesion.
- Foster loyalty and commitment.
- Build spirit and confidence.
- Instill discipline.
- Take care of subordinates.
- Lead small group physical fitness training.
- Develop and mentor subordinates.

Knowledge

- Concept of team building (FM 22-102).
- Principles of leadership (FM 22-100).
- Factors of leadership (FM 22-100).

- Human stress factors (FM 22-100).
- Customs and traditions of unit (first sergeant).
- Promotion criteria through corporal (AR 600-200).
- Prerequisites for PLDC (AR 351-1).
- Company-level disciplinary actions (UCMJ, AR 27-10, FM 27-14, and FM 27-1).
- Physical fitness training (FM 21-20 and unit master fitness trainer).

Technical and Tactical Proficiency
Skills

- Qualify with individual weapon.
- Demonstrate proficiency with crew-served weapons and equipment.
- Perform skill level one to standard.
- Perform Common Tasks skill level one to standard.
- Be proficient in land navigation and map reading.
- Use MILES (Multiple Integrated Laser Engagement System).
- Train and lead small group collective tasks.
- Perform PMCS (preventive maintenance checks and services) on individual and small group weapons and equipment.

Knowledge

- Basic rifle marksmanship (FM 23-9).
- Operation, characteristics, and employment of team weapons and equipment.
- MOS skill level one tasks and standards (Soldiers Manual).
- Common Tasks skill level one (STP 21-1 and 21-24).
- Fundamentals of land navigation and map reading (FM 21-26).
- Preventive measures against environmental health hazards (medics).
- Operation of MILES.
- Small-group collective tasks (mission training plans).
- Common leader combat skills.
- Equipment operator's manual (TM-10 series).

Decision Making
Skills

- Interpret information and make decisions affecting small groups.
- Use problem-solving process.
- Use ethical decision-making process.
- Exercise initiative in tactical situations.

Knowledge

- Problem-solving process (FM 22-100 and FM 22-101).
- Ethical decision-making process (FM 22-100).

Planning
Skills

- Plan small group and individual training.
- Use backward planning process.

Knowledge

- Planning principles (FM 25-100).
- Training schedules and event plans (FM 25-101).
- Team/section training objectives.
- Backward planning process (FM 22-100).

Use of Available Systems
Skill

- Use and control automated systems at small group level.

Knowledge

- Automated systems applicable to small group.

Professional Ethics
Skills

- Lead by example.
- Practice Professional Army Ethic.
- Demonstrate high moral standards.

Knowledge

- Professional Army Ethic (FM 100-1).
- Soldierly qualities (FM 100-1).

Physical Fitness Training

The real value of being physically fit is as clear today as it was on distant battlefields long—and not so long—ago. In April 1942, for example, Japanese soldiers were on the verge of overwhelming desperate American and Filipino defenders on the Bataan Peninsula of Luzon in the Philippines. Thousands of weary defenders fought until they had literally nothing left to fight with, then surrendered. The September 1989 issue of *Soldiers* magazine described what happened to 35,000 of the valiant soldiers: "They were herded and marched 200 miles from Bataan to Camp O'Donell in central Luzon. Some 900 Americans perished, butchered where they fell. News of the 'Bataan death march' raced through the islands." Only the strongest, most enduring soldiers survived the ordeal.

During one grim episode of the Korean War, U.S. soldiers who were exhausted during an infamous wintertime retreat decided to quit, sit alongside the road, and wait for the enemy to arrive and take them prisoner. Enemy soldiers did arrive—and they shot American after American in the back of the head. The U.S. men were so tired and mentally whipped that they just gave up and waited for the enemy to kill them.

In Vietnam, hardier soldiers from the 101st Airborne Division assaulted an enemy-infested hill 11 times—as portrayed in the movie "Hamburger Hill"—captured it, and destroyed the entrenched enemy. As strategically empty as the victory was, it nevertheless showed the willpower and gut-tough abilities of lean warriors who would not quit.

During recent conflicts in the Caribbean, Panama, and Southwest Asia, U.S. casualties were minimized and victory was virtually assured, largely because our nation deployed physically fit, determined soldiers into the combat zones.

Mental toughness is an additional benefit of physical fitness. Soldiers who fought, won, and survived in Grenada, Panama, Kuwait, and Iraq can attest to the value of physical strength and mental endurance. Soldiers today are more "fit to fight" than ever before.

Infantrymen, medics, cooks, combat support specialists, mechanics, tankers, engineers, artillerymen, air defenders, military police, supply clerks—everyone, regardless of the job in the active Army, Army National Guard, or Army Reserve—serves on the same team. Each soldier on the total Army team is expected to get and stay prepared because a call to arms may sound without warning.

According to official Army policy, soldiers must train to accomplish their wartime Mission Essential Task List (METL). A unit METL includes all of its critical wartime tasks. So, soldiers should have in their physical training programs events that fully prepare them to accomplish METL, or wartime, tasks.

In an artillery unit, one physically demanding METL task might be, "Load 202-pound, eight-inch explosive projectiles into howitzer." In an armored unit, a METL task could be, "Remove, repair, and replace a track pad on a disabled M-1 tank." An airborne infantry METL might include,

"On order, parachute at night with full combat load from a C-141 jet aircraft, then move on foot to find, close with, and kill the enemy." By now you should fully grasp the critical importance of linking physical training to the accomplishment of a unit's METL. Commanders do.

The Army chief of staff, Gen. Gordon Sullivan, has a saying he used often in 1992 to describe both his feelings and professional position regarding what happened to a soft Army task force suddenly thrust into war in Korea. He exclaimed, "No more Task Force Smiths!" which is to say the Army will train properly to maintain a high level of readiness.

Physical Fitness Tools

Graduates of the Army Master Fitness Trainers Course conduct physical training programs aimed at critical wartime task accomplishment. Master Fitness Trainers (MFTs) use the four MFT Battle Competencies, the five Components of Fitness, and the seven Principles of Exercise to encourage, develop, and maintain high levels of physical readiness in units. These program tools come from AR 350-15, *The Army Physical Fitness Program*; FM 21-20, *Physical Fitness Training*; AR 600-9, *The Army Weight Control Program*; and the *Master Fitness Trainer Course Workbook*. MFTs also make sure that a five- to seven-minute warm-up precedes each exercise period, and a five- to seven-minute cool-down follows each period. The warm-up and cool-down help ensure that muscles are stretched properly before exercise to reduce the possibility of injury and that the heart safely slows to a normal rate after exercise.

The Four MFT Battle Competencies

The four MFT battle competencies are *train the trainer, conduct unit fitness assessments, analyze the unit METL and design an appropriate physical fitness program*, and *teach soldiers to understand their bodies*.

Train the trainer means to teach commanders and NCOs to use the master fitness physical training approach and philosophy. A *unit fitness assessment*, the second competency, helps the MFT take a "snapshot" of a unit's current overall physical condition. The MFT uses medical profiles, Army Physical Fitness Test results, the commander's guidance, and other information to conduct an assessment. Based on this, the MFT designs a METL-oriented physical training program. Programs often run from eight weeks to six months to enable units to achieve the required level of fitness. It is likely that your own unit is conducting an MFT-style training program—or should be, especially if it is a combat arms, combat support, or combat service support unit.

The unit MFT also helps soldiers learn to train and use muscles and muscle groups correctly, to diet properly, to combine safe diet reduction and exercise plans to reduce body fat, and to avoid health risks by eliminating smoking, drinking, or other harmful habits.

The Five Components of Fitness

The President's Council on Physical Fitness defines fitness as "a reflection of the ability to work with vigor without undue fatigue, with energy left over for meeting unforeseen emergencies." The components of fitness give soldiers the ability to handle military emergencies. The components are cardiorespiratory endurance, muscular strength, muscular endurance, flexibility, and body composition.

Cardiorespiratory endurance enables the body to deliver nutrients and remove waste at the cellular level. Muscular strength is applying the greatest amount of force possible in a single movement. Muscular endurance is the ability to perform repeated movements with moderate resistance for given periods of time. Flexibility is the ability to move joints of your body through their entire range of motion. Body composition deals with the proportion of lean body mass (muscle, bone, and essential organ tissue) to body fat.

The Seven Principles of Exercise

PROVRBS (pronounced "proverbs") — progression, regularity, overload, variety, recovery, balance, and specificity — are the principles behind a proper physical training program. These principles lead to a positive training effect each time you exercise and to physical excellence. Violate any one and your program will be less rewarding.

The intensity of each successive exercise period must gradually be increased so the body will improve (progress). In terms of safe improvement, a 10 percent increase in cardiorespiratory and muscular ability every 10 days is recommended. That is, you should strive to reduce your elapsed time on a run by about 10 percent every 10 days to two weeks until you achieve excellence. You should try to increase the number of endurance-related exercises such as pushups and sit-ups by about 10 percent during the same period, and you should push and pull toward the same level of improvement in muscular strength during the period.

Exercise must be performed at routine (regular) intervals, at least three to five times weekly, to provide a training effect. Soldiers must also rest, sleep, and eat properly on a regular basis.

Overloading means going for the "max" during each exercise session, and doing so safely to achieve a positive training effect. It means working your heart at a relatively high percentage of its maximum capacity, based on your current physical condition, sex, and age. This is called the training heart rate, and your local MFT can help you determine what yours is so you can train at the proper intensity when running or doing other aerobic exercises.

Overloading also means working to muscle failure when doing muscular strength or endurance routines. Where pushups and sit-ups are concerned, it means using several timed sets (such as a 60-second set, followed by a 20-second rest, followed by a 45-second set, followed by a 20-second rest, followed by a 30-second set, and doing as many repetitions per set as possible). Over time, as the soldier becomes more and more fit, the training heart rate intensity is increased and the timed sets are lengthened.

Variety means breaking up the weekly training routine with various exercises to reduce boredom and increase motivation. A program can include different kinds of runs, such as ability group runs, Indian runs, fartlek (a Swedish term meaning "speed play") runs, interval training, circuit training, slow distance runs, fast continuous runs, relays, and so forth. Strength and endurance workouts can be outdoors or at the gym and include free weights, Nautilus machines, Kaiser or pneumatic machines, universals, mat routines, partner-resisted exercises, timed sets, sandbag circuits, and so forth. Of course, units should train collectively, so periodic cohesion runs and extended rectangular formation routines should be included.

Recovery means providing 24- to 48-hour rests between exercising the same muscles. It also means hard days of training should be alternated with easier days, or alternate the muscles exercised each day. Improper recovery leads to muscle fatigue, which can cause injury. During rest periods, muscle damage is repaired and waste is metabolized.

Balance means balancing the principles of exercise so that they lead to the five components of fitness. It means that, as you progress through your exercise program, you should balance upper-body and lower-body routines, back muscle and abdomen routines, and rest and recovery periods. It means balancing endurance runs with sprints so you can run fast and far, as long as possible. Don't focus so much exercise on one part of the body that other parts are neglected. Remember that image, or "disco muscles," are not important. You want to achieve a high level of overall fitness.

The last principle, specificity, means doing what the balance principle seems to tell you to avoid—working on a specific ability. Specificity, however, means working on specific muscles and muscle groups or on a specific kind of run to deal with areas that clearly need improvement. Suppose you were an infantry scout who had real trouble climbing over tall obstacles. You would need to focus on your lack of upper-body climbing strength and do so without violating the principles of exercise. By adding a rope-climbing routine to your overall exercise program, you would comply with the principles of exercise and overcome a specific METL-related deficiency.

Most soldiers will be required to participate in an organized physical training program. The program will undoubtedly emphasize the "big three" of the Army's Physical Fitness Test—pushups, sit-ups, and running—but it should also offer a variety of calisthenics and individual fitness training. Many unit PT programs also offer team sports, which both support physical fitness goals and enhance unit esprit.

As previously stated, working on an exercise program should be a regular, but gradual, process. If you fail to stick to a maintenance program, you can soon find yourself right back where you started—out of condition.

Individual exercise programs are generally more successful when you use the "buddy system." Not only is there an increased safety factor in case one of you is hurt while exercising, but the encouragement of another soldier can keep the program progressing.

Common-sense safety rules should be applied. Use exercise equipment only after proper instruction, wear appropriate reflective gear when jogging at night, and wear proper footgear during exercise. Keep a record of the exercise program—seeing how far you've come can be a great source of encouragement.

Weight Control

A soldier should look trim and neat, not only through proper care of the uniform but also through proper weight control. The Army places such high priority on weight control that a bar from reenlistment or separation proceedings will be enacted against soldiers not meeting minimum Army standards. Involuntary separation from service will be enacted if a soldier has been unsuccessful in meeting Army weight standards after spending six months in the Army Weight Control Program. In addition, overweight soldiers will not be considered for promotion and will be denied enrollment in professional military or civilian schooling.

Regulations of the Army Weight Control Program aim to ensure that all soldiers are physically able to perform under the most strenuous combat conditions and that all soldiers maintain a trim military appearance.

Although all personnel are encouraged to strive for a stringent percentage of body fat (20 percent for males; 28 percent for females), a more lenient maximum allowable body fat percentage has been established by age group and sex.

Age Group	Sex	Percentage of Body Fat
17–20	M	20
	F	30
21–27	M	22
	F	32
28–39	M	24
	F	34
40+	M	26
	F	36

In addition to the maximum body fat composition, the Army has established a maximum weight, based on height, age group, and sex. (See accompanying table.)

All personnel must be weighed at the time of the Army Physical Fitness Test or at least every six months. In addition, body fat composition testing is required whenever a supervisor feels that a soldier's appearance suggests excessive body fat. Soldiers who exceed either maximum body fat percentage or maximum weight limits will enter a weight control program that includes nutritional training and exercise programs that are administered by health officials. Weight loss and body fat goals are established, and monthly weigh-ins are required.

Few exceptions to these standards are allowed. A commander may approve an extension of enlistment, however, for a soldier with a temporary medical condition that precludes weight loss and who is currently under a doctor's care; or for a pregnant soldier, fully qualified for reenlistment except for exceeding weight requirements. Commanders may allow reenlistment for an overweight soldier only if a medically documented condition precludes that soldier from attaining the required standard and a disability separation would not be appropriate.

Diet and Nutrition

The Army's concern about weight control and body fat composition highlights the need for adequate information on proper diet and nutrition. A healthy diet includes a wide variety of foods; a low percentage of empty calories from "junk foods"; only small amounts of fat, sugar, salt, and alcohol; and adequate amounts of complex carbohydrates and fiber. Increased awareness of the importance of nutrition has led to alterations in food preparation in Army dining halls. New menus incorporate a 25-percent reduction in salt and a reduction in the frequency that fried foods are offered (baked and roasted versions of the same items are featured

Weight for Height Table

Weight (in pounds)

Height (in inches)	Male by Age Group				Female by Age Group			
	17–20	*21–27*	*28–39*	*40+*	*17–20*	*21–27*	*28–39*	*40+*
58	—	—	—	—	109	112	115	119
59	—	—	—	—	113	116	119	123
60	132	136	139	141	116	120	123	127
61	136	140	144	146	120	124	127	131
62	141	144	148	150	125	129	132	137
63	145	149	153	155	129	133	137	141
64	150	154	158	160	133	137	141	145
65	155	159	163	165	137	141	145	149
66	160	163	168	170	141	146	150	154
67	165	169	174	176	145	149	154	159
68	170	174	179	181	150	154	159	164
69	175	179	184	186	154	158	163	168
70	180	185	189	192	159	163	168	173
71	185	189	194	197	163	167	172	177
72	190	195	200	203	167	172	177	183
73	195	200	205	208	172	177	182	188
74	201	206	211	214	178	183	189	194
75	206	212	217	220	183	188	194	200
76	212	217	223	226	189	194	200	206
77	218	223	229	232	193	199	205	211
78	223	229	235	238	198	204	210	216
79	229	235	241	244	203	209	215	222
80	234	240	247	250	208	214	220	227

instead). Other changes include the posting of calories contained in all menu items and the availability of salad bars when at all possible.

Even the order in which foods are presented has come under the scrutiny of Army regulations. To encourage the soldier to make sensible diet choices, salads and fresh fruits are presented first, then soups, entrées, hot vegetables, starches, and breads. Desserts, with their high sugar and low nutritional value, are held back until the soldier has had a chance to fill his tray with other choices.

Selecting foods from the basic food groups is a good starting place for a balanced diet. The fruit and vegetable group provides fiber, minerals, and vitamins, especially when fresh selections are made instead of canned or frozen; the raw form is the most nutritious. At least four and as many as nine servings a day should come from this group.

The bread and cereal group provides carbohydrates the body needs for energy. Whole-grain selections provide significant amounts of fiber, as well as iron and vitamins. At least four servings a day are needed.

Protein-rich foods, such as poultry, fish, eggs, and red meats, provide minerals in addition to protein. Beans, peas, soybeans, and lentils are other excellent sources of protein. The American diet overemphasizes meats. Ideally, only two servings a day should be consumed, and then they should be about three ounces each. By that standard, one 12-ounce steak is a two-day supply of meat.

Dairy foods provide protein, in addition to calcium (especially important to women), phosphorus, and vitamins. Skim milk is recommended over whole milk; 2-percent is an acceptable alternative. Yogurt and cheeses add variety to the dairy group. Three servings a day are adequate.

Many books available commercially provide nutritional information for the health-conscious and the dieter. Using common sense is the best approach to dieting, however, and fad diets, or diets that emphasize only one or two food choices, are not sensible.

Exercise combined with a sensible diet leads to weight control. All three concepts must be viewed as an integrated package. Even more important, all three must be viewed in light of their impact on your overall physical fitness.

Army Physical Fitness Tests

The Army's Physical Fitness Test consists of three events—pushups, sit-ups, and running, in that order—to test your endurance, strength, and cardiorespiratory efficiency. Taking part in a regular exercise program will help you to improve your test performance.

The first event is a two-minute pushup test, which measures the strength and endurance of the chest and shoulder muscles and of the triceps. The pushups must be properly completed to be counted as valid repetitions. The starting position is as follows:

- Hands are placed a comfortable distance apart.
- The body must remain in a generally straight line.
- Arms are straight and fully extended.
- Feet may be up to 12 inches apart.

To execute a repetition, bend your elbows, evenly lowering your body until your upper arms are parallel with the ground. Then straighten your arms until they are fully extended. Throughout the repetition, your body should remain generally straight and your hands and feet must not break contact with the ground. Only your hands and feet may touch the ground during this exercise. If you fail to maintain proper form for the entire repetition, it will not be counted.

The second event is a two-minute sit-up test, which measures the strength of the abdominal and flexor muscles. To assume the starting position for this exercise, do the following:

- Lie flat on your back.
- Bend your knees so that your feet are flat on the ground and a 90-degree angle is formed by the upper and lower portions of your legs.
- Place your feet together or up to 12 inches apart.
- Clasp your hands behind your head with your fingers interlocked.

To execute a correct repetition, raise your body to the vertical position, with the base of your neck above the base of the spine, and then lower your body so your back touches the ground. The repetition will not be counted if you fail to reach the vertical position, arch or bow your back, raise your buttocks off the ground, fail to keep your fingers interlocked and behind your head, or allow your knees to exceed a 90-degree angle. Another soldier will assist you during this exercise by holding your feet firmly on the ground.

The final event, a two-mile run, measures your aerobic and leg muscle endurance. Walking is discouraged during the running event, but it is not unauthorized. The shorter the time period needed to complete the run, the higher the score.

The accompanying table lists the requirements for each of the three events according to sex and age group. The first number in each pair of requirements is the minimum time or number of repetitions a soldier must achieve in order to earn a passing score of 60 points. The second number indicates the achievement needed to earn the maximum score of 100 points.

A soldier with a limiting physical condition, or medical "profile," may be medically exempted from doing one, two, or all three of the primary events. To receive passing credit for the fitness test, however, a soldier must successfully complete either the primary aerobic event (the two-mile run) or one of three alternate aerobic events.

Standards for the Army Physical Fitness Test

Age Group	Pushups*	Sit-ups*	Run**
Men			
17–21	42/82	52/92	15:54/11:54
22–26	40/80	47/87	16:36/12:36
27–31	38/78	42/82	17:18/13:18
32–36	33/73	38/78	18:00/14:00
37–41	32/72	33/73	18:42/14:42
42–46	26/66	29/69	19:06/15:06
47–51	22/62	27/67	19:36/15:36
52+	16/56	26/66	20:00/16:00
Women			
17–21	18/58	50/90	18:54/14:54
22–26	16/56	45/85	19:36/15:36
27–31	15/54	40/80	21:00/17:00
32–36	14/52	35/75	22:36/18:36
37–41	13/48	30/70	23:36/19:36
42–46	12/45	27/67	24:00/20:00
47–51	10/41	24/64	24:30/20:30
52+	9/40	22/62	25:00/21:00

*Number of repetitions
**Minutes: seconds

Source: DA Form 705, APFT Scorecard, *May 87*

The alternate aerobic events are the 2.5-mile walk, 6.2-mile bicycle ride (using one gear), or 800-yard swim. Like the primary aerobic event, the alternates are timed based on the soldier's age and sex. Unlike the primary event, though, the alternates are not scored. Instead, a soldier is credited with passing or failing based upon whether he or she completes an alternate event in the prescribed time.

For example, a 36-year-old male with a physical profile against running may choose to do the 2.5-mile walk. He must complete the walk in no more than 35½ minutes to pass—and he must pass the pushup and sit-up events to pass the fitness test.

Medical profiles can be confusing. If you have a profile, consult with your unit first sergeant or master fitness trainer well in advance of the mandatory semi-annual fitness test. Doing so will ensure that you have adequate time to train on an alernate aerobic event prior to the test.

References

AR 27-10, *Military Justice*
AR 350-15, *The Army Physical Fitness Program*
AR 600-9, *The Army Weight Control Program*
AR 670-1, *Wear and Appearance of Army Uniforms and Insignia*
FM 21-20, *Physical Fitness Training*
FM 21-26, *Land Navigation and Map Reading*
FM 22-5, *Drill and Ceremonies*
FM 22-100, *Military Leadership*
FM 22-101, *Leadership Counseling*
FM 22-102, *Soldier Team Development*
FM 23-9, *M16A1 and M16A2 Rifle Marksmanship*
FM 25-101, *Battle Focused Training*
FM 100-1, *The Army*
STP 21-1-SMCT, *Soldiers Manual of Common Tasks*

3

Educational Opportunities

One active-duty first sergeant today remembers how hard it was to take college night school courses when he was a private in the infantry in 1974. Time and again, he would get permission from his commander, enroll, pay tuition, buy books, and begin to attend classes—only to find that course completion would not be possible because of conflicting military duties. Eighteen years later, with two college degrees under his belt, the senior NCO had this advice for college-bound junior soldiers: "Do not quit."

You can excel at soldiering—complete your mandatory and voluntary military training and other job-related requirements—and also continue your civilian education. You should *stay* enrolled in trade school or college if you desire to remain highly competitive for promotion and career-enhancing assignments.

Army Education Centers

Make an appointment—it is vital—to speak with a counselor at your

Your post's Army Education Center offers a variety of services

local Army Education Center (AEC). If you want to earn a trade school certificate or college degree, you should discuss the following:

- An evaluation of credit based upon any previous school or college course work, work experience, MOS and formal military training, and college-level testing.
- On-post or nearby school certification or degree programs, or extension or independent study programs, and how to get enrolled.
- Use of education benefits, tuition assistance, or other financial assistance.

AEC counselors are wonderful, informative, overworked people. They can help you identify both long- and short-range educational goals. You are required to attend counseling sessions at the AEC when you in-process at a new post. The counselors have diagnostic tests and interest inventories to help you analyze your aptitudes and interests. They can also provide the most current information on the educational programs available at your new duty station. And they can explain your Montgomery GI Bill benefits (under Chapter 30, Title 38, U.S. code). The benefits are highlighted in Department of Veterans Affairs Pamphlet 22-90-2, *Summary of Education Benefits*, dated June 1990.

Counselors can help you apply for tuition assistance, grants, loans, or other financial aid. Before discussing money matters, however, visit the education center and request a copy of the pamphlet "Financial Aid from the U.S. Department of Education" for the current academic year. The pamphlet includes a section for soldiers who were receiving federal student aid when called to active duty to support Operation Desert Shield/Desert Storm.

AEC officials can also tell you about the Mind Extension University (MEU). According to a MEU Public Affairs Office release distributed during mid-1992, the MEU offers televised (in the United States) or videotaped (overseas) undergraduate and graduate degree instruction from a coalition of 20 major colleges and universities.

If you cannot get quality information through your local AEC (because of remote duty or some other reason), obtain a copy of the *Army Veterans Education Guide*. The 1990 edition, available free at AECs, has 17 relevant articles, listings of state agencies involved with GI Bill benefits, a glossary of college terms, tear-out postcards for admission information to various technical schools and colleges, and a school and college directory. If your AEC does not have the guide, obtain it by calling (914) 632-7771, or outside the 914 area code, (800) 433-7771; or write to School Guide Publications, 210 North Avenue, New Rochelle, NY 10801.

The *Blue Book* is another valuable and free source of information for the soldier-student. This is actually a five-volume hardbound set of college listings, requirements, enrollment data, prerequisite criteria, points of contact, locations, degree programs, and much more. AEC counselors maintain and refer daily to the current edition. Previous editions often are filed in the post MOS library and are readily available.

As by now you can see, AECs are the organ through which the Army provides an integrated system of educational courses, from the high school and college preparatory level to post-master's work.

Testing, guidance and counseling, and course work, both on- and off-post, at vocational and college levels are available through AECs. Whether stationed in the United States or overseas, you have a wide variety of offerings. As a minimum, AECs provide resources such as an MOS library, testing services, the Servicemembers' Opportunity Colleges

(SOC), career counseling, and skill development programs for language, MOS, and occupationally oriented courses.

Some educational programs allow you to participate during duty hours; others require attendance on your own time. For instance, you can attend certain vocational courses or MOS-related training, including the Basic Skills Education Program (BSEP), the Advanced Skills Education Program (ASEP), and the Job Skills Education Program (JSEP), during duty hours; language training, including English as a second language or mission-required language training in preparation for an upcoming PCS overseas, can be scheduled during duty hours. Most programs, however, involve your off-duty time, during lunchtime, evening, or weekend hours.

Education benefits are not restricted to active duty personnel. Several programs are available to help you pursue your educational goals after returning to civilian life. Other programs aid your spouse and children.

Credit by Examination

In addition to nationally recognized achievement tests needed for entrance into some colleges, such as the Scholastic Aptitude Test (SAT) and the American College Testing (ACT) program, the Army Continuing Education System (ACES) provides a variety of testing programs through which you can receive college credit without ever entering the classroom.

The Defense Activity for Nontraditional Education Support (DANTES) is one such program. DANTES offers the means by which you can receive college credit for knowledge acquired through experience, personal reading, or independent study. DANTES also offers self-study courses to help you prepare for tests you may wish to take. You are not required to pay for any DANTES tests, but your dependents must pay a nominal fee.

A wide variety of testing programs are available through DANTES. First, the College Level Examination Program (CLEP) covers general exams that measure achievement in five areas: English composition, social studies, natural sciences, humanities, and mathematics. You can earn a full year of college credit (30 semester hours) through the general CLEP tests. Also available through CLEP are about 40 subject exams in areas such as business, history, science, and languages. For each successfully passed exam, you can earn three semester hours of credit.

Another testing program that DANTES offers is the Subject Standardized Test (DSST). The DSSTs cover vocational and technical subject areas as well as those included in more traditional college work. You can select from some 55 tests in fields as diverse as auto mechanics, forestry, and carpentry. Vocational-technical or college credits are awarded for the DSSTs, each of which has been evaluated by the American Council on Education (ACE). An ACE Guide has been developed advising colleges and universities not only on minimum scores that should be acceptable for earning college credit through the testing program, but also on credit that should be awarded for the successful completion of military schools.

The American College Testing Proficiency Examination Program (ACT/PEP) offers about 50 exams in subject areas such as nursing, management, finance, marketing, and accounting. The DANTES ACT/PEP program offers series in these areas, as well. For instance, there are tests for three levels of courses in marketing alone.

Also within the DANTES program, soldiers may take the Graduate Management Admission Test (GMAT), Law School Admission Test (LSAT), National Teacher Examinations (NTE), and the Automotive Service Excellence (ASE) Examinations.

Soldiers, many of whom now have undergraduate degrees, may also take general and subject Graduate Record Examinations (GRE). The GRE General Examination often is required for admission to graduate school. GRE Subject Examinations may serve the same purpose, and may also contribute greatly to completion of undergraduate degree requirements. For example, the 200-question, three-hour GRE Sociology Examination is worth 30 semester hours—15 lower level, 15 upper level. Students enrolled at some colleges may receive the full 30 semester hours and credit for a concentration in sociology if their score meets their college's grading standard.

Soldiers may also enter the Institute for Certification of Computer Professionals (ICCP) Program through DANTES. DANTES has agreements with 27 nationally recognized certification programs, including the ICCP. The ICCP is highlighted here because computer literacy (Use of Available Systems) is one of the Nine Leadership Competencies soldiers strive to develop. (See chapter 2.)

For a complete listing of DANTES college and vocational certification examinations, visit your education center and ask for DANTES brochure 1218, *DANTES Examination Programs—A Profitable Experience.*

Another convenient, effective way to earn college credit by examination is through the Annenberg Project, which is offered jointly through the Annenberg Project and the Corporation for Public Broadcasting. Like other DANTES offerings, this program is for soldiers who cannot attend resident college classes, are on temporary duty, work odd shifts, want to save tuition expenses, or want to complete their degree requirements sooner. The Annenberg Project includes selected college courses on audio and videotapes, supplemented with textbooks and study guides. Soldiers read a chapter in a study guide, view or listen to the related tape, then read the related chapter in the textbook.

In one Annenberg Project course, "War and Peace in the Nuclear Age," the student reads a chapter in the guide for about 30 minutes, views a related videotape for an hour, then reads the related chapter in the textbook for about an hour. The course covers 13 chapters, and so takes about 33 hours to complete. If a soldier can spare a few hours a day for two weeks (or only a few hours a week for a couple of months), he or she can complete the course and learn something new, take the corresponding DANTES examination, and earn three semester hours of college credit.

According to DANTES literature titled *Ten Steps to Success with the Annenberg Project,* successful independent learners tend to be in the rank of specialist or higher, have one or more years of college, have completed military correspondence courses, have specific degree goals, and are mature. Dedicated privates can also be successful independent learners who save time and money—and earn college degrees earlier in life.

Correspondence Courses

There are ways for every soldier in the Army to further his or her education. Even the soldier assigned to the most remote duty site, or the one who is required to pull shift work, has the opportunity to pursue an education through correspondence courses. DANTES offers numerous independent study courses from fully accredited civilian colleges and universities. Students complete reading assignments and exercises, submit the work for evaluation, correspond with a professor, and, in the end, take one or more examinations through the education center. Credits earned through correspondence courses equal those earned by other students in a normal classroom environment.

The major difference is the extra discipline required by the student to work diligently at the assignments without the benefit of specific deadlines and the watchful eye of a professor. Tuition assistance applies to correspondence courses under the same rules that apply to standard college courses.

MILPO Testing

Army personnel, or MILPO (Military Personnel Office), testing is also offered at education centers. Army personnel tests are used to select applicants for entry into the active Army, Army National Guard, or Army Reserve; to select applicants for appointment as commissioned or warrant officers; to initially or subsequently classify enlisted personnel; and to select personnel for special training and assignment.

Included in this category are the Armed Forces Classification Test, commonly used to modify an individual's GT (General Technical) score; the Officer Selection Battery for soldiers seeking admission to Officer Candidate School; and the Defense Language Proficiency Tests, which are available for about 50 languages.

MOS Library

Mentioned previously in this chapter, the MOS Library is a valuable source of information that too often is underused. In it soldiers will find computer hardware and software, books and tapes that comprise the Annenberg Project, other DANTES material, Army regulations and field manuals (these may be signed out), other Army literature, editions of the college *Blue Book*, school and college literature, language tapes and books, and many other reference materials that support military and civilian education. The trained librarians there are more than helpful to novice researchers.

Financial Aid

Tuition Assistance

Most soldiers are eligible for some level of tuition assistance. Tuition assistance can be used only to offset the costs of tuition; fees, books, and other costs cannot be paid for through this program.

Two rates are currently in effect for tuition assistance:

- 100 percent for courses leading to a high school diploma.
- 75 percent for all other soldiers.

Enlisted soldiers who receive tuition assistance do not incur any additional service obligation, nor does the use of tuition assistance reduce other educational benefits (Montgomery GI Bill, VEAP, ACF) that may be available to the soldier.

If a soldier withdraws from a course, neglects to make up an incomplete grade within 120 days, or fails a course due to non-attendance, the Army will require the soldier to pay back the tuition assistance.

Scholarships, Loans, and Grants

The federal government also supports higher education through student aid programs that include grants (money that does not have to be repaid) and loans. A counselor at the AEC or at the financial affairs office of the university you attend is in the best position to provide current information about financial aid. Requesting such aid can be a time-consuming task, but the effort is frequently rewarded by additional money for your education.

Military and veterans' organizations often offer scholarships. The American Legion, the Association of the U.S. Army, and the Society of the First Division are a few of the many organizations that provide scholarships to college-bound men and women. Eligibility requirements vary, so interested soldiers should contact each organization directly for details.

Scholarships from private organizations frequently go unawarded — not because of lack of funds, but because of lack of applicants. Requirements for private scholarships can be sweeping in scope, or surprisingly narrow. For instance, one national organization provides money to women studying any phase of business, science, engineering, or professional studies. Another private scholarship can be awarded only to residents of New Jersey who have worked for a specified period of time as a golf caddy.

Digging out information on the thousands of scholarships available can be a time-consuming, frequently frustrating process, but the rewards can be most satisfying. The AEC, university financial affairs office, and the public library all have information that can be of help. Books are published annually that list organizations with money to give away in the form of educational scholarships. Many of these scholarships can also be used by your spouse or children.

The best advice is to start early. Application deadlines are as varied as the qualifications themselves.

Montgomery GI Bill

Soldiers enlisting in the Army after 1 July 1985 are eligible for the Montgomery GI Bill. A participatory program, the Montgomery GI Bill automatically covers all eligible recruits unless they specifically decline enrollment from the program. (Disenrollment is an irrevocable decision, so you should consider carefully before choosing this option.) For the first 12 months of active duty, $100 is deducted from the soldier's pay. The nonrefundable deductions become your contribution to the education fund. You make no further contributions after the first year.

To be eligible for benefits, a soldier must have completed high school or earned a GED prior to separation from active duty and have received an honorable discharge. In addition, you must meet one of the following criteria for time in service:

- Three years active duty.
- Two years active duty and four years in the Selected Ready Reserve or National Guard.
- At least 20 months service prior to being discharged because of a hardship, a service-connected disability, a pre-existing medical condition, or a reduction in forces.
- Two years active duty if the initial term of service was for less than three years. (These participants receive reduced monthly benefits.)

If you are unsure about your eligibility, consult with your post's education counselor.

Benefits under the Montgomery GI Bill are based on time in service. With two years of active duty, the maximum basic benefit is $9,000. Two years of active duty plus four years in the Selective Reserve increase the maximum to $10,800. This same figure applies to soldiers serving at least three years on active duty.

Additional benefits are also available to some soldiers through the New Army College Fund (ACF). To be eligible, soldiers must be eligible for the Montgomery GI Bill, must have completed their high school studies before entering the Army, must have scored a 50 or above on the AFQT, and must have enlisted in a critical MOS. (ACES counselors can advise you on the current list of critical MOSs.) The New ACF is also based on time served on active duty. Combining the basic benefits of the Montgomery GI Bill with the additional benefits of the New ACF can raise the total educational benefits to $25,200 for the soldier who spends four years on active duty in a critical MOS.

Schooling Availability

Almost all Army installations provide on-post educational courses at various levels — high school and college preparatory, vocational and technical, associate degree level, and baccalaureate degree level. Many posts offer master's and post-master's college course work as well. All institutions providing educational opportunities to soldiers on military installations must be accredited by the appropriate agencies. These off-campus programs are recognized in the same manner as programs taken on a college campus.

SOC and SOCAD/BDFS

The Army has developed two programs to aid you in your quest to attain a college degree: Servicemembers' Opportunity Colleges (SOC) network and Servicemembers' Opportunity Colleges Associate Degree/ Bachelor's Degree for Soldiers program (SOCAD/BDFS).

The SOC network removes many of the obstacles soldiers had faced when trying to complete degree requirements within the framework of frequent military moves. Problems of lost credit hours, varying degree requirements, and limited numbers of transfer hours were minimized through the SOC network. Member colleges recognize the special needs of the soldier by doing the following:

- Establishing liberal entrance requirements.
- Limiting or waiving residency requirements.
- Accepting nontraditional credits (generally at the levels recommended by the ACE Guide), including MOS experience and formal service school completion.
- Allowing more transfer hours.
- Scheduling classes at times and locations that accommodate the needs of the soldier.

At the associate degree level, the Army offers special opportunities through SOCAD. SOCAD course work applies to associate degree programs related to military specialties. Soldiers receive college credit for what they have learned through the Army, and they enhance their Army careers by improving their military skills through civilian training. SOCAD/BDFS institutions agree to the same guidelines as the more general SOC program, and they offer additional benefits as well. An official evaluation is made of the soldier's nontraditional credit sources, using a standardized form accepted by all SOCAD/BDFS institutions. The soldier chooses one SOCAD/BDFS school as the "home institution." Once he or she meets the limited residency requirement at the home institution, he or she is free to complete the requirements at other SOCAD/BDFS schools within his or her chosen curriculum.

The Bachelor's Degree for Soldiers (BDFS) program, an extension of SOCAD, is designed to allow servicemembers to earn a four-year degree while still meeting their service obligations. More than 200 military installations are involved in the BDFS program, and course offerings are varied. Among programs currently offered are accounting, computer studies, corrections, criminal justice, general business, liberal arts, management, and public administration.

Basically, SOCAD/BDFS schools make earning college degrees much easier for you. With the Army's increasing emphasis on education, this benefit will enhance your promotion potential.

College Programs and Locations

Before a PCS move or before requesting a particular assignment or location, it would be beneficial to the soldier pursuing a degree to know the availability of schooling at the new site. Many colleges offer courses on-post, at least on a limited basis. If an institution is close to the installation, it sometimes offers certain popular courses on site but will require students enrolling in smaller or more specialized courses to attend classes on campus.

Schooling Overseas

Overseas assignments are served by contract institutions. In Europe, for instance, some colleges provide vocational, technical, associate, and baccalaureate programs for all Army installations. Others provide graduate programs as well, although there is overlap among the groups. Overseas assignments are listed only by regions.

Europe

Army education centers in Europe serve the military community. The educational program is a comprehensive package, with services provided to soldiers in even the most remote of the caserns and garrisons. A few colleges provide technical certificate and baccalaureate degree programs throughout Europe: Big Bend Community College, Central Texas College, and City Colleges of Chicago. Embry-Riddle Aeronautical University and the University of Maryland also offer baccalaureate programs. Graduate programs are also plentiful. Embry-Riddle Aeronautical University, Ball State University, Boston University, the University of Oklahoma, and the University of Southern California offer degree programs at the master's level. Boston University expands its curriculum to post-master's work, as well. A soldier's choices of graduate (master's and post-master's) programs are somewhat more limited.

As with stateside assignments, soldiers have a wealth of educational opportunities at the high school and Basic Skills Education Program (BSEP) levels.

Japan/Okinawa

Educational opportunities in Japan and Okinawa are more limited than those in Europe. A soldier can still participate in college preparatory programs, however, and language programs include German and Japanese.

The University of Maryland serves this region and offers associate and baccalaureate degrees.

At the master's degree level, the University of Oklahoma and the University of Southern California offer programs. Post-master's programs are not available.

Panama

Soldiers stationed in Panama can take advantage of a full range of course work at the college preparatory level, including BSEP and English as a Second Language (ESL). Vocational/technical training is also available, as is Spanish instruction.

Universities offer a wide range of programs in the area. Florida State University offers certificates and baccalaureate degrees. The Panama Canal College offers certificate programs and associate degrees. Nova University provides baccalaureate and master's degree programs, and the University of Oklahoma offers master's degrees.

Puerto Rico

The on-post educational opportunities in Puerto Rico are quite limited. A full curricular range is available, however, from the associate level to the post-master's level for students willing to travel to off-post campuses located from three to fifty miles from Fort Buchanan.

Only two skill development programs offer certificates on-post. These are Los Angeles Community College and the Manpower Business Training Institute. College preparatory programs on-post include BSEP and ESL. Language training is available in Spanish and German. Off-post universities include Bayamon Central University, Catholic University, Inter-American University, Sacred Heart University, University of Puerto Rico, and World University.

South Korea

Soldiers stationed in South Korea can take advantage of a full range of educational opportunities without leaving the post, whether they are assigned in the northern region (Camp Red Cloud or Camp Greaves), in the southern region (Camp Pusan), or at any of the 12 other camps in between. College preparatory courses, languages (German, Japanese, and Korean), BSEP, and ESL are offered.

Central Texas College offers certificates and associate degrees. The only other associate degree program is offered by the University of Maryland. The University of Maryland also provides opportunities at the baccalaureate level. At the graduate level, two schools are available—the University of Oklahoma and the University of Southern California. Post-master's programs are not available.

4

Excelling

Every day, somewhere in the Army, soldiers are being recognized for outstanding performance. Although these soldiers are from different units and hold different MOSs, they all have one characteristic in common — motivation. Motivation to be the best soldier you can be, skilled and knowledgeable in your assigned duties and in a variety of military subjects, is the way to achieve excellence as a soldier. This excellence will be reflected in your evaluation reports and rewarded by opportunities for recognition and promotion.

Promotions

Moving up through the ranks is important to every soldier. Promotions mean more than an increase in pay. They represent recognition for a job well done, a vote of confidence in future potential, and an increase in responsibility and leadership opportunities. The Army uses promotions not only to fill spaces with qualified soldiers but also to provide career progression for the individual and to recognize those soldiers best qualified to fill higher positions of authority.

The primary qualification for promotion is the mastering of skills needed to perform the duties in the new grade. Technical expertise in the soldier's field of specialization is a consideration in the promotion process, but personal traits, professionalism as a soldier, and leadership are not overlooked. Before you can expect to be promoted, you must be highly proficient in your present grade and level of responsibility.

A soldier may meet all of the minimum time-related requirements for promotion, but may not be ready to assume the higher grade. If the soldier is not recommended for promotion by the commander once he has met minimum eligibility (without waivers), the supervisor is required to counsel the soldier on those areas that are deficient. With weaknesses thus identified, the soldier can begin the process of improvement, setting goals in self-improvement and training, which can lead to a more satisfying military career.

Promotion to Private E-2

The only promotion in the Army that can be said to be automatic is the promotion to private E-2. Once a soldier has been on active duty in the Army for six months, he or she is promoted, unless such promotion is blocked for a serious cause by the unit commander (see Nonpromotable Status in this chapter). Local commanders can, however, promote a deserving soldier faster. Accelerated promotions can be given to a soldier with four months of time in service. The number of these promotions is limited. Not more than 20 percent of privates E-2 who are assigned or attached to a given unit may have less than six months' active duty time.

Training advancements are another manner in which a soldier may be accelerated more quickly than normal. Soldiers in Advanced Individual Training (AIT) or One-Station Unit Training (OSUT) who are assigned to the Fast Track Leader Development Program receive additional instruction during their initial training and, upon completion of four months' service, may be advanced to private E-2. In certain common MOSs, fast track advancements to private first class are authorized.

Promotion to Private First Class

After the initial promotion to private E-2, no other promotions are automatic or mandatory. Promotions to private first class are given on the authority of the unit commander, and accelerated schedules are still possible.

For normal promotion consideration, a soldier must have 12 months of time in service and four months of time in pay grade E-2 to be considered for promotion to private first class. The four months of time in grade can be reduced to two months if the time-in-service requirements are met. No restrictions exist on the time-in-grade reductions.

Accelerated promotions are possible at the discretion of the unit commander when an outstanding soldier has at least six months in service and two months in grade. Only 20 percent of the soldiers assigned or attached to a unit may be privates first class with less than 12 months of service.

Promotion to Specialist and Corporal

Advancement to specialist and corporal is also usually awarded by the unit commander. Normal and accelerated promotions are still possible. The most significant difference between this promotion and earlier promotions is that the soldier may be required to meet a local selection board and to have taken the SDT.

Without any waivers, a soldier can be promoted to specialist or corporal after 24 months in service and six months in grade as a private first class. Half of the time-in-grade requirement can be waived without restrictions.

Outstanding performance can again be recognized through accelerated promotions, with a minimum time-in-service requirement of 12 months and a minimum time-in-grade requirement of three months. Only 20 percent of the soldiers attached or assigned to a unit may hold the specialist or corporal rank with less than 24 months of service.

When time-in-service waivers are to be considered, local commanders can choose to convene a selection board to identify the soldiers most qualified to receive accelerated promotions. Soldiers appearing before the board who are not selected for promotion must be counseled on which areas need improvement. A Report of Board Proceedings and a recommended promotion list must be prepared and maintained in the unit files. (For more information on boards, see *Promotion Boards* and *Board Appearances* in this chapter.)

Promotions to Sergeant and Staff Sergeant

Promotions to sergeant and above are based on an Army-wide point system. Headquarters, Department of the Army, (HQDA) determines the needs of the Army by grade and MOS and establishes promotion cutoff scores accordingly. Cutoff scores for both primary and secondary zone promotions are announced, authorizing commanders to promote the best qualified soldiers Army-wide in each MOS. Only colonels and above are authorized to award promotions to sergeant and staff sergeant.

To qualify for promotion to sergeant and staff sergeant, soldiers must meet certain time-in-service, time-in-grade, and other requirements and appear before a promotion selection board. Waivers are permitted on some requirements, such as time in service and time in grade, but no more than two waivers may be granted to an individual. The requirements for a soldier to be in a promotable status, have the recommendation of the unit commander, and appear before a promotion selection board cannot be waived.

Waivers, which permit promotion from the secondary zone, are reserved for the truly exceptional soldier and must be approved personally by the promotion authority. Promotion from the secondary zone is counted as one of the two allowable waivers.

Secondary zone promotions can be compared to accelerated promotions at the lower grades and are intended to serve as an incentive, a goal for soldiers "who strive for excellence and whose accomplishments, demonstrated capacity for leadership, and marked potential warrant promotion ahead of their peers" (AR 600-200).

To be eligible for consideration for promotion to sergeant, a soldier must have served eight months as a specialist or corporal. For promotion to staff sergeant, the time-in-grade requirement at sergeant is 10 months. Half of the time-in-grade requirement may be waived.

For primary zone consideration for promotion to sergeant, the soldier must have 36 months in service; for secondary zone consideration, the time-in-service requirement is reduced to 24 months. For promotion to staff sergeant, the time-in-service requirements are 84 months (seven years) for the primary zone and 60 months (five years) for the secondary zone. Soldiers can appear before a promotion selection board up to three months before time-in-service requirements are met.

The minimum education requirement for promotion to sergeant and above is a high school diploma or GED equivalent. College course work is rewarded with extra points during the promotion board's review. All soldiers meeting promotion boards must also have completed the NCOES course appropriate for their rank (PLDC for sergeant, BNCOC for staff sergeant). If trends continue, future requirements for promotion for senior NCOs may include an associate degree as the minimum.

Certain MOSs require security clearances or security investigations. In such cases, regulations define levels of clearance required for each rank. Therefore, soldiers must meet the clearance requirements for the grade to which they wish to be promoted. In other words, no soldier can be promoted to sergeant without already having the security clearance appropriate to that grade. No waiver can be granted for security clearances, although an interim clearance may be used if a full clearance is not yet available.

Physical qualifications are also required. Having a permanent physical profile does not restrict a soldier's promotion potential, provided the soldier has been reclassified into an MOS where he meets the physical demands of that occupational specialty. The physical qualifications requirement merely means that the soldier must be able to perform the duties of the MOS and grade for which he seeks promotion. A soldier who does not meet the weight or body fat requirements listed in AR 600-9, the *Army Weight Control Program*, will not be considered for promotion. This requirement may not be waived.

A soldier may be disqualified for promotion based on "moral or administrative" reasons. These include having a court-martial conviction, being AWOL, or having lost time, if any of these occurred during the current term of enlistment.

Waivers may not be granted for the service-remaining obligation. To be promoted to sergeant, a soldier must have three months remaining before his or her expiration of time in service (ETS). To be promoted to staff sergeant, the soldier must have 12 months remaining. Soldiers can extend or reenlist to meet the service-remaining obligation. If a bar to reenlistment or extension exists, the soldier cannot be promoted.

A "position vacancy" at the next higher grade at a local unit is not required. Promotions to sergeant and staff sergeant are based on Army-wide needs.

Promotion Boards

This section includes some general information on the makeup and governance of promotion boards, but soldiers meeting a board for the first time are advised to carefully read the *Board Appearances* section in this chapter.*

Promotion boards are usually convened by the 15th of each month in which soldiers have been recommended for promotion consideration. No prescreening boards can be held before the full promotion board to determine promotion eligibility. By regulation, promotion boards are limited to questions only; other boards can have hands-on requirements, such as Common Task Testing or PT testing.

Each promotion board must have at least one member of the same sex

---

*Another helpful resource when preparing for promotion board appearances is *Soldier's Study Guide, 2nd edition*, by CSM Walter J. Jackson, USA (Ret.). (Harrisburg, Pa.: Stackpole Books, 1993.)

BOARD MEMBER APPRAISAL WORKSHEET
For use of this form, see AR 600-200; the proponent agency is MILPERCEN

NAME (Last, First, MI)	RECOMMENDED GRADE	PRESENT PMOS	RECOMMENDED CPMOS

BOARD INTERVIEW AND EVALUATION

AREAS OF EVALUATION	POINT SPREAD				TOTAL
	AVERAGE	ABOVE AVERAGE	EXCELLENT	OUTSTANDING	
1. PERSONAL APPEARANCE, BEARING AND SELF-CONFIDENCE	1-15 POINTS	16-20 POINTS	21-25 POINTS	26-30 POINTS	
2. ORAL EXPRESSION AND CONVERSATIONAL SKILL	1-15 POINTS	16-25 POINTS	26-30 POINTS	31-35 POINTS	
3. KNOWLEDGE OF WORLD AFFAIRS	1-10 POINTS	11-15 POINTS	16-20 POINTS	21-25 POINTS	
4. AWARENESS OF MILITARY PROGRAMS	1-10 POINTS	11-15 POINTS	16-20 POINTS	21-25 POINTS	
5. KNOWLEDGE OF BASIC SOLDIERING (Soldier's Manual). (See note)	1-15 POINTS	16-25 POINTS	26-35 POINTS	36-45 POINTS	
6. SOLDIER'S ATTITUDE (includes leadership and potential for advancement. Trends in performance, etc.).	1-15 POINTS	16-25 POINTS	26-35 POINTS	36-40 POINTS	
TOTAL POINTS AWARDED					
(MAXIMUM 200 POINTS)					

NOTE: Questions concerning the knowledge of basic soldiering will be tailored to include land navigation, survival, night operations, inclement weather operations, adverse environment and terrain.

REMARKS:

I DO _____ DO NOT _____ RECOMMEND THE SOLDIER FOR PROMOTION

RANK/SIGNATURE OF BOARD MEMBER	DATE

DA FORM 3356
MAR 85

EDITION OF NOV 80 IS OBSOLETE.

Board Member Appraisal Worksheet

as soldiers appearing before the board. In addition, at least one minority ethnic group should be represented on the board, whether or not any soldiers being considered for promotion that month are members of minority ethnic groups. No board can be made up entirely of servicemembers from minority ethnic groups, however.

Board members are appointed to the board by the promotion authority (a field grade officer responsible for promoting soldiers at a given command level). A president of the board, usually the senior member, must be appointed. If the president has voting authority, the voting members must be odd in number so that a tie can never occur. If the president does not have voting authority, he will serve as the tie-breaker in the event a tie vote should occur among voting members. All voting members and the president must be of at least one grade higher than the grade for which selections are being made. Boards can be made up of all officers (commissioned and warrant officers) or can be a mixture of enlisted and officer members. Once a board is convened, each board member must be present to review every candidate for promotion.

The *recorder,* who takes notes on the proceedings, is a board member who has no voting authority; consequently, he or she does not have to be of a grade higher than the promotion grades being considered. Qualifications for the recorder include familiarity with Army personnel procedures. Ideally, the recorder should be from the organization's Personnel Support Center (PSC).

Every board member independently evaluates each soldier, using DA Form 3356 *(Board Member Appraisal Worksheet).* Members rate soldiers through a point system for six broad areas of evaluation:

- Personal appearance, bearing, and self-confidence.
- Oral expression and conversational skill.
- Knowledge of world affairs.
- Awareness of military programs.
- Knowledge of basic soldiering.
- Soldier's attitude, including leadership, potential for advancement, and trends in performance.

For each category, point spreads are given for soldiers rated as average, above average, excellent, and outstanding. The board members first decide which general rating the soldier merits, and then where in the allowable point spread to place the soldier. For instance, a soldier rated "excellent" on oral expression and conversational skill could be awarded 26 to 30. Once a board member had determined the general "excellent" rating, he or she would have to refine that rating further with a numerical score within the allowable spread.

PROMOTION POINT WORKSHEET

For use of this form, see AR 600-8-19; the proponent agency is ODCSPER

1. TYPE	2. DATE
☐ a. Initial ☐ b. Reevaluation ☐ c. Recomputation	

DATA REQUIRED BY THE PRIVACY ACT OF 1974

3. NAME	4. SSN	5. GRADE

6. CURRENT ORGANIZATION	7. SRB MOS	8. PMOS	9. RECOMMENDED GRADE/CPMOS

SECTION A - RECOMMENDATION

10. FROM (Commander)	11. THROUGH (Promotion Authority)	12. TO (PSC)

13. Under the provisions of AR 600-8-19, chapter 3 (Active Army); AR 140-158, chapter 3 (USAR); or NGR 600-200, chapter 6 (ARNG) (check one of the following):

  a. Recommend the above-named soldier for promotion/reevaluation to the grade indicated. (Complete lines 13b (1) - (6) and send to the promotion authority.)

  b. Request the following information be used in the next scheduled recomputation of promotion points. (Complete lines 13(b)(2) - (6) and send to the PSC).

(1) Waivers required (maximum of two allowed)		(2) Most recent individual assigned weapon qualification		(d) DATE
	(a) Time in Service	(a) Expert		
	(b) Time in Grade	(b) Sharpshooter		
	(c) SQT score (59 or below)	(c) Marksman		

(3) Most recent Physical Fitness Test Scores (Minimum score of 60 in each event.)		(4) (a) SOLDIER'S CURRENT SQT SCORE	(4) (b) DATE
	(a) Situps	(5) I certify (Must check one of the following on all recommendations):	
	(b) Pushups	(a) That the soldier has taken an SQT during the most recent test period.	
	(c) Two-Mile Run		
	(d) Total	(e) DATE	(b) That the soldier has not taken an SQT due to no fault of his/her own.

14. REMARKS

  (c) That the soldier failed to take an SQT during the most recent test period due to his/her own fault.

  (6) PROMOTION POINTS AWARDED TO SOLDIER FOR DUTY PERFORMANCE (Maximum 200 points)

15a. SIGNATURE BLOCK OF COMMANDER	15b. SIGNATURE OF COMMANDER	15c. DATE

16a. SIGNATURE BLOCK OF PROMOTION AUTHORITY	16b. SIGNATURE OF PROMOTION AUTHORITY	16c. CHECK ONE ☐ Approved ☐ Disapproved	16d. DATE

SECTION B - ADMINISTRATIVE POINTS

		POINTS GRANTED
1.	DUTY PERFORMANCE - MAXIMUM 200 POINTS (Enter points awarded by Commander for duty performance on promotion recommendation (See Section A, item (13b(6).))	
2.	SKILL QUALIFICATION TEST (SQT) - MAXIMUM 200 POINTS	POINTS GRANTED
a.	Enter the soldier's latest SQT score from the Individual Soldier's Report (ISR), or TSO data, if the score is 60 or higher ⟶ x 2 =	
b.	Enter the number of promotion points granted under the no fault provision.	

DA FORM 3355, APR 91   DA FORM 3355, MAR 85 IS OBSOLETE

Promotion Point Worksheet

3. Awards and Decorations - *Maximum 50 Points*. List and multiply the number of awards received by the number of points authorized for the award as explained in the instructions.

	x	=			x	=			x	=
	x	=			x	=			x	=
	x	=			x	=			x	=

Total Points Granted ⟶

4. Military Education - *Maximum 150 Points*

5. Civilian Education - *Maximum 100 Points*

6. Military Training - *Maximum 100 Points*

5. Civilian Education								6. Military Training	
								a. Marksmanship	
								b. Physical Fitness Test	
Total Points Granted ⟶								c. Total Points ⟶	

7. I certify that the above administrative points shown have been accurately extracted from appropriate records and promotion points indicated are correct.

a. SIGNATURE OF RESPONSIBLE OFFICIAL	b. GRADE	c. DATE	d. SIGNATURE OF RECOMMENDED INDIVIDUAL

SECTION C- TOTALS

Note - *Only the fractional total promotion points in item 3 of this section will be rounded off to the nearest whole number.* A fraction of 5/10 or higher will be rounded up to the next higher whole number. A fraction of 4/10 or less will be rounded down to the next lowest whole number.

		GRANTED
1.	TOTAL ADMINISTRATIVE POINTS - *MAXIMUM 800 POINTS* (Total of items 1 through 6, Section B.)	
2.	TOTAL BOARD POINTS - *MAXIMUM 200 POINTS*	
3.	TOTAL PROMOTION POINTS - *MAXIMUM 1,000 POINTS* (Add items 1 and 2.)	

4. I certify that the total points shown have been accurately extracted from appropriate records and promotion list points indicated are correct.

a. SIGNATURE OF BOARD RECORDER	b. GRADE	c. DATE

5. I certify that the soldier has been recommended for promotion by a valid promotion board.

a. SIGNATURE BLOCK OF PROMOTION AUTHORITY	b. SIGNATURE	c. DATE BOARD PROCEEDINGS WERE APPROVED

6. STATEMENT (Use only when a recommendation is disapproved, when a soldier is not selected by the board, or when the soldier cannot be added to the recommended list due to not attaining the minimum required points.)

"I have been counseled on my promotion status and deficiencies."

a. SIGNATURE OF SOLDIER	b. DATE	c. TYPED OR PRINTED NAME OF COUNSELOR
		d. SIGNATURE OF COUNSELOR

PAGE 2, DA FORM 3355, APR 91

*U.S. Government Printing Office: 1991 — 281-485/40257

Promotion Point Worksheet (continued)

There are 1,000 total points possible for soldiers being evaluated for promotion to sergeant and staff sergeant. Only 200 of these points are awarded by the board; the remaining 800 are administrative points. Each board member awards the soldier up to 200 points. After all board members have evaluated the soldier, the recorder will pick up the forms, tally the vote from the section marked "do/do not recommend the soldier for promotion," and report the majority vote to the president. The president will break the tie if one exists. The recorder then averages the scores of the board (on DA Form 3357) so that the soldier is given a single composite score of not more than 200 from the board's evaluation.

The administrative points are also entered on DA Form 3355 by the recorder; 800 administrative points are the maximum attainable. Administrative points are awarded for the following, listed in order of maximum points possible:

- Duty performance, as awarded by the soldier's commander through the promotion recommendation.
- SDT scores of 60 or above.
- Military education, including NCOES educational courses and other military individual training courses (Ranger School, Special Forces Qualification Course, and correspondence courses).
- Military training, including PT test scores and marksmanship qualification.
- Civilian education.
- Awards and decorations.

Soldiers who are competing for promotions to sergeant must attain a total score of 450 in order to be added to the list of recommended promotions, and they must be recommended by the majority of the board. Soldiers competing for promotions to staff sergeant cannot be added to the list without a total score of 550. The recommended list for promotion will list soldiers by MOS, pay grade, and zone. Within appropriate groups, soldiers will be listed in descending order based on total points.

Promotions are made from this list. Although orders can be issued with future effective dates, soldiers are not eligible for promotion until the first day of the third month following the date of selection. For example, soldiers meeting the board on 15 January are eligible for promotion on 1 April.

Since cutoff scores are established by HQDA separately for each zone, soldiers are transferred on the list from secondary zone to primary zone when they meet the necessary time-in-service requirements. On the first day of a soldier's 33rd month of active duty, his or her name may be

SERVICE SCHOOL ACADEMIC EVALUATION REPORT

For use of this form, see AR 623-1; the proponent agency is MILPERCEN.

DATE

1. LAST NAME - FIRST NAME - MIDDLE INITIAL	2. SSN	3. GRADE	4. BR	5. SPECIALTY/MOSC

6. COURSE TITLE	7. NAME OF SCHOOL	8. COMP

9. TYPE OF REPORT	10. PERIOD OF REPORT (Year, month, day)	11. DURATION OF COURSE (Year, month, day)
☐ RESIDENT	From: Thru:	☒ From: Thru:
☐ NONRESIDENT	12. EXPLANATION OF NONRATED PERIODS	

13. PERFORMANCE SUMMARY

*a. ☐ EXCEEDED COURSE STANDARDS
   (Limited to 20% of class enrollment)

b. ☐ ACHIEVED COURSE STANDARDS

*c. ☐ MARGINALLY ACHIEVED COURSE STANDARDS

*d. ☐ FAILED TO ACHIEVE COURSE STANDARDS

Rating must be supported by comments in ITEM 16.

14. DEMONSTRATED ABILITIES

a. WRITTEN COMMUNICATION
☐ NOT EVALUATED   ☐ UNSAT   ☐ SAT   ☐ SUPERIOR

b. ORAL COMMUNICATION
☐ NOT EVALUATED   ☐ UNSAT   ☐ SAT   ☐ SUPERIOR

c. LEADERSHIP SKILLS
☐ NOT EVALUATED   ☐ UNSAT   ☐ SAT   ☐ SUPERIOR

d. CONTRIBUTION TO GROUP WORK
☐ NOT EVALUATED   ☐ UNSAT   ☐ SAT   ☐ SUPERIOR

e. EVALUATION OF STUDENT'S RESEARCH ABILITY
☐ NOT EVALUATED   ☐ UNSAT   ☐ SAT   ☐ SUPERIOR

(SUPERIOR/UNSAT rating must be supported by comments in ITEM 16)

15. HAS THE STUDENT DEMONSTRATED THE ACADEMIC POTENTIAL FOR SELECTION TO HIGHER LEVEL SCHOOLING/TRAINING?

☐ YES   ☐ NO   ☐ N/A   *(A "NO" response must be supported by comments in ITEM 16)*

16. COMMENTS *(This item is intended to obtain a word picture of each student that will accurately and completely portray academic performance, intellectual qualities, and communication skills and abilities. The narrative should also discuss broader aspects of the student's potential; leadership capabilities, moral and overall professional qualities. In particular, comments should be made if the student failed to respond to recommendations for improving academic or personal affairs)*

17. AUTHENTICATION

a. TYPED NAME, GRADE, BRANCH, AND TITLE OF PREPARING OFFICER | SIGNATURE

b. TYPED NAME, GRADE, BRANCH, AND TITLE OF REVIEWING OFFICER | SIGNATURE

18. MILITARY PERSONNEL OFFICER

a. FORWARDING ADDRESS *(Rated student)*

b. DISTRIBUTION

☐ STUDENT   ☐ UNIT CDR *(P/B NCOES only)*
☐ STUDENT'S OFFICIAL MILITARY RECORDS

DA FORM 1 NOV 77 **1059**   EDITION OF 1 JUL 73 IS OBSOLETE.   8-0478-003

Service School Academic Evaluation Report

transferred from a secondary zone to a primary zone on the promotion list if the promotion being considered is for sergeant. Three months from then (the 36th month), the soldier is eligible for promotion. During the interim three months, the soldier's promotion would be based on the cutoff point for the secondary zone. For promotion to staff sergeant, a soldier's name is moved from the secondary zone to the primary zone in the 81st month, but he or she must still be considered under the point cutoff score for secondary zone until the first day of the 84th month.

Each soldier who appears before a promotion selection board and is not recommended for promotion must be counseled. The individual with promotion authority may choose to counsel the soldier or may appoint another individual to do so. DA Forms 3355, 3356, and 3357, used by the board in its considerations, are to be employed in counseling the soldier. The counselor should point out ways in which the soldier can improve his promotion potential. After the counseling session, both the counselor and the soldier must sign DA Form 3355, which is then filed with the complete board proceedings.

Even after you are on the promotion list, you may request a reevaluation if your administrative points have increased by at least 50. The increase in points must be due to a higher SDT score (or CTT or CE if the SDT was not available); additional awards or decorations; or increases in military or civilian education, or in military training. Soldiers requesting reevaluation may elect to appear before the board, but they are not required to do so.

A new evaluation of the soldier by the board is completely independent of the previous evaluation. Before requesting a reevaluation, a soldier must sign a statement indicating that he or she understands that the evaluation by the new board is final; and that if the new board does not recommend promotion, or awards fewer board points so that the soldier no longer falls within the promotion cutoff score, he or she will then be removed from the promotion list.

The soldier who elects not to appear before the board will have his or her administrative points adjusted and will be eligible for promotion using the higher point total on the first day of the third month after reevaluation. During the interim period, the soldier can still be promoted based on the previous point score.

When administrative points are increased by fewer than 50 points, a soldier may request reevaluation if he or she has been on the list for a minimum of six months. Under these circumstances, however, it is mandatory that the soldier appear before the board a second time. The same criteria apply: the soldier can be removed from the list if not recommended for promotion by the board or if the board awards fewer points and the soldier then does not meet the cutoff score.

Soldiers removed from the promotion list through reevaluation can be considered for promotion by future boards. Such consideration is processed in the same manner as the initial evaluation — initiated through the commander's recommendation.

Placement on a promotion roster does not necessarily mean a quick promotion is ahead. Soldiers may be on the list for more than a year before being promoted. Under such cases, administrative points are recalculated annually without request by the soldier and without action by the board. Soldiers review the recomputation for accuracy and completeness. New scores are added to the next published promotion roster and, like initial scores, become effective three months after being updated on the list. In the interim the soldier can be promoted based on the old score.

Merit Promotions

The Department of the Army recognizes that high cutoff scores have an adverse effect on morale and retention. In some balanced and overstrength MOSs, the cutoff score for promotion is 999 points, effectively blocking promotions in those MOSs. Under the merit promotion system, if an MOS has not been authorized regular Army promotions for a year or more, then one merit promotion per month will be given to the soldier in the MOS with the highest number of promotion points.

In fields in which the specialty is overstrength, the merit system provides an opportunity for truly outstanding junior soldiers to advance.

Promotions under Unusual Circumstances

Once on the promotion list, a soldier may still be promoted while on TDY or on special duty or assignment. The commander of the unit to which the soldier is temporarily attached must verify the soldier's eligibility before promoting him or her. The promotion is not to be withheld simply because the soldier is not at the regularly assigned duty station.

Likewise, soldiers reassigned prior to promotion, who are already on the promotion list, are to be added to the promotion list at the new assignment based on the board recommendation from the previous assignment. No board action is required for this transaction.

If a soldier becomes eligible for promotion to sergeant or staff sergeant by meeting the cutoff score while in transit between assignments, he or she will be promoted at the new assignment by the promoting authority there. This differs somewhat for promotions to private E-2 through corporal; these soldiers are promoted by the Commander, PERSCOM, if they meet eligibility, without waiver, while in transit status.

Commanders of local medical facilities will promote soldiers hospitalized with serious illnesses or injuries received in the line of duty when those soldiers become eligible to be promoted from the recommended list. This ruling applies to privates first class who are recommended by their unit commanders for promotion to specialist or corporal, as well as to specialists, corporals, or sergeants on the list for promotion to sergeant or staff sergeant.

Nonpromotable Status

The fact that a soldier has received a commander's recommendation for promotion or has been placed on a promotion list does not guarantee promotion. Under certain circumstances, a soldier can be assigned nonpromotable status or removed from a promotion standing list. No promotion will then be made, regardless of previous decisions, until this designation, or "flag," is removed.

A soldier becomes nonpromotable ("flagged") when he or she:

- Is AWOL.
- Is in civilian or military confinement (placed under arrest or in a jail).
- Has deserted.
- Is ill or injured *not in the line of duty.*
- Is under court-martial charges.
- Is serving a court-martial sentence, including a suspended sentence.
- Is undergoing proceedings that may result in other than honorable discharge.
- Has received a Report for Suspension of Favorable Personnel Actions (DA Form 268).
- Is being considered for a DA Form 268 by an officer having general court-martial (or higher) authority.
- Is recommended for reclassification due to inefficiency or disciplinary reasons. (A letter must be sent to the promotion authority under this condition before the soldier is nonpromotable.)
- Is being punished under Article 15, even if the punishment is suspended.
- Is not qualified for reenlistment.
- Cannot receive an appropriate security clearance or favorable security investigation for the promotion grade for which he is being considered.

- Is recommended for a reduction in grade. (A letter must be sent to the promotion authority before the soldier is nonpromotable; then the promotion authority must decide whether to convene a board to consider the reduction in grade.)
- Fails to take the SDT through his or her own fault.
- Does not have necessary qualifications or formal training required for his or her career specialty.
- Exceeds the Army weight standards or the body fat requirements.
- Fails the semi-annual APFT, but does not have a medical exemption such as a physical profile.
- Has not taken the APFT during the past six months (exceptions are made for circumstances beyond the control of the individual).

A soldier may be removed from nonpromotable status when the following conditions are met, as applicable: confinement ends; the court-martial sentence or Article 15 punishment is completed; proceedings against the soldier are completed but do not result in a discharge; Army weight and body fat requirements are met; or necessary tests, clearances, or qualifications are achieved.

Other conditions for removal from nonpromotable status apply for special cases. Reports for Suspension of Favorable Personnel Actions (flags) contain an effective time frame; when the suspension is over, the soldier is again promotable. Soldiers being reclassified must compete under their new MOS classification; the nonpromotable status applies to the old MOS specialty. Soldiers failing to take the SDT through their own fault are again promotable once they take the test. If, however, the SDT is no longer available for their MOS, these soldiers may have to wait up to one year before regaining promotable status.

Board Appearances

Boards are standard procedure within the Army structure for the selection of the best-qualified individuals for promotions and awards, and school and training selection. In addition to promotion boards, local boards are held to recommend soldiers for Soldier or NCO of the Month. Boards are convened at the Department of the Army level to consider senior NCOs for promotion, schools, separation, and assignments.

You may have the opportunity to appear before a Soldier of the Month board before you are eligible to meet a promotion board. Although board guidelines vary slightly from post to post, most Soldier of the Month boards are created to identify and recognize individual soldiers who have demonstrated exemplary conduct, efficiency, appearance, and overall military performance. Generally, specialists and below compete for Soldier of the Month, and corporals, sergeants, and staff sergeants compete for NCO of the Month. Often, however, promotable specialists will also compete on the NCO boards. These boards are normally composed of three or more voting members; frequently the first sergeant of the headquarters company for the post serves as board president.

Appearing before a board is an excellent way to demonstrate your potential. The ability to go before a Soldier of the Month board and present yourself as a knowledgeable and highly confident soldier marks you as someone ready for better things. Your leaders remember the achievers.

Many young soldiers shy away from appearing before boards until they must report to a promotion board. This is the wrong attitude; the worst that can happen at a board is that you won't come out in first place. Every time you appear before a board you increase your knowledge and experience, and you make yourself visible to those who can help you get ahead.

Since board appearances play such an important role in the advancement of your Army career, it is in your best interest to prepare for them carefully.

Getting Ready

The proper attitude is essential when preparing for a board appearance. You should pay special attention to your appearance, knowledge, and personal conduct long before the board convenes. Boards evaluate your performance as a soldier as well as your presentation at the board.

Thorough preparation requires careful study of a variety of subjects.* You should be prepared to answer questions on military subjects, traditions, your chain of command and NCO support channel, and current events. You must also take time to prepare your uniform properly, as discussed later in this section.

Practice aloud reciting from memory such things as the three general orders, the code of conduct, your unit motto, and other "instant recall" types of questions. This will help you build confidence because you will be able to express what you are thinking.

On the day before the board, get a fresh haircut. If you have a mustache or sideburns, make sure that they are well within the limits of the regulation.

---

*A helpful resource is *Soldier's Study Guide, 2nd edition*, by CSM Walter J. Jackson, USA (Ret.). (Harrisburg, Pa.: Stackpole Books, 1993).

One last tip: Get a good night's sleep the evening before the board. Pulling an all-nighter is unlikely to improve your performance at the board. If you have prepared properly, it will be unnecessary for you to spend extra hours studying. If you aren't prepared, the extra hours won't help.

What to Study

Since each board is different, it is impossible to create a definitive list of topics from which the questions will be derived. However, three board areas stand out: general military subjects, MOS job skill knowledge, and current events.

General Military Knowledge

A partial list of general military subjects would include the following:

Adverse Environment and Terrain	Military Customs/Courtesies
Code of Conduct	Military Intelligence
Drills & Ceremonies	Military Justice (UCMJ)
Field Sanitation	Military Tactics
First Aid	Military Unit History
Flags	M16 Rifle
Geneva Convention	NBC Operations
Guard Duty	Night Operations
Inclement Weather Operations	Supply (economy)
Leadership	Survival
Map Reading	

Although the list appears large, you probably know more than you think. By hitting the books for some refresher study well in advance of your board appearance, you will be prepared and confident of your knowledge. Start by studying the *Soldier's Manual of Common Tasks* (STP-21-1 SMCT) for your skill level. Other useful material will be found in the following FMs:

- FM 100-1, *The Army.*
- FM 22-102, *Soldier Team Development.*
- FM 100-5, *Operations.*
- FM 22-100, *Military Leadership.*
- FM 22-101, *Leadership Counseling.*
- FM 22-5, *Drill and Ceremony.*

- FM 21-20, *Physical Fitness Training.*
- FM 23-9, *M16A1 and M16A2 Rifle Marksmanship.*
- FM 25-100, *Training the Force.*
- FM 25-101, *Battle Focused Training.*

MOS Job Skill Knowledge

You should take special care to review the *Soldiers Manual* for the appropriate skill level. Be familiar with your own job book and the requirements of your current MOS skill level. In addition, the job description of the next higher grade for your MOS (as provided in AR 611-201) is an excellent source of study before meeting the board.

Current Events

Current events topics can include any local, state, national, or international event that has been reported frequently in the newspapers, broadcast media, or newsmagazines. Good sources for keeping abreast of current events are *USA Today,* a national newspaper providing coverage of national and international news; *Army Times,* for military news; the local newspaper, for community affairs; and the post newspaper and unit bulletin board for matters even closer to home. You can supplement your reading by listening to both local and national news broadcasts.

Don't wait until a few days before the board convenes to start following current events. "Cramming" will only leave you confused and nervous during your appearance before the board.

Preparing the Uniform

An impeccably dressed soldier makes a positive first impression that can be persuasive. Therefore, great care should be taken with the uniform.

Be sure to consult AR 670-1, *Wear and Appearance of Army Uniforms and Insignia.* You should also refer to AR 672-5-1, *Military Awards*; and to AR 672-8, *Manufacture, Sale, Wearing, and Quality Control of Heraldic Items.* You may, depending on the unit you are assigned to, also need to check DA Pams 672-1 and 672-3, *The Unit Citation and Campaign Participation Credit Registers, WWII and Korea.* To make sure your uniform is fitted properly, you may check TM 10-277, *Fitting of Army Uniforms and Footwear.*

Often a soldier will put a set of Class A uniforms aside for special occasions, such as boards or parades. Make sure that your uniform is clean and pressed and that it is properly fitted. If possible, you should carry the uniform to the board site and dress there, 30 minutes before your scheduled appearance before the board. After dressing, you shouldn't sit down.

Don't pull a loose thread from your uniform. You may cause a seam to open or a button to fall off. Loose threads should be cut off. Also, a few paper clips dropped in the uniform pocket can avert an embarrassing moment if one of the button backings breaks right before you are to report to the board.

Check to make sure that you have the proper awards, unit crests, and patches and that they are correctly placed on the uniform. Carry a few small erasers to replace insignia or ribbon backings if they should be lost.

Finally, do not eat, drink, or smoke once you have put on your uniform. A spill or a few crumbs from a doughnut, or foul smell, could ruin your hours of preparation.

Reporting to the Board

On the day of the board, most candidates are extremely nervous. But if you are well prepared and confident, you can relax and expect success.

Candidates should knock on the door of the board room and enter when directed. When approaching the president of the board, use distinct, crisp movements. Generally, the president of the board will be flanked by other board members. You should come to attention in front of the president, render a hand salute (holding it until returned by the president), and report. The next move should be directed by the president.

Responding to the Board

All board members will evaluate the candidate on his or her military bearing, uniform and appearance, oral presentation, and knowledge of general topics such as chain of command, current events, and Army programs. In addition, each board member will ask the candidate several specific questions covering a wide range of military subjects. Only the member asking the specific question will evaluate the candidate's response.

Candidates should preface responses to board members with the proper rank of the individual (i.e., "sergeant major," "first sergeant," or "sergeant," as appropriate).

Remember these tips when reporting to the board or answering questions:

- Speak in a firm, clear voice.
- Do not mumble.
- Do not use profanity.

- When you are addressed, look at the questioner and maintain eye contact when you give your answer.
- If you don't know the answer to a question, don't try to bluff through it. An incorrect or made-up answer is more damaging than an honest, straightforward, "Sergeant, I do not know the answer to your question."
- Be conscious of, and avoid, any nervous habits you might have. Bouncing your knees, overused gestures, and fingerpointing should be avoided.

Dismissal by the Board

Once the president has indicated that the board has concluded its questioning, the candidate should come to attention in front of the president, render a hand salute, hold the salute until it is returned by the president, and then exit the room and close the door. Crisp movements during the exit create a final positive image.

After exiting the room, you should not discuss questions with other candidates. Doing so only gives an advantage to the competitors.

Noncommissioned Officer Evaluation Reporting System

No other document affects soldiers' careers as much as DA Form 2166-7, the *Noncommissioned Officer Evaluation Report* (NCOER). NCOERs are prepared for all noncommissioned officers, sergeant through command sergeant major. Corporals and below do not receive an NCOER. Corporals are "evaluated" using the NCOER Counseling Form, DA Form 2166-7-1. Every junior soldier should become familiar with the NCOER, however, because it lists evaluated traits every good soldier should possess. Ask your personnel sergeant for a blank NCOER form and study it—ask your supervising NCO about it—to give yourself an edge on your future as an NCO.

The purpose of the NCOER is to evaluate duty performance, professionalism, and advancement potential. Through this system the senior enlisted leadership for the Army is determined and developed. The NCOER is used in conjunction with other qualifications and the needs of the Army to determine a broad spectrum of actions directly influencing soldiers' careers. Among these actions are promotions, school selections, MOS classifications, and future assignments.*

*Helpful information on how to make the most of a career as an NCO can be found in *NCO Guide, 4th edition* revised by Frank Cox. (Harrisburg, Pa.: Stackpole Books, 1992.)

PART I - ADMINISTRATIVE DATA

a. NAME (Last, First, Middle Initial)			b. SSN		c. RANK		d. DATE OF RANK	e. PMOSC

| f. UNIT, ORG., STATION, ZIP CODE OR APO, MAJOR COMMAND | | | | | | g. REASON FOR SUBMISSION | |

h. PERIOD COVERED		i. RATED MONTHS	j. NON-RATED CODES	k. NO. OF ENCL	l. RATED NCO COPY (Check one and Date)		m. PSC Initials	n. CMD CODE	o. PSC CODE
FROM	THRU				1. Given to NCO	Date			
YY MM	YY MM				2. Forwarded to NCO				

PART II - AUTHENTICATION

a. NAME OF RATER (Last, First, Middle Initial)	SSN	SIGNATURE	
RANK, PMOSC/BRANCH, ORGANIZATION, DUTY ASSIGNMENT			DATE

b. NAME OF SENIOR RATER (Last, First, Middle Initial)	SSN	SIGNATURE	
RANK, PMOSC/BRANCH, ORGANIZATION, DUTY ASSIGNMENT			DATE

c. RATED NCO: I understand my signature does not constitute agreement or disagreement with the evaluations of the rater and senior rater. Part I, height/weight and APFT entries are verified. I have seen this report completed through Part V. I am aware of the appeals process (AR 623-205).	SIGNATURE	DATE
d. NAME OF REVIEWER (Last, First, Middle Initial) SSN	SIGNATURE	
RANK, PMOSC/BRANCH, ORGANIZATION, DUTY ASSIGNMENT		DATE

e. ☐ CONCUR WITH RATER AND SENIOR RATER EVALUATIONS   ☐ NONCONCUR WITH RATER AND/OR SENIOR RATER EVAL (See attached comments)

PART III - DUTY DESCRIPTION (Rater)

a. PRINCIPAL DUTY TITLE	b. DUTY MOSC

c. DAILY DUTIES AND SCOPE (To include, as appropriate, people, equipment, facilities and dollars)

d. AREAS OF SPECIAL EMPHASIS

e. APPOINTED DUTIES

f. Counseling dates from checklist/record	INITIAL	LATER	LATER	LATER

PART IV - VALUES/NCO RESPONSIBILITIES (Rater)

a. Complete each question. (Comments are mandatory for "No" entries; optional for "Yes" entries.)

		YES	NO
1. Places dedication and commitment to the goals and missions of the Army and nation above personal welfare.	1		
2. Is committed to and shows a sense of pride in the unit - works as a member of the team.	2		
3. Is disciplined and obedient to the spirit and letter of a lawful order.	3		
4. Is honest and truthful in word and deed.	4		
5. Maintains high standards of personal conduct on and off duty.	5		
6. Has the courage of convictions and the ability to overcome fear - stands up for and does, what's right.	6		
7. Supports EO/EEO	7		

V A L U E S

PERSONAL
Commitment
Competence
Candor
Courage

ARMY ETHIC
Loyalty
Duty
Selfless Service
Integrity

Bullet comments

DA FORM 2166-7, SEP 87   REPLACES DA FORM 2166-6, OCT 81, WHICH IS OBSOLETE

NCO Evaluation Report

RATED NCO'S NAME (Last, First, Middle Initial)	SSN	THRU DATE

PART IV (Rater) - VALUES/NCO RESPONSIBILITIES

Specific Bullet examples of "EXCELLENCE" or "NEEDS IMPROVEMENT" are mandatory.
Specific Bullet examples of "SUCCESS" are optional.

b. COMPETENCE

- o Duty proficiency; MOS competency
- o Technical & tactical; knowledge, skills, and
  abilities
- o Sound judgment
- o Seeking self-improvement; always learning
- o Accomplishing tasks to the fullest capacity;
  committed to excellence

EXCELLENCE	SUCCESS	NEEDS IMPROVEMENT	
(Exceeds std)	(Meets std)	(Some)	(Much)
☐	☐	☐	☐

APFT	HEIGHT/WEIGHT

c. PHYSICAL FITNESS & MILITARY BEARING

- o Mental and physical toughness
- o Endurance and stamina to go the distance
- o Displaying confidence and enthusiasm;
  looks like a soldier

EXCELLENCE	SUCCESS	NEEDS IMPROVEMENT	
(Exceeds std)	(Meets std)	(Some)	(Much)
☐	☐	☐	☐

d. LEADERSHIP

- o Mission first
- o Genuine concern for soldiers
- o Instilling the spirit to achieve and win
- o Setting the example; Be, Know, Do

EXCELLENCE	SUCCESS	NEEDS IMPROVEMENT	
(Exceeds std)	(Meets std)	(Some)	(Much)
☐	☐	☐	☐

e. TRAINING

- o Individual and team
- o Mission focused; performance oriented
- o Teaching soldiers how; common tasks,
  duty-related skills
- o Sharing knowledge and experience to fight,
  survive and win

EXCELLENCE	SUCCESS	NEEDS IMPROVEMENT	
(Exceeds std)	(Meets std)	(Some)	(Much)
☐	☐	☐	☐

f. RESPONSIBILITY & ACCOUNTABILITY

- o Care and maintenance of equip./facilities
- o Soldier and equipment safety
- o Conservation of supplies and funds
- o Encouraging soldiers to learn and grow
- o Responsible for good, bad, right & wrong

EXCELLENCE	SUCCESS	NEEDS IMPROVEMENT	
(Exceeds std)	(Meets std)	(Some)	(Much)
☐	☐	☐	☐

PART V - OVERALL PERFORMANCE AND POTENTIAL

a. RATER. Overall potential for promotion and/
or service in positions of greater responsibility.

AMONG THE BEST	FULLY CAPABLE	MARGINAL
☐	☐	☐

e. SENIOR RATER BULLET COMMENTS

b. RATER. List 3 positions in which the rated
NCO could best serve the Army at his/her
current or next higher grade.

_____

_____

_____

c. SENIOR RATER. Overall performance	1 2 3 4 5 Successful Fair Poor	d. SENIOR RATER. Overall potential for promotion and/or service in positions of greater responsibility.	1 2 3 4 5 Superior Fair Poor

NCO Evaluation Report (continued)

Evaluation Procedures

In order for the NCOER to have as positive an influence as possible on your career, it is important that you understand the criteria used in the evaluation and the way in which the evaluation is conducted and reviewed. The basic areas evaluated are daily performance of duties, professionalism as a soldier, and personal traits. The evaluation includes your weaknesses as well as your strengths, abilities, and potential.

According to DA Circular 623-88-1, the NCOER is designed to be comprehensive, accurate, complete, thoughtful, and fair in its appraisal. The general philosophy is *not* one of expecting perfection from each servicemember but rather of fostering an environment for continuous professional development and growth.

The evaluation process must include career development counseling by the rater. This mandatory initial and quarterly counseling is vital because it provides the best way for you to increase your understanding of what is expected of you. The counseling will be documented on the *NCO Counseling Checklist/Record,* DA Form 2166-7-1. Through counseling on a regular basis before the evaluation is given, you will be informed of precisely what the Army and your superiors expect of you, and you will have ample time to improve areas identified as weaknesses.

Each NCO's evaluation is carefully monitored by the soldier's chain of command. Some commands firmly enforce the mandatory NCOER counseling requirements; others do not, unfortunately. If you are in the latter type of command, bring the matter to the attention of your chain of command, beginning with your immediate supervisor. Soldiers who are not counseled properly are not rated properly, generally speaking. If you are a corporal or sergeant and are not counseled within the first 30 days of arrival at your new duty station (and quarterly thereafter), your rater will have real difficulty documenting your accomplishments on the NCOER, or NCOER Counseling Form, if you are a corporal.

The rater must have been the first-line supervisor of the rated soldier for at least three months and must be senior to the rated soldier either by grade or by date of rank. A senior rater and a reviewer are involved in the process in order to keep the NCOER as objective as possible and to evaluate the rated NCO's potential for future service. In the event the NCO disagrees with the evaluation, an appeals process is available.

The chain of command/supervision is the most common model for the rating chain. Indeed, by DA Circular 623-88-1, the rating chain should correspond as nearly as possible to the chain of command within the organization. The rating chain, by name or duty position, is also required to be published and posted within the unit, so that each soldier knows in advance who will be his rater, senior rater, and reviewer. In addition, DA

NCO COUNSELING CHECKLIST/RECORD

For use of this form, see AR 623-205; the proponent agency MILPERCEN

NAME OF RATED NCO	RANK	DUTY POSITION	UNIT

PURPOSE: The primary purpose of counseling is to improve performance and to professionally develop the rated NCO. The best counseling is always looking forward. It does not dwell on the past and on what was done, rather on the future and what can be done better. Counseling at the end of the rating period is too late since there is no time to improve before evaluation.

RULES:

1. Face-to-face performance counseling is mandatory for all Noncommissioned Officers.
2. This form is for use along with a working copy of the NCO-ER for conducting NCO performance counseling and recording counseling content and dates. Its use is mandatory for counseling all NCOs, CPL thru SFC/PSG, and is optional for counseling other senior NCOs.
3. Active Component. Initial counseling must be conducted within the first 30 days of each rating period, and at least quarterly thereafter. Reserve Components. (ARNG, USAR). Counseling must be conducted at least semiannually. There is no mandatory counseling at the end of the rating period.

CHECKLIST – FIRST COUNSELING SESSION AT THE BEGINNING OF THE RATING PERIOD

PREPARATION

1. Schedule counseling session, notify rated NCO.
2. Get copy of last duty description used for rated NCO's duty position, a blank copy of the NCO-ER, and the names of the new rating chain.
3. Update duty description (see page 2).
4. Fill out rating chain and duty description on working copy of NCO-ER. Parts II and III.
5. Read each of the values/responsibilities in Part IV of NCO-ER and the expanded definitions and examples on page 3 and 4 of this form.
6. Think how each value and responsibility in Part IV of NCO-ER applies to the rated NCO and his/her duty position.
Note: Leadership and training may be more difficult to apply than the other values/responsibilities when the rated NCO has no subordinates. Leadership is simply influencing others in the accomplishment of the mission and that can include peers and superiors. It also can be applied directly to additional duties and other areas of Army community life. Individual training is the responsibility of all NCOs whether or not there are subordinates. Every NCO knows something that can be taught to others and should be involved in some way in a training program.
7. Decide what you consider necessary for success (a meets standards rating) for each value/responsibility. Use the examples listed on pages 3 and 4 of this form as a guide in developing your own standards for success. Some may apply exactly, but you may have to change them or develop new ones that apply to your situation. Be specific so the rated NCO will know what is expected.
8. Make notes in blank spaces in Part IV of NCO-ER to help when counseling.
9. Review counseling tips in FM 22-101.

COUNSELING

1. Make sure rated NCO knows rating chain.
2. Show rated NCO the draft duty description on your working copy of the NCO-ER. Explain all parts. If rated NCO performed in position before, ask for any ideas to make duty description better.
3. Discuss the meaning of each value/responsibility in Part IV of NCO-ER. Use the trigger words on the NCO-ER, and the expanded definitions on pages 3 and 4 of this form to help.
4. Explain how each value/responsibility applies to the specific duty position by showing or telling your standards for success (a meets standards rating). Use examples on pages 3 and 4 of this form as a start point. Be specific so the rated NCO really knows what's expected.
5. When possible, give specific examples of excellence that could apply. This gives the rated NCO something special to strive for, Remember that only a few achieve real excellence and that real excellence always includes specific results and often includes accomplishments of subordinates.
6. Give rated NCO opportunity to ask questions and make suggestions.

AFTER COUNSELING

1. Record rated NCO's name and counseling date on this form.
2. Write key points made in counseling session on this form.
3. Show key points to rated NCO and get his initials.
4. Save NCO-ER with this checklist for next counseling session.

CHECKLIST – LATER COUNSELING SESSIONS DURING THE RATING PERIOD

PREPARATION

1. Schedule counseling session, notify rated NCO, and tell him/her to come prepared to discuss what has been accomplished in each value/responsibility area.
2. Look at working copy of NCO-ER you used during last counseling session.
3. Read and update duty description. Especially note the area of special emphasis; the priorities may have changed.
4. Read again, each of the values/responsibilities in Part IV of NCO-ER and the expanded definitions and examples on pages 3 and 4 of this form; then think again, about your standards for success.
5. Look over the notes you wrote down on page 2 of this form about the last counseling session.
6. Think about what the rated NCO has done so far during this rating period (specifically, observed action, demonstrated behavior, and results).
7. For each value/responsibility area, answer three questions: First, what has happened in response to any discussion you had during the last counseling session? Second, what has been done well?; and Third, what could be done better?
8. Make notes in blank spaces in Part IV of NCO-ER to help focus when counseling. (Use new NCO-ER if old one is full from last counseling session).
9. Review counseling tips in FM 22-101.

DA FORM 2166-7-1, AUG 87

NCO Counseling Checklist/Record

COUNSELING

1. Go over each part of the duty description with rated NCO. Discuss any changes, especially to the area of special emphasis.

2. Tell rated NCO how he/she is doing. Use your success standards as a guide for the discussion (the examples on pages 3 and 4 may help). First, for each value/responsibility, talk about what has happened in response to any discussion you had during the last counseling session (remember, observed action, demonstrated behavior and results). Second, talk about what was done well. Third, talk about how to do better. The goal is to get all NCOs to be successful and meet standards.

3. When possible, give examples of excellence that could apply. This gives the rated NCO something to strive for, REMEMBER, EXCELLENCE IS SPECIAL, ONLY A FEW ACHIEVE IT! Excellence includes results and often involves subordinates.

4. Ask rated NCO for ideas, examples and opinions on what has been done so far and what can be done better. (This step can be done first or last).

AFTER COUNSELING

1. Record counseling date on this form.

2. Write key points made in counseling session on this form.

3. Show key points to rated NCO and get his initials.

4. Save NCO-ER with this checklist for next counseling session. (Notes should make record NCO-ER preparation easy at end of rating period).

COUNSELING RECORD

DATE OF COUNSELING	RATED NCO's INITIALS	KEY POINTS MADE
INITIAL		
LATER		
LATER		
LATER		

DUTY DESCRIPTION (PART III of NCO-ER)

The duty description is essential to performance counseling and evaluation. It is used during the first counseling session to tell rated NCO what the duties are and what needs to be emphasized. It may change somewhat during the rating period. It is used at the end of the rating period to record what was important about the duties.

The five elements of the duty description:

1 & 2. Principal Duty Title and Duty MOS Code. Enter principal duty title and DMOS that most accurately reflects actual duties performed.

3. Daily Duties and Scope. This portion should address the most important routine duties and responsibilities. Ideally, this should include number of people supervised, equipment, facilities, and dollars involved and any other routine duties and responsibilities critical to mission accomplishment.

4. Area of Special Emphasis. This portion is most likely to change somewhat during the rating period. For the first counseling session, it includes those items that require top priority effort at least for the first part of the upcoming rating period. At the end of the rating period, it should include the most important items that applied at any time during the rating period (examples are preparation for REFORGER deployment, combined arms drills training for FTX, preparation for NTC rotation, revision of battalion maintenance SOP, training for tank table qualification, ITEP and company AMTP readiness, related tasks cross-training, reserve components annual training support (AT) and SIDPERS acceptance rate).

5. Appointed Duties. This portion should include those duties that are appointed and are not normally associated with the duty description.

NCO Counseling Checklist/Record (continued)

VALUES: Values are what soldiers, as a profession, judge to be right. They are the moral, ethical, and professional attributes of character. They are the heart and soul of a great Army. Part IVa of the NCO-ER includes some of the most important values. These are: Putting the welfare of the nation, the assigned mission and teamwork before individual interests; Exhibiting absolute honesty and courage to stand up for what is right; Developing a sense of obligation and support between those who are led, those who lead, and those who serve alongside; Maintaining high standards of personal conduct on and off duty; And finally, demonstrating obedience, total adherence to the spirit and letter of a lawful order, discipline, and ability to overcome fear despite difficulty or danger.

Examples of standards for "YES" ratings:

- Put the Army, the mission and subordinates first before own personal interest.
- Meet challenges without compromising integrity.
- Personal conduct, both on and off duty, reflects favorably on NCO corps.
- Obey lawful orders and do what is right without orders.
- Choose the hard right over the easy wrong.
- Exhibit pride in unit, be a team player.
- Demonstrate respect for all soldiers regardless of race, creed, color, sex, or national origin.

COMPETENCE: The knowledge, skills and abilities necessary to be expert in the current duty assignment and to perform adequately in other assignments within the MOS when required. Competence is both technical and tactical and includes reading, writing, speaking and basic mathematics. It also includes sound judgment, ability to weigh alternatives, form objective opinions and make good decisions. Closely allied with competence is the constant desire to be better, to listen and learn more and to do each task completely to the best of one's ability. Learn, grow, set standards, and achieve them, create and innovate, take prudent risks, never settle for less than best. Committed to excellence.

Examples of standards for "Success/Meets Standards" rating:

- Master the knowledge, skills and abilities required for performance in your duty position.
- Meet PMOS SQT standards for your grade.
- Accomplish completely and promptly those tasks assigned or required by duty position.
- Constantly seek ways to learn, grow and improve.

Examples of "Excellence":

- Picked as SSG to be a platoon sergeant over twelve other SSGs.
- Maintained SIDPERS rating of 98% for six months.
- Scored 94% on last SQT.
- Selected best truck master in annual battalion competition.
- Designated Installation Drill Sergeant of Quarter.
- Exceeded recruiting objectives two consecutive quarters.
- Awarded Expert Infantryman Badge (EIB).

PHYSICAL FITNESS AND MILITARY BEARING: Physical fitness is the physical and mental ability to accomplish the mission – combat readiness. Total fitness includes weight control, diet and nutrition, smoking cessation, control of substance abuse, stress management, and physical training. It covers strength, endurance, stamina, flexibility, speed, agility, coordination and balance. NCOs are responsible for their own physical fitness and that of their subordinates. Military Bearing consists of posture, dress, overall appearance, and manner of physical movement. Bearing also includes an outward display of inner-feelings, fears, and overall confidence and enthusiasm. An inherent NCO responsibility is concern with the military bearing of the individual soldier, to include on-the-spot corrections.

Examples of standards for "Success/Meets Standards" rating:

- Maintain weight within Army limits for age and sex.
- Obtain passing score in APFT and participate in a regular exercise program.
- Maintain personal appearance and exhibit enthusiasm to the point of setting an example for junior enlisted soldiers.
- Monitor and encourage improvement in the physical and military bearing of subordinates.

Examples of "Excellence":

- Received Physical Fitness Badge for 292 score on APFT.
- Selected soldier of the month/quarter/year.
- Three of the last four soldiers of the month were from his/ her platoon.
- As Master Fitness Trainer, established battalion physical fitness program.
- His entire squad was commended for scoring above 270 on APFT.

NCO Counseling Checklist/Record (continued)

LEADERSHIP: Influencing others to accomplish the mission. It consists of applying leadership attributes (Beliefs, Values, Ethics, Character, Knowledge, and Skills). It includes setting tough, but achievable standards and demanding that they be met; Caring deeply and sincerely for subordinates and their families and welcoming the opportunity to serve them; Conducting counseling; Setting the example by word and act/deed; Can be summarized by BE (Committed to the professional Army ethic and professional traits); KNOW (The factors of leadership, yourself, human nature, your job, and your unit); DO (Provide direction, implement, and motivate). Instill the spirit to achieve and win: Inspire and develop excellence. A soldier cared for today, leads tomorrow.

Examples of standards for "Success/Meets Standards" rating:

- Motivate subordinates to perform to the best of their ability as individuals and together as a disciplined cohesive team to accomplish the mission.
- Demonstrate that you care deeply and sincerely for soldiers and welcome the opportunity to serve them.
- Instill the spirit to achieve and win; Inspire and develop excellence through counseling.
- Set the example: BE, KNOW, DO.

Examples of "Excellence":

- Motivated entire squad to qualify expert with M-16.
- Won last three platoon quad inspections.
- Selected for membership in Sergeant Morales Club.
- Inspired mechanics to maintain operational readiness rating of 95% for two consecutive quarters.
- Led his squad through map orienteering course to win the battalion competition.
- Counseled two marginal soldiers ultimately selected for promotion.

TRAINING: Preparing individuals, units and combined arms teams for duty performance; The teaching of skills and knowledge. NCOs contribute to team training, are often responsible for unit training (Squads, Crews, Sections), but individual training is the most important, exclusive responsibility of the NCO Corps. Quality training bonds units: Leads directly to good discipline; Concentrates on wartime missions; Is tough and demanding without being reckless; Is performance oriented; Sticks to Army doctrine to standardize what is taught to fight, survive, and win, as small units when AirLand battle actions dictate. "Good training means learning from mistakes and allowing plenty of room for professional growth. Sharing knowledge and experience is the greatest legacy one can leave subordinates."

Examples of standards for "Success/Meets Standards" rating:

- Make sure soldiers-
  a. Can do identified common tasks.
  b. Are prepared for SQT and Commander's Evaluation.
  c. Develop and practice skills for duty position.
  d. Train as a squad/crew/section.
- Identify and recommend subordinates for professional development courses.
- Participate in unit training program.
- Share knowledge and experience with subordinates.

Examples of "Excellence":

- Taught five common tasks resulting in 100% GO on Annual CTT for all soldiers in directorate.
- Trained best howitzer section of the year in battalion.
- Coached subordinates to win consecutive soldier of month competitions.
- Established company Expert Field Medical Badge program resulting in 85% of all eligible soldiers receiving EFMB.
- Distinguished 1 tank and qualified 3 tanks in platoon on first run of tank table VIII.
- Trained platoon to fire honor battery during annual service practice.

RESPONSIBILITY AND ACCOUNTABILITY: The proper care, maintenance, use, handling, and conservation of personnel, equipment, supplies, property, and funds. Maintenance of weapons, vehicles, equipment, conservation of supplies, and funds is a special NCO responsibility because of its links to the success of all missions, especially those on the battlefield. It includes inspecting soldier's equipment often, using manual or checklist; Holding soldiers responsible for repairs and losses; Learning how to use and maintain all the equipment soldiers use; Being among the first to operate new equipment; Keeping up-to-date component lists; Setting aside time for inventories; and Knowing the readiness status of weapons, vehicles, and other equipment. It includes knowing where each soldier is during duty hours; Why he is going on sick call, where he lives, and his family situation; It involves reducing accidental manpower and monetary losses by providing a safe and healthful environment; It includes creating a climate which encourages young soldiers to learn and grow, and, to report serious problems without fear of repercussions. Also, NCOs must accept responsibility for their own actions and for those of their subordinates.

Examples of standards for "Success/Meets Standards" rating:

- Make sure your weapons, equipment, and vehicles are serviceable, maintained and ready for accomplishing the mission.
- Stop waste of supplies and limited funds.
- Be aware of those things that impact on soldier readiness e.g., family affairs, SQT, CTT, PQR, special duty, medical conditions, etc.
- Be responsible for your actions and those of your subordinates.

Examples of "Excellence":

- His emphasis on safety resulted in four tractor trailer drivers logging 10,000 miles accident free.
- Received commendation from CG for organizing post special olympics program.
- Won the installation award for Quarters of the Month.
- His constant instruction on maintenance resulted in six of eight mechanics earning master mechanic badges.
- Commended for no APCs on deadline report for six months.
- His learn and grow climate resulted in best platoon ARTEP results in the battalion.

NCO Counseling Checklist/Record (continued)

Pamphlet 623-205, *The NCOER System "In Brief,"* should be made available to the NCO when he or she is counseled during the rating period.

The NCOER System, then, follows these key steps in the evaluation process:

- The initial face-to-face counseling session between the rated NCO and the rater to establish expectations and set goals.
- Quarterly follow-up counseling to review progress.
- Execution of NCOER by the rater.
- Evaluation by senior rater focusing on the rated NCO's potential for future service.
- Objective overwatch conducted by the reviewer throughout the process.
- An appeals process, if the soldier so requests.

Additional Reports

NCOERs are normally submitted annually, 12 months after promotion to sergeant or 12 months after the last report. Several circumstances require additional NCOERs. Change-of-rater reports are submitted in the following circumstances:

- The rater retires, dies, or is relieved. (In the event the rater is relieved, the senior rater will complete both the rater's and the senior rater's portions of the NCOER.)
- The soldier's expiration of term of service (ETS) occurs, unless he or she has immediately reenlisted with no break in service.
- The rated soldier transfers.
- The soldier is serving on special assignment or TDY, outside of the supervision of the normal rater, for a period of 90 days or more.
- The soldier is in a military or civilian school for a period of 90 days or more. (School evaluations are made on the *Academic Evaluation Report,* DA Form 1059.)
- The rated NCO is reduced in rank to specialist or below.
- When requested by the rater or the rated NCO prior to retirement.

Optional complete-the-record reports are submitted under special circumstances. When a soldier is in the primary or secondary zone of consideration for a Department of the Army centralized promotion board, or is being considered for selection to a military or civilian school, and has not yet been rated for his current duty assignment but has been in that assignment for at least six months, the rater may submit a complete-the-record report so that the soldier's personnel file is up-to-date before the board's review.

Relief-for-cause reports are submitted when a soldier is removed from his or her assignment because "personal or professional characteristics, conduct, behavior, or performance of duty warrant removal in the best interest of the US Army" (AR 600-20, para. 3-13). Relief from duty must be preceded by counseling by the rater, allowing the soldier time to correct deficiencies. Temporary suspension from assigned duties does not warrant a relief-for-cause report. The narrative portion of such a report must clearly define the reasons for the action taken and must specify that the soldier has been notified of the reasons. The minimum rating period is 30 days, although this minimum can be waived by a general officer or an officer with courts-martial authority over the soldier; cases in which such a waiver would be considered are only those cases where clear-cut misconduct is evident and warrants such action.

Information an NCOER Cannot Include

Since the NCOER has such wide-ranging influence on your career, restrictions have been placed on types of information that can be included. For instance, if a soldier voluntarily enrolls in the Army Alcohol and Drug Abuse Prevention and Control Program (ADAPCP), that information cannot be included in his or her NCOER. This does not mean that poor performance due to the alcohol or drug problems cannot be noted in the evaluation. On the other hand, if the supervisor identifies the problem and requires the soldier's entrance into the program, the soldier can then be identified in the NCOER as having the problem. Such identification must be based on information obtained from sources outside of the ADAPCP. Once a soldier has been so identified in an NCOER, subsequent evaluations should highlight successful rehabilitation as a credit to the soldier.

The servicemember is protected from the inclusion of unproven derogatory information in an NCOER. This pertains to investigations or legal proceedings that have not been completed and to criminal accusations that resulted in a not-guilty verdict. Further, no unfavorable comments are allowed in an NCOER concerning the zeal with which a soldier performs duties such as the Equal Opportunity NCO or counsel to the accused in a court-martial.

Comments related to the soldier's race, color, religion, sex, or national origin are also inappropriate. In addition, no mention can be made of the fact that a soldier received an Article 15; the misconduct that resulted in the Article 15 can, however, be noted.

Generally, the NCOER should not contain classified information.

Those NCOERs that do contain such information must be properly marked and must contain downgrading instructions.

Appeals

An appeals system exists to ensure fairness to the soldier, protect the Army's interests, and prevent unjustified attacks on the integrity or judgment of rating officials. In the event that you disagree with an NCOER, you may take one of two actions: request a commander's inquiry or begin an appeal, as directed by DA Circular 623-88-1, chapter 4, and Appendix G.

Technically, a request for a commander's inquiry is not an appeal; you are simply asking the commander to investigate an inaccurate evaluation before it becomes a matter of permanent record. Such inquiries are limited to problems with the clarity of the report, information presented as fact in the report, conduct of the rated soldier and the rater during the evaluation process, and compliance with regulations governing NCOERs. A commander's inquiry may not be used to document a difference of opinion between the rater and the reviewer or senior rater with regard to the soldier's performance or potential, or between the commander and the rating officials.

Use of the commander's inquiry is not necessarily the first step in processing an appeal, although it is often used as such. The two processes — the commander's inquiry and the appeals process — are separate, distinct procedures. Invoking one process places no limitations on beginning the next, nor is one course of action a prerequisite for the other.

The burden of proof rests with the soldier making the appeal. The mere allegation of error or injustice does not constitute proof. Once an NCOER is filed in your permanent record, it is presumed to be administratively correct, to have been prepared by the proper officials, and to represent the considered opinions and impartial judgments of rating officials at the time they were prepared. Clear and convincing evidence must be submitted to cause alteration, replacement, or withdrawal of a report from a soldier's permanent file. Therefore, the decision to appeal an evaluation should not be made lightly. Frequently, clear and convincing evidence may be difficult to obtain, and in many cases, the soldier making the appeal may be unable to analyze his or her own case objectively.

In most cases, appeals are originated by the rated soldier. Another individual may make an appeal on behalf of the rated soldier, but only after the rated soldier has been notified in person or in writing and given the opportunity to submit statements pertaining to the case. Rating officials who claim second thoughts about ratings previously made have no grounds for submitting an appeal on behalf of the rated soldier. A rating official may not submit an appeal based on typographical errors or administrative oversight.

The appeals process handles two basic types of problems: administrative corrections to an NCOER and substantive corrections — claims of injustice, bias, prejudice, or inaccurate evaluations. Administrative errors are the easiest to prove because they often involve data recorded elsewhere. Substantive errors — errors in accuracy, judgment, or fairness — are much more difficult to prove. Since there are no records or documents that show prejudice or bias, such claims are based, for the most part, on evidence from third parties — persons other than the rater or the soldier being rated, who have knowledge of the soldier's performance during the rating period in question.

An appeal, which should be submitted in the form of a military letter, can contest either the full evaluation report or only specific parts of the comments included. All evidence submitted must be relevant to the claim made in the appeal, and documents must be either originals or certified true copies of originals. Statements by third parties must clearly identify the third party's relationship to the soldier during the time period in question.

No time limitations exist on the filing of an appeal, but as time elapses between the evaluation and the appeal, it becomes increasingly difficult to document errors, especially errors in judgment. Time can erode the credibility of the evidence submitted, so prompt submission of an appeal is in the soldier's best interest.

If you feel an appeal of an NCOER is in order, consult DA Circular 623-88-1 and your chain of command for assistance.

5

Moving On

"I'm so short, you can close the door and I'll walk under it."

"Yeah? Well, I'm so short that if I jumped off a chair, I wouldn't hit the ground for a week."

"Short!" The well-known yell and related jokes generally mean that a soldier is about to separate or to make a permanent-change-of-station (PCS) move. In the latter case, "Short!" also signals to all within earshot that the Army personnel pipeline is about to flow—from a losing command to a gaining command.

Moving is as certain to soldiers as death and taxes. Soldiers either move out or move on. Every day, across the nation and abroad, thousands of soldiers are preparing to move or are in the process. In some "space imbalanced" MOSs (those with 55 percent or more of their authorized positions overseas), moves come about every two years. In most others, moves are less frequent, about every three years.

The first PCS move is always memorable.

Pack, turn in field gear, clear dozens of agencies, get medically screened, accomplish processing for overseas movement (POM), say good-byes, wrap up final military tasks, ship the privately owned vehicle (POV), fill out mail cards, turn in meal and weapons and NBC mask cards—rush, rush, rush. A move means turmoil, both when departing one duty station and when arriving at another. Turmoil can be reduced to virtual insignificance if a soldier is properly prepared to move and understands the Army assignment system.

Assignment Procedures

Moves occur for two major reasons. First, military readiness depends on having the right people with the right qualifications in the right place. Soldiers are constantly upgrading their skills and "outgrowing" their present jobs. Secondly, the United States maintains Army bases all over the world. Some locations are more desirable than others. Since all installations must be maintained regardless of the lifestyle they offer, a rotation system works to equalize desirable and hardship assignments among all soldiers.

Enlisted Personnel Assignment System

Where you live and work is determined by the Army's Enlisted Personnel Assignment System. The principal goal of the assignment system is to meet personnel requirements for the Army. The secondary goals are to:

• Equalize desirable and undesirable assignments by reassigning the most eligible soldier from those of similar MOSs and grade.
• Equalize the hardship of military service.
• Meet the personal desires of the soldier.
• Assign each soldier so that he or she will have the greatest opportunities for professional development and promotion advancement.

Normally, Personnel Support Centers (PSCs) submit requisitions, stating the number of personnel needed and the requirements for each MOS and grade, to Total Army Personnel Command (PERSCOM) in Alexandria, Virginia. The requisitions are based on the stations' projected gains and losses in personnel. PERSCOM branch assignment NCOs then compare lists of available soldiers to the requisitions.

Soldiers become available for reassignment when they are awarded an initial or a new MOS; when they volunteer for reassignment; when they complete schooling or training; or when they complete an overseas tour, a stabilization period, or the normal "turn-around time" in CONUS. (Each MOS has an established period that is considered normal for a soldier to spend stateside before being assigned an additional overseas position.)

The Enlisted Distribution Assignment System (EDAS) matches available soldiers against requisitions based on their grade, MOS, skill level,

PERSONNEL ACTION

For use of this form, see DA PAM 600-8 and AR 680-1; the proponent agency is MILPERCEN.

DATA REQUIRED BY THE PRIVACY ACT

Authority: Title 5, section 3012; Title 10, U.S.C. E.O. 9397. Principal Purpose: Use by service member in accordance with DA Pamphlet 600-8 when requesting a personnel action on his/her own behalf (Section III). Routine Uses: To initiate the processing of a personnel action being requested by the service member. Disclosure: Voluntary. Failure to provide Social Security Number may result in a delay or error in processing of the request for personnel action.

THRU: (Include ZIP Code)	TO: (Include Zip Code)	FROM: (Include ZIP Code)
		COMMANDER.

SECTION I - PERSONAL IDENTIFICATION

NAME (Last, first, MI)	GRADE OR RANK/PMOS (Enl only)	SOCIAL SECURITY NUMBER

SECTION II - DUTY STATUS CHANGE (Proc 9-1, DA Pam 600-8)

The above member's duty status is changed from _____

_____ to _____

_____ effective _____ hours _____ 19 ____

SECTION III - REQUEST FOR PERSONNEL ACTION

I request the following action:

TYPE OF ACTION	Procedure		TYPE OF ACTION	Procedure
Service School (Enl only)			Reassignment Married Army Couples	
ROTC or Reserve Component Duty			Reclassification	
Volunteering For Oversea Service			Officer Candidate School	
Ranger Training			Assgmt of Pers with Exceptional Family Members	
Reasgmt Extreme Family Problems			Identification Card	
Exchange Reassignment (Enl only)			Identification Tags	
Airborne Training			Separate Rations	
Special Forces Training/Assignment			Leave - Excess/Advance/Outside CONUS	
On-the-Job Training (Enl only)			Change of Name/SSN/DOB	
Retesting in Army Personnel Tests			Other (Specify)	

SIGNATURE OF MEMBER (When required)	DATE

SECTION IV - REMARKS (Applies to Sections II, III, and V) (Continue on separate sheet)

SECTION V - CERTIFICATION/APPROVAL/DISAPPROVAL

I certify that the duty status change (Section II) or that the request for personnel action (Section III) contained herein -

☐ HAS BEEN VERIFIED   ☐ RECOMMEND APPROVAL   ☐ RECOMMEND DISAPPROVAL
        ☐ IS APPROVED   ☐ IS DISAPPROVED

COMMANDER/AUTHORIZED REPRESENTATIVE	SIGNATURE	DATE

DA FORM 4187 DEC 82   EDITION OF FEB 81 WILL BE USED.   COPY 1

Personnel Action Request Form

and current ETS. In addition, Skill Qualification Identifiers (SQI) and Additional Skill Identifiers (ASI) are considered. The number of months since the last PCS and the number of months since serving in an overseas assignment are other major considerations, as is the soldier's availability month compared to the requirement month. Finally, the soldier's areas of preference are considered. It should be noted, however, that the preference of the individual soldier can only be honored if the needs of the Army are also served by making the desired assignment. Scores are devised based on these criteria, and then the scores are used in making the final assignment decisions.

When an assignment is likely to cause severe family hardship, the soldier can request a deferment or deletion from the assignment. Most extreme problems are further complicated when the move is to be to a dependent-restricted overseas assignment. (Deferments and deletions are discussed fully later in this chapter.)

Soldiers can also request an early arrival. Requests should be made directly to PERSCOM when the soldier has been assigned to a short-tour overseas area; when the request is for an early arrival in excess of 60 days; or when the need for the request occurs while the soldier is TDY or en route to the new assignment. Requests for early arrivals of less than 60 days can be approved by the installation commander at the soldier's current assignment if the upcoming assignment is to a long-tour overseas area.

An application for deletion or curtailment of an overseas assignment can be made while the soldier is on leave in CONUS. Once the soldier discovers that the problem can be resolved only by remaining in CONUS, the soldier should then go to the nearest Army installation or activity that has a personnel or administrative office and request the reassignment through that office. If it is not possible to go to an Army installation, the soldier should telephone Headquarters, Department of the Army (HQDA DAPC-EPS-E) during duty hours. That number is (202) 325-7730 (DSN 221-7730). HQDA can then advise the soldier of further action he or she may need to take.

The New Manning System

One of the most difficult experiences a young soldier faces is that of reporting to a new outfit in a new location, making new friends, and getting to know new NCOs and officers. The New Manning System (NMS) is designed to minimize this turbulence in the Army's replacement system.

The two key components of the NMS are the U.S. Army Regimental System (USARS, covered in AR 600-82) and the Cohesion, Operational

NEW MANNING SYSTEM

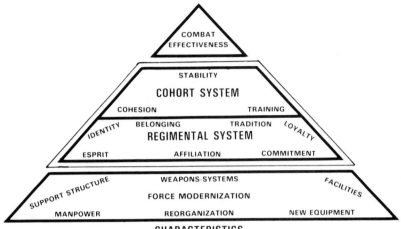

COHORT

- MORE STABLE UNIT ENVIRONMENT
- REDUCED PERSONNEL TURBULENCE
- EXTENDED SOLDIER-LEADER INTERFACE
- REDUCED ORGANIZATIONAL TURBULENCE
- GREATER STRUCTURAL COMPATABILITY

REGIMENTAL SYSTEM

- RECURRING ASSIGNMENTS
  - SAME UNITS
  - SAME LOCATIONS
  - SAME PEERS
- INCREASED PROFESSIONAL SPECIALIZATION
- GREATER SENSE OF BELONGING IDENTITY
- INCREASED PREDICTABILITY
- INCREASED FAMILY SUPPORT

Readiness, and Training System (COHORT, covered in AR 600-83). Together, the two elements of the NMS encourage soldiers to identify with their units, minimize personnel instability, and enhance the unit's operational readiness.

Until the 1950s, regiments were tactical organizations. Under the USARS, a group of like battalions in CONUS and overseas is given the same regimental designation. The regiments are formed to allow affiliation and recurring assignments to the same units and geographical locations. Each soldier is given the opportunity to affiliate with a regiment during his or her first enlistment.

The goal of the COHORT unit replacement system is to keep units together during their life cycles, thus increasing unit cohesion and a sense of attachment to an organization. The effect of this system is that certain programs for which soldiers are normally eligible are not available to soldiers in COHORT units until the completion of the unit's life cycle. Specific examples include:

- Airborne training (unless the COHORT unit is an airborne unit).
- Hometown recruiting.
- Officer Candidate School.
- Ranger School.
- Assignment exchanges ("swapping").
- Assignment outside of the unit to establish joint domicile. (The spouse of a COHORT-assigned soldier may seek reassignment to the location of the NMS unit in order to establish joint domicile.)

The initial training of soldiers assigned to COHORT units generally occurs in an OSUT environment, except for specialty positions (e.g., communications and administration) that require special training. The soldiers will then be moved as a unit from their training post to the unit location.

At the new post, NCO and officer cadres are linked up with the new troops. If the unit is to be CONUS-based during its life cycle, the soldiers will continue to train as a unit until the cycle is complete. At the end of the unit's life cycle, soldiers who are eligible to separate from the service may do so; those remaining in the service will go on to other assignments.

COHORT companies or batteries that are going to a short-tour area spend 24 months in the United States preparing for deployment; those headed for long-tour areas remain in CONUS for 18 months. The cadre and the soldiers stay together for the entire three-year life of the unit. At the end of the unit's cycle, the soldiers either separate from the Army or are reassigned to other units.

Soldiers with family members may, if the unit serves in an area where accompanied tours are authorized, apply for permission to take their families overseas. To do this, however, the soldier must have sufficient time remaining to serve an accompanied tour in the area of assignment. If the soldier does not have sufficient time remaining, then he or she must extend the tour overseas beyond the life of the unit. After the unit stands down, the soldiers with time remaining to serve overseas are reassigned within the theater to complete their overseas tours.

Exchanging Assignments

Commonly called "swapping," exchanging assignments is one way you can control where you live and work. The process is simple in principle, but it is not always so simple to implement.

Two soldiers in different locations must agree to exchange assignments. Both must be the same pay grade and be serving in the same MOS, with similar qualifications. In addition, all commanders involved must agree to the swap. Requests for an assignment exchange cannot be made directly to the commander at the location where the soldier would like to be assigned; each soldier must work out the arrangements on a person-to-person basis with another soldier wanting to be assigned to the present location of the first. Official correspondence and government mailing cannot be used in making arrangements for an assignment exchange.

Once arrangements have been made, one of the soldiers must submit a request to his or her installation commander. If he or she approves the request, that commander then coordinates the action with the installation commander of the second soldier. If one spouse of a married Army couple receives authorization for a swap, the other spouse may not request reassignment to reestablish a joint residence at the new duty station. Also, soldiers already on orders for a new assignment will not be authorized an assignment exchange.

The soldiers must pay all expenses incurred by the relocation, since the Army will not move the families of soldiers exchanging assignments. In addition, any travel time needed is counted as ordinary leave.

An excellent source of information on possible stateside swaps can be found in the weekly issues of *Army Times*. In a "want-ad" format, *Army Times* lists soldiers by MOS, rank, name, and address — and includes those areas in which the soldier would be interested. If another soldier is interested in the location/assignment of the individual listed in the ad, all contact information is readily available.

Assignment of Married Army Couples

Special consideration can be afforded to married couples when both individuals are members of the Army. Specifically, the Army has established a voluntary Army couples program, which provides consideration for joint assignments. Such joint assignments, of course, must be consistent with the needs of the Army. The Army's objective in the Married Army Couples (MAC) program is that 90 percent of the soldiers enrolled in the program will automatically receive joint assignments. Soldiers married to members of other branches of the military are not eligible for the MAC program.

Once a couple has enrolled in the program, consideration for joint assignment is continuous and computerized. Whenever one member is under consideration for a PCS move, the spouse is also considered for assignment to the same installation, command, or general area. While consideration is automatic, assignment is not. An Army spouse cannot be assigned if he or she does not meet all necessary qualifications and is not in an MOS and grade in which a valid Army requirement exists at the proposed assignment. Of course, the needs of the Army must be of primary consideration in any reassignment. Married Army couples are still required to fulfill their individual military obligations regardless of their own assignment location or that of their spouse.

Joint overseas assignments are sometimes more difficult to obtain than joint CONUS assignments. There are several reasons for this. First, the overseas major command must give its permission for the joint assignment. If the couple has minor dependents, such permission is more difficult to obtain for isolated tours or hazardous areas where facilities are not available for dependent care. Hawaii is almost impossible for a joint assignment because so many slots are reserved there through guaranteed assignments for reenlisting and recruiting efforts. Joint assignments to Germany, Italy, and elsewhere may be easier to get.

Whenever possible, married Army couples can receive concurrent overseas assignments, if they so desire. Ideally, they would be assigned to the same overseas command, or at least to the same general location. If such assignments are not possible, PERSCOM will give consideration to a request that each spouse serve a short-term tour in different locations but at the same time. In this manner, joint assignments after the short tour are facilitated.

If both members of an Army couple are assigned to overseas tours but one spouse arrives at a later date than the other, the soldier with the earlier date eligible for return from overseas (DEROS) may normally extend his or her tour to coincide with the later DEROS of the spouse. The spouse who arrives later determines when the Army couple returns to CONUS.

Problems can be avoided in the MAC program if couples follow a few basic rules. First, they should enroll in the MAC program as soon as possible. (Newly married Army couples are advised to join the MAC program within the first 60 days after they are married.) Once one servicemember has received orders, it is too late for the couple to enroll. They may, however, initiate a request for joint domicile, which can be handled through PERSCOM on a manual, rather than computerized, basis.

To enroll in the MAC program, one of the soldiers must fill out a *Personnel Action Request,* DA Form 4187, through his or her PSC. After the PSC clerk verifies the marriage, one Standard Installation/Division Personnel Reporting System (SIDPERS) transaction is completed, listing names and Social Security numbers of both spouses, in addition to their current assignments. One transaction updates the master files for both soldiers. Under the following circumstances, both soldiers must fill out DA Form 4187 and two transactions must be made:

- If the Army couple has married, but they carry different surnames. (Usually this occurs when the wife elects to retain her maiden name.)
- If the Army couple consists of one officer and one enlisted soldier. (Since assignments for officers and for enlisted soldiers are handled through different offices, two transactions are required.)

The soldiers involved should inform the PSC clerk of the necessity of filing two transactions under these circumstances.

Divorces can also cause problems for the MAC program. Unless one of the divorced soldiers completes paperwork to remove the couple's names from the MAC program, they will continue to receive joint assignments.

The MAC program functions only for computer-generated assignments. If one soldier reenlists for a guaranteed assignment, the other spouse will not receive a joint assignment under the MAC program.

The soldiers involved are then left with three options:

- The couple may request a joint domicile, providing certain time-on-station (TOS) requirements have been met and the gaining command has a valid need for the spouse's MOS.
- The couple may request a permissive assignment to establish a joint domicile. The moving spouse must have served between 12 and 24 months at his current station, and the move will be conducted at no cost to the government.
- The soldiers may seek an exchange of assignments with a third party. Although such swaps may be approved, they do not constitute authorization for establishment of joint domicile.

Overseas Assignments

The primary role of soldiers stationed overseas is the same as that of their stateside counterparts — to fulfill mission requirements. Overseas assignments, however, carry additional roles that should not be overlooked.

Foreign nationals get their principal opinions of the United States through the Americans they see — often soldiers and dependents living overseas. These Americans become unofficial ambassadors. It is not a job they may choose to decline; it is forced upon them by their very location in the foreign country. Poor conduct by a soldier can result in being returned to the United States under punitive action; poor conduct on the part of

A German child gets a special treat from a friendly Army radio-telephone operator

dependents can result in the overseas commander requiring the early involuntary return of dependents to the United States.

The role of ambassador can be complicated by the differing customs and lifestyles in overseas communities. By accepting and adjusting to different social concepts and beliefs, the soldier can gain the respect of the host countrymen. A positive attitude toward differing customs goes a long way toward making adjustment easier. It might be helpful for the soldier to recall that his or her customs seem as strange to the foreign nationals as their customs seem to him or her. Further, their pride in their heritage is every bit as strong as the soldier's pride in the United States.

Overseas assignments are an integral part of the military lifestyle. If you have adequate information and preparation, such tours can be very satisfying and can prove to be the highlight of your career. Clearly, some overseas assignments are more desirable than others, but Army regulations (AR 614-30) emphasize the need for "equitable distribution of overseas assignments, considering both desirable and undesirable locations."

Which assignments are "desirable" is a debatable subject. One soldier may consider a particular location to be ideal, a true paradise. Another may consider the same duty to be nearly intolerable. The best advice you can follow is to gather factual information but reserve judgment. Keeping a positive attitude before and after arriving "in country" can be key to making your first overseas tour an enjoyable experience.

Tour Length

Although the Army will decide where you will be assigned, you have an impact on how long the tour will be. Basically, command-sponsored tours (when family members are authorized to accompany the service-member) are longer than unaccompanied tours. Length of tour varies with location and dependent status. In addition, the length of overseas tours of soldiers who have no dependents depends on whether they have obtained career status. Generally, soldiers in their first three-year enlistment are not considered to have career status and can therefore serve a shorter overseas tour in many cases. A complete list of overseas tours is found in AR 614-30, Appendix B.

The Family Care Plan

All soldiers whose dependents would be unable to care for themselves in the absence of the servicemember must file a *Family Care Plan* (DA Form 5305-R) with their unit commander. The military requires such a plan so that the soldier and his or her family will be prepared in the event that he or she is assigned or deployed in a military emergency to a re-stricted overseas location.

Examples of soldiers who must file a *Family Care Plan* include those who are:

- Single parents.
- Pregnant and residing without their spouses.
- Married to another servicemember.
- Caring for adult, non-spouse dependents (e.g., parents).
- Likely to be deployed.

Once the soldier completes the *Family Care Plan,* the form and such attachments as special powers of attorney for guardianship, certificates of acceptance of guardianship, ID card applications (as necessary), and ap-propriate military pay allotment authorizations will be approved by the servicemember's commander to ensure that the plan is workable in the soldier's absence.

The plan must be updated if the soldier's family situation changes; in any case, the plan must be reviewed annually.

Soldiers who fail to maintain a *Family Care Plan* may be counseled, barred from reenlistment, given nonjudicial punishment under Article 15 of the UCMJ, or separated from the service. If a soldier on orders for an overseas assignment fails to prepare a plan, he or she will not be reassigned until the plan is completed or will be considered for involuntary separation. The issues involved in family care planning are complex, so you should consult with your Chain of Command, the Judge Advocate General's (JAG) office, and the post Finance and Accounting Office (FAO).

Accompanied and Unaccompanied Tours

Soldiers who have dependents have a choice in many instances of taking their families overseas. If you choose an accompanied tour, but have insufficient time remaining on your current enlistment to serve its entire length, you are required to extend or reenlist prior to the actual move. The reenlistment "window" is eight to three months prior to ETS.

Sometimes a soldier is not sure whether it is better to choose an accompanied or unaccompanied tour. If undecided, you can possibly retain some options by selecting the accompanied tour and then going overseas originally unaccompanied. If, after arriving at the new assignment and assessing the situation, you decide it is better for your family *not* to make the move, you can request a change in tour from accompanied to unaccompanied. Although the overseas commander is authorized to approve such a request, the request must be made within six months for shorter tours and 12 months for longer tours.

The opposite scenario is not quite so easy. If you originally select an unaccompanied tour and later decide you'd prefer an accompanied tour, you may have difficulty making that change. Family members can join you overseas, traveling at their own expense, and then you may request command sponsorship. You must have enough time remaining on your current enlistment, however, to serve the accompanied tour length, or have 12 months of remaining service after the family arrives — whichever is longer. Once the family members have been approved as command-sponsored, their travel expenses for their return trip to the United States will be paid by the government. If, however, you do not secure command sponsorship for your dependents, you will be responsible for financing their stay abroad and trip home.

In some overseas areas, no accompanied tours are allowed. Servicemembers sometimes decide to bring the family along at personal expense in a non–command-sponsored status. Such a decision can have serious consequences. No government housing will be available; non–command-sponsored individuals are not allowed to use the commissary and post exchange; and dependents will not be authorized to attend Department of Defense Dependents Schools (DODDS). In the event of a need for evacuation of family members, the Noncombatant Evacuation Operation (NEO) program will not be specifically structured to support non–command-sponsored family members. You should carefully weigh these factors before deciding to take your family.

When an unaccompanied tour is the first selection, the service family is entitled to a government-paid move, including transportation of dependents and household goods, to another location of their choice within the continental United States. Government-paid moves to Alaska, Hawaii, Puerto Rico, or other U.S. territory are sometimes possible.

Although deciding whether to take family members overseas is never easy, you can receive counseling on this decision through several sources. The Army Community Services (ACS) Office can advise the family on financial matters and how an accompanied tour may affect its financial situation. The legal office can provide advice on any legal matters that may be more complicated when the servicemember is overseas. Counseling of a more general nature can be obtained through the Army chaplain or the unit's first sergeant.

Marital status sometimes changes while the servicemember is overseas. Such a change can affect the length of tour. If military members acquire dependents (i.e., through marriage) and request command sponsorship for the new dependents, the overseas commander may approve sponsorship only if the servicemember has sufficient time remaining on his enlistment to serve an accompanied tour. Newly acquired family members with command sponsorship can travel to the United States at government expense. On the other hand, if a servicemember is divorced and does not retain physical custody or financial responsibility for dependents, he or she will be considered to have no dependents, and the tour length will be adjusted appropriately. Similar adjustments to tour length can be made when two married servicemembers have joint domicile overseas and one spouse separates from the service, thus becoming classified as a dependent.

Pregnant Servicewomen

How pregnancy affects overseas tours depends on when the soldier finds out she is pregnant. If the pregnancy and recovery period will last for more than 90 days beyond the reporting date, the soldier's orders will be deleted. Otherwise, her assignment will be deferred. The deferment will not normally last more than six weeks beyond the end of the woman's hospital stay. Exceptions to this policy can be granted through Headquarters, Department of the Army, at HQDA (DAPC-EPA-C), Alexandria, VA 22331. If joint domicile has already been approved and if the soldier can obtain a clearance for overseas travel from military medical authorities, a local commander (colonel or higher) can approve the request. Under no circumstance, however, will a pregnant servicemember be allowed to travel overseas after the seventh month of pregnancy.

When a soldier becomes pregnant while overseas, her tour sometimes must be curtailed. For instance, if a noncombatant evacuation is ordered, pregnant servicewomen who have reached the seventh month of pregnancy will have their tours curtailed and be evacuated. The tours of soldiers in earlier stages of pregnancy may be curtailed on an individual basis. Such curtailments are based on the ability of the soldier to perform her duties, medical availability of both prenatal and postnatal care, proximity to hostilities, and danger to the welfare of the unborn child (e.g., inadequate resources such as housing, child care, or infant food). In addition, the overseas tours of single soldiers who have reached the seventh month of pregnancy may be curtailed if their scheduled DEROS is less than six months from the expected date of delivery.

Also, if the soldier would be required to involuntarily extend her tour for more than 90 days on a long tour or for more than 60 days on a short tour, based on travel restrictions and her expected delivery date, her tour will be curtailed and she will be returned to the United States. However, six weeks after the birth of her child and subsequent release from inpatient status, the servicewoman may be reassigned overseas if she had not completed a sufficient amount of her tour to be credited with a completed tour.

The bar to assignment overseas based on failure to meet weight requirements (in accordance with AR 600-9, the *Army Weight Control Program*) applies to pregnant soldiers. This means that a servicemember whose tour was curtailed because of pregnancy cannot return overseas unless her weight is within Army standards six weeks after the birth of her child. This requirement also applies to soldiers requesting exceptions based on joint domicile or for other reasons. If the pregnant soldier is not within Army weight standards, the exception must be disapproved.

Deferments, Deletions, and Curtailments

Quite logically the Army desires to keep deferments, deletions, and curtailments of overseas assignments to a minimum. All can tend to adversely affect personnel readiness. They will be granted occasionally, however, mostly for compassionate reasons.

Deferments are temporary delays in the PCS date, usually for less than 90 days. Except for emergency situations, deferments must be requested within 30 days of receiving assignment instructions. If the assignment instructions are for one of the Army's six light infantry divisions, the request for deferment must be submitted within 15 days after receiving instructions.

When a deletion is approved, the soldier normally will be stabilized at the present assignment for up to one year or until the problem for which the deletion was approved has been resolved.

The following are examples of reasons for deferments or deletions. There are a number of other such conditions.

Deferments of not more than 90 days may be granted when a family member other than a spouse or child dies within 90 days of the scheduled overseas movement date. Deletions are usually approved when the servicemember's spouse or child dies after the servicemember receives assignment instructions.

When a family member requires hospitalization of less than 90 days, deferments can be granted. In more severe cases when hospitalization is expected to extend beyond 90 days, a deletion can be approved. Terminal illness of a family member, where death is expected within a year, is another reason for deletion. A domestic hardship, in which the presence of the soldier can result in a permanent solution, can be a valid reason to request a deferment, as can a scheduled court date or a pending child custody resolution in a divorce, legal separation, or desertion case. Documented cases of abuse of the servicemember's child or rape of the servicemember's spouse can be the basis for deletions when the presence of the servicemember is essential to resolve associated problems.

Although pregnancy of the servicemember is a cause for deletion, pregnancy of a spouse is not. Deferments may be granted when the spouse is between the eighth week before scheduled delivery and the sixth week of post-natal recovery as of the date the soldier is scheduled to report to an overseas assignment.

Training is another valid reason for either deferment or deletion from an overseas assignment. If, after selection for NCOES course attendance, a soldier receives overseas assignment instruction, the assignment can be deferred for up to 90 days to allow the servicemember to attend or complete training. The assignment can be deleted for more than 90 days for the same cause or for preselection to attend Officer Candidate School (OCS).

If a soldier has tested positive for the human immunodeficiency virus (HIV), the orders will be revoked. If a family member tests positive for HIV, a deletion may be authorized based on compassionate or hardship reasons associated with the medical condition because HIV causes Acquired Immunodeficiency Syndrome (AIDS).

Other situations that may be traumatic to the servicemember are not, in and of themselves, considered valid conditions for deferments. Among these situations are divorce, legal separation, family members' allergies that would be aggravated in the overseas climate, financial problems, problems associated with home ownership, or the recent award of child custody under court orders. In this last case, the soldier would be expected to execute the appropriate arrangements for a Family Care Plan.

Once the soldier is overseas, his or her tour can be curtailed for some of the same reasons approved for deferment or deletion. The death of an immediate family member can be cause for curtailment, as can urgent health problems of a family member living with the soldier overseas. Health problems that necessitate the return of family members to the United States are not, however, necessarily causes for curtailment of the soldier's overseas tour. When family members must return from overseas before the servicemember, the soldier may request an adjusted length of tour based on his unaccompanied status. A pregnant soldier may have her tour curtailed, as detailed previously.

Volunteering

Instead of waiting for the Army to assign you to an overseas post, you may choose to volunteer for such an opportunity. Although no volunteer is guaranteed an assignment, volunteering increases the chances that you will get an assignment that suits your needs and desires. The Army benefits from its volunteer program by identifying soldiers who are highly motivated about their new assignments.

Approval for voluntary overseas assignments is based on the number and types of vacancies that exist (or are projected to exist) at the overseas location. To be eligible to volunteer, a soldier must not have already received orders for overseas duty. In addition, the soldier must have completed 24 months of service at the current duty station. This time-on-station (TOS) requirement may be waived depending on the status of the volunteer. Current exceptions include students at schools in a PCS status, trainees, and patients in medical hold status, who may apply at any time but will not be reassigned until after they complete training or are released from medical hold status; soldiers with soldier spouses, who may apply with 6 months' TOS in order to establish joint domicile overseas; soldiers holding a space-imbalanced MOS (SIMOS); and first-term soldiers, who may apply with 12 months TOS.

Soldiers who are overweight, pending trial or results of special or general court-martial, under investigation for criminal or subversive activities, or being processed for involuntary separation from the service are not qualified for overseas service.

Once overseas, the soldier may also volunteer for extension of his or her tour and for intertheater and intratheater transfers. (Involuntary extensions and transfers are sometimes necessary as well.) If the voluntary extension is approved and the soldier subsequently requests a cancellation of the extension, that request could be disapproved by the overseas commander. If the servicemember has already begun serving the extension, a request for cancellation of the extension cannot be approved.

Regulations governing requests for extension are detailed. For most long tours, the request must be approved no later than 12 months before the scheduled DEROS. Junior enlisted personnel (privates through corporals) can shorten that period to 6 months before DEROS if assigned to a long tour in Europe, unless that assignment is with Allied Command Europe, in which case the 12-month deadline holds. If language training is required for the Allied Command Europe position, the 12-month deadline is expanded for all soldiers to a period of 12 months *plus* the length of language training desired. Time periods for short-tour extensions change to 6 months before DEROS, and then only if reassignment instructions have not already been received. Short tours in Korea and Fort Greely, Alaska, have even shorter deadlines — 4 months before DEROS, and again, only if reassignment instructions have not already been received.

Normally any length of extension between 6 and 18 months can be approved for each extension request. Extensions for Allied Command Europe can be between 6 and 12 months, however. Shorter extensions can be approved by the overseas commander for the servicemember whose dependents, living at the overseas assignment, are restricted from travel because of advanced pregnancy of the wife, recent birth of a child, or serious illness of a dependent.

Voluntary extensions expand the time that a soldier spends at a single location. Also possible are voluntary intertheater and intratheater transfers, which extend the overseas time but at a new location. An intertheater transfer is an overseas transfer from one theater to another; an intratheater transfer is from one location to another within the same theater.

Overseas theaters encompass the following geographic areas: Africa and Middle East Asia area (AMEA); European area (EURA); Far East and Pacific area (FEPA); and South American and Caribbean area (SACA).

For intertheater transfers, a soldier must complete the current overseas tour he or she is serving before being reassigned, but the request for voluntary transfer should be submitted no later than 5 months before DEROS for short tours and no later than 10 months before DEROS for long tours. Requests are submitted on DA Form 4187, Personnel Action Request. A complete tour will be served at the new assignment.

For voluntary intratheater transfers, a soldier must serve a complete tour at the new assignment but does not necessarily have to complete the tour at the current assignment before being transferred. All voluntary transfers must fill a valid vacancy and must not necessitate two PCS moves within one fiscal year.

Extending a long tour through the Overseas Extension Incentive Program can mean extra money or benefits. If your MOS is designated by PERSCOM as a space-imbalanced or shortage MOS, or if the normal turnaround time between the States and overseas assignments is less than 24 months for your MOS, you are eligible for the program. Extending adds $80 a month to your salary or it provides you with either 30 days' nonchargeable leave or 15 days' nonchargeable leave and space-required travel to and from the States. See your local PSC office for the most current list of qualifying MOSs.

Homebase and Advance Assignment Program

Servicemembers in the rank of sergeant and above are eligible to participate in the Homebase and Advance Assignment Program (HAAP). Under HAAP a soldier's current stateside assignment is considered his homebase. When the individual receives an overseas assignment to a 12-month short-tour, dependent-restricted area, he or she is returned to the homebase assignment area, once the overseas assignment is completed, when at all possible. If a return to the homebase is not possible, the soldier is at least informed of the assignment that will follow the overseas short tour *before* leaving the overseas location.

Soldiers assigned to 18-month unaccompanied tours overseas may participate in the homebase portion of HAAP if their rank is sergeant or above and if reassignment to the homebase is possible. The advanced assignment portion of HAAP is not available to them.

Voluntary extensions by the soldier will automatically cancel any pre-arranged HAAP assignment.

PCS Moves

Thorough preparation is the key to any successful move. It is important to start planning for a permanent change of station (PCS) move as soon as you receive your orders; waiting until the last few weeks before the packers show up is an invitation to disaster.*

Preparing for the Move

Your first stop after receiving PCS orders should be at your Transportation Office. Make an appointment to talk with the counselors about your move as soon as possible. They will be able to update you on current regulations, restrictions, and household goods weight allowances under the Joint Travel Regulations (JTR).

The post Army Community Services (ACS) Office should also be contacted. ACS Relocation Assistance will assist you in planning your move; it also provides a resource at your new post for temporary loan of various household items until your household goods arrive.

A popular option with soldiers who are moving from one CONUS station to another is to execute a do-it-yourself move, commonly referred to as a DITY move. Working with your Transportation Office, you may be allowed to move your household goods on your own.

A soldier applies through the Transportation Office to make a DITY move. Upon approval, the Transportation Office computes the amount that a commercial mover would charge for the move. You are then advanced 80 percent of that estimate. If you can execute the move for less than the 80 percent figure, you may keep the difference. If the cost of the move is between 80 and 100 percent of the commercial charges, then the Army reimburses you for that amount. You pay any costs in excess of what a commercial carrier may charge. Depending on your particular circumstances, the DITY program may be the best way for you to move.

Regardless of how you move, these tips can help to make it easier:

- Develop a checklist of the key steps in the moving process. This should include a personal "back planning" timetable for making sure that the move happens on time.
- Make sure that you have extra copies of your PCS orders and any amendments. A minimum of 20 copies should be in your possession.
- Meet with your mover to discuss such things as insurance, packing, packing material removal, and any special circumstances regarding your move.

---

*A helpful resource on moving and many other topics of interest to soldiers with families is *Today's Military Wife*, 2nd edition, by Lydia Sloan Cline. (Harrisburg, Pa: Stackpole Books, 1992.)

- Arrange to have your phone and cable television disconnected. If you live off-post, ensure that the other utility services are notified.
- Notify the post office of the change in your address. When the move is caused by military orders, the post office cannot charge additional postage to forward your mail.
- Make your move an opportunity to sort out and dispose of any personal possessions that you no longer use. This will keep excess weight charges to a minimum. (See *Weight Allowances* in this chapter.)
- Set aside any important papers or documents (e.g., passports, immunization records, birth certificates, and marriage licenses) that you will need during your travel to the new post. Don't let the movers pack these documents.
- Talk with your family about the move. A move can be less traumatic for children if they know where they are going, what is going to happen during the move, and what life will be like when they get to their new home.
- If you have a pet, make sure that it will be welcome at your new duty station. Animals may not be moved or quarantined at government expense, so be prepared for the extra cost. Check with the post veterinarian or the local animal shelter for advice on moving your pet. Before acquiring pets, soldiers should take into consideration the frequent moves and barracks restrictions that are part of the military lifestyle.

Weight Allowances

Unless you're making a DITY move, the government hires movers to pack and move your possessions for you. You will be given a weight allowance—a maximum weight of goods that can be moved and/or stored at government expense—based on rank, whether the move is within CONUS or overseas, and the length of the tour.

You will have to separate your belongings into three categories: unaccompanied baggage, household goods, and storage. Unaccompanied ("hold") baggage is a small shipment of things sent ahead to the new duty station so that you can set up basic housekeeping when you arrive. Enlisted soldiers are authorized 500 pounds.

Household goods include furniture and everything else you want to ship. The accompanying table gives general guidelines for weight allowances for household goods, but your transportation counselor will give you specifics for your situation.

Storage applies to overseas moves, since you usually can't ship every-

Weight Allowances for Household Goods
(In Pounds)

	Unaccompanied		Accompanied
Pay Grade	Long Tour	Short Tour	
E-1	700	150	5,000
E-2	700	150	5,000
E-3	700	150	5,000
E-4 (less than 2 years' service)	800	350	7,000
E-4 (2 + years' service)	800	350	8,000
E-5	1,000	500	9,000

thing you own; the government will pay to store these excess items, up to your maximum weight allowance.

In addition, you can ship a privately owned vehicle (POV)—a car, truck, or motorcycle—overseas, if POV shipment is authorized for the area where you will be stationed.

Moving Overseas

The Army operates several programs designed to make overseas moves easier, but perhaps the most valuable is the sponsorship program. Once you have received orders, you should be contacted by an assigned sponsor from the new unit. If no contact is initiated, you should write to the first sergeant at the new location and request a sponsor. Sponsors provide individuals with details about the unit, civilian economy, housing, educational and family support facilities, and other information to make the move more comfortable.

Another important program is the Overseas Orientation Program, a normal part of the out-processing procedure. All personnel on overseas assignment orders are required to attend the orientation; family members are also encouraged to attend, whether or not they will be accompanying the servicemember overseas. Three films are normally a part of this orientation: "Going Our Way," which presents information on travel; "Personal Affairs," which covers topics such as wills, insurance, powers of attorney, records, and files; and "Travel Entitlements," which introduces soldiers to various entitlements available to them.

Normal details involved with any PCS are magnified in importance with an overseas move. Getting an overseas sponsor and attending the orientation program with your dependents can help you manage your move more effectively.

One detail you should attend to as soon as possible after you get your orders is obtaining passports for yourself and your dependents. Each military installation stateside has a passport office where you can obtain the necessary forms. Although passports are not required for military personnel in most cases, it is highly advisable to obtain one. Passports are necessary if soldiers wish to travel on leave in the overseas area. Dependents must have passports in order to accompany the servicemember overseas.

When traveling to your overseas duty station, you must keep a number of documents in your immediate possession at all times. Among them are your military ID card, two ID tags (dog tags), a copy of your reassignment orders, a Request and Authorization for Leave (if appropriate), your passport (if required), military records packet, an immunization record (PHS Form 731), and the Travelope and/or airline ticket. In addition, you must take your basic issue of military clothing and uniforms, as well as eyeglass inserts for the protective field mask if vision so necessitates.

The Travelope (DA Form 4600) gives important information on travel and port of call. You should pick up your Travelope (and airline ticket if appropriate) at least four days prior to the scheduled port of call date. If you are taking leave before going overseas, you should get the Travelope before leaving the stateside installation.

While traveling overseas, you should carry all prescribed medications on your person or in carry-on luggage—don't pack them in unaccompanied baggage or household goods. You should also keep medicines in their proper pharmaceutical containers, carry copies of the prescriptions, and check to see that all such medications are properly recorded in your family's individual health records. (Health records should be in the possession of the person carrying the medication.)

Overseas Travel with Dependents

Depending on the projected availability of housing at the overseas duty station, a soldier's family may or may not be able to travel with him or her when the soldier goes overseas, even if the soldier is serving an accompanied tour. Three possibilities for travel exist: concurrent travel, deferred travel, or disapproved travel.

Concurrent travel means the family travels with the servicemember.

This option is generally approved if housing is expected to be available within 60 days after the family's arrival. If the projected availability is between 61 and 140 days, the family's travel will be deferred until housing is available. Families in government quarters at the current assignment will be allowed to retain those quarters for up to 140 days if deferred travel is approved. Families living off-post may either stay at the current location with no movement of household goods or move to a temporary location, provided the household goods have been divided into those awaiting shipment overseas and those being placed in storage.

When the projected waiting period for overseas housing is greater than 140 days, family travel will be disapproved. This does not mean that the family cannot join the servicemember at a later date. Once the servicemember arrives at the new assignment and locates adequate housing for his or her dependents, he or she may request family travel. If housing does not become available, the servicemember may request that the length of tour be adjusted to an unaccompanied tour.

Concurrent travel for family members can be based on the availability of temporary housing with a friend or relative in the overseas area, provided the friend or relative is not occupying government quarters. The soldier must secure a statement from the individuals providing the temporary housing acknowledging that the servicemember's family may live with them until they are able to find housing for themselves. The soldier then forwards this statement, with a request for concurrent family travel, to the overseas commander. In addition, the soldier should indicate the availability of such quarters when completing the reassignment processing.

There is one other method of ensuring concurrent travel. If the soldier's family has been denied concurrent travel based on the projected availability of housing, the soldier's sponsor may be able to locate housing on the civilian economy for the incoming family. This is not, however, an easy task.

First, the sponsor and the new soldier rarely are personally acquainted, and their choices in housing may vary greatly. Second, the sponsor has no obligation to undertake such a search and may not agree to do so. The soldier would have to request assistance from the sponsor, provide the sponsor with the necessary power of attorney to sign the rental or lease contract for the stateside soldier, and, of course, provide any money required to complete the arrangements. In addition, the housing located by the sponsor would have to be approved as adequate by the Housing Referral Office overseas. Once this approval was obtained, the family members could be granted concurrent travel.

Managing Expenses

The financial implications of a PCS move can be enormous. For a complete discussion of the financial circumstances of your move, consult with the Finance and Accounting Office (FAO), the Transportation Office, and the PSC. Make sure that you understand fully what the costs of the move are going to be before you begin the move.

To help offset the costs of PCS moves, the Army offers a number of special allowances. These include the Dislocation Allowance, which is equal to two months' BAQ, and per diem allowances, which pay for food and lodging while in transit to the new duty station. Both are discussed fully in chapter 7. Other applicable allowances are the Mileage Allowance, Temporary Lodging Allowance, and Temporary Lodging Entitlement.

The Mileage Allowance, known officially as MALT, is paid to service-members who drive to their new duty station. The amount paid to you depends on the number of dependents, the distance traveled, the type of vehicle you use in your move, and the number of vehicles you are authorized to take.

Temporary Lodging Allowance (TLA) is used to offset the cost of temporary housing at a new duty station overseas. Temporary Lodging Entitlement (TLE) provides for temporary housing before signing out of your current post in CONUS or after signing into a new CONUS duty station. Soldiers going overseas may be eligible for both TLA and TLE. The factors that determine TLA and TLE are complex, so you should consult with the FAO and Housing Office about your particular situation.

If necessary, you can request an advance on your pay to cover moving expenses. Advance pay is a loan that may be drawn for up to three months' pay, but must be repaid within a year. In cases of extreme hardship, the repayment period may be extended to 24 months. Advance pay may only be used to cover the legitimate costs of a relocation, not to pay for vacation trips or used as a no-interest loan from the government.

You may also seek reimbursement for miscellaneous expenses such as turnpike tolls, taxi or limousine service, official calls, and passport costs. Be sure to keep receipts and present them to the FAO when reporting to your new station.

Handling Emergencies

As with any journey, unexpected events may occur en route to the new duty station. You should be aware of the procedures to follow and the support services available in case of medical, financial, or other emergencies.

Medical Care

Medical emergencies that arise for either the servicemember or accompanying dependents should be handled through military hospitals, if at all possible, when the individuals are en route to a new assignment, especially overseas. Most maps clearly mark military facilities. If the servicemember is hospitalized, it is critical that proper authorities be notified. The treatment facility should contact both the Red Cross and the soldier's Military Personnel Center Personnel Assistance Point (PAP). The PAP should be listed on the Travelope, DA Form 4600. These authorities should be notified of the soldier's location, the nature of the illness or injury, and the anticipated length of hospitalization. The PAP can advise the soldier on what actions to take on release from the treatment facility.

If no military hospital is nearby and the illness or injury is an emergency, you should seek medical attention from civilian sources. If the treatment is not an emergency, but is elective in nature, the cost of treatment will usually not be reimbursed by the government. The same rules apply for dependents of the servicemember. If the soldier must pay for emergency medical treatment, he or she should get a detailed bill showing diagnosis, treatment, costs, and whether the treatment was routine or emergency in nature. A claim for reimbursement of medical costs should then be submitted to military officials or Civilian Health and Medical Program of the Uniformed Services (CHAMPUS) as soon as possible.

Medical emergencies could arise when the soldier (and dependents) have already left the United States but have not yet arrived at the new assignment location overseas. If in a foreign country and no U.S. military medical facilities are available, the soldier should contact the nearest U.S. embassy or consulate for advice.

Non-government friends and relatives visiting a soldier overseas may be treated at military facilities, but the soldier must reimburse the government for the cost of the treatment.

Financial Crisis

Soldiers en route to an overseas assignment who find themselves without funds for transportation to their port of call should first contact the FAO at the nearest military installation. With proper military ID, reassignment orders, and individual pay records (from the records packet), you may be able to receive casual pay. Such pay would later be deducted from standard end-of-month pay. If casual pay cannot be arranged, your next sources of help are (in order) the American Red Cross, the nearest Army Community Service where referral can be made to the Army Emergency Relief (AER) Office, and the nearest military transportation office, on a military post or base. Once overseas, the soldier in financial crisis should contact the nearest U.S. military installation for help, or the U.S. embassy or consulate if no military installations are located within that country.

Lost Airline Tickets

A lost airline ticket can become a financial crisis. The first step you should take to resolve this problem is to contact the commercial carrier on which the ticket was to be used and request a replacement ticket. If this cannot be arranged, the Travelers Aid office located in many major terminals may be able to help. Travelers Aid specifically serves military travelers. The final step is to contact the PAP, calling either collect or DSN ("AUTOVON"), if available, and requesting aid and instructions. If the soldier is in a foreign country when he loses the ticket, U.S. military installations, the embassy, or a consulate are the sources of aid available.

Family Crisis

Serious illness or death of an immediate family member can create the need for an emergency leave request. Immediate family members include mother, father, spouse, child, brother, or sister. The request should be made directly to the assigned PAP by calling collect or DSN, if available. In addition, contacting the American Red Cross, so that it can verify the emergency, can aid the soldier in expediting the request for emergency leave. The local Red Cross should contact the soldier's PAP after verification.

Lost or Stolen Documents

Soldiers should be especially careful to keep ID cards, passports, and other important documents in a safe place while in transit. If you are traveling by commercial carrier, keep these items on your person or in carry-on luggage; never pack them in checked baggage. It is also a good idea to place a copy of your reassignment orders in each piece of luggage before the trip begins to expedite recovery of lost baggage.

A missing ID card should be reported to military police at the nearest military installation, as well as to the local police in the area where the card was lost or stolen. The Adjutant General's Office at the nearest military post may be able to issue a new ID card if the soldier can provide copies of military personnel records and reassignment orders. In each case, however, the servicemember should report the problem to the PAP as well.

Lost military pay records can result in a delay in receiving pay. The PAP is again the primary authority that needs to be notified. A loan can possibly be arranged through the AER once the soldier arrives at the new duty station. Lost immunization records, health records, or dental records should also be reported to the PAP. If the losses occur after the soldier has left the United States, the new unit commander is the primary individual to be notified.

6

Looking Sharp

The axiom "You can't tell a book by its cover" may be true in many circumstances, but a soldier is frequently judged by his or her appearance. A soldier's military presence, professionalism, self-discipline, and esprit de corps are all reflected in daily grooming habits and appearance.

The Army places great emphasis on a well groomed, neat appearance. The way you look does influence the opinions of both superiors and peers. Commanders and NCOs, who have significant impact on the promotions of their soldiers, are tasked by the Army to ensure that military personnel under their command maintain a neat and soldierly appearance. Regulations remind them that "A vital ingredient of the Army's strength and military effectiveness is the pride and self-discipline that American soldiers bring to their Service" (AR 670-1). The soldier's appearance becomes a reflection of that pride. In that light, it is the military duty of the soldier to maintain a soldierly appearance at all times. Appearance is greatly affected by physical fitness, weight control, and care for uniform standards.

General Regulations
Grooming

Good grooming is essential for a neat, soldierly appearance. Soldiers should pay special attention to regulations governing hairstyles, facial hair, and cosmetics.

The basic Army standard is that the hair be neat, clean, and of an appropriate length and style so that it does not interfere with the proper wearing of headgear or protective masks. Dyes, tints, and bleaches are permissible, provided the resulting color occurs naturally in human hair. Faddish or extreme hairstyles are considered inappropriate for the soldier, as are hairstyles that appear ragged or unkempt.

The male soldier must wear a style with a tapered appearance. While block-cut fullness in the back is permitted in moderation, the overall look must project a tapered effect. The length of the hair must be such that, when combed, it neither touches the ears or eyebrows nor the collar. Closely cut hair at the back of the neck can touch the collar, but the length of the hair cannot.

The female soldier must also choose a style with a neat appearance, not excessive or extreme. Her hair may not fall over her eyebrows, but it may touch the top of the collar at the back of the neck. Hairnets are not authorized unless required for health or safety reasons. (In such cases, hairnets will be provided free of cost.) Any barrettes, clips, or pins used in the hair must be transparent or the same color as the soldier's hair. In addition, such hair-holding devices must be placed inconspicuously in the hairstyle. No hair ornaments, such as beads or colorful barrettes, may be worn while in uniform.

Wigs or hairpieces may be worn by either male or female soldiers, although the rules differ somewhat. For either, the hairpiece must be of a natural human-hair color. The style must comply with all regulations affecting natural hair. For male soldiers, a wig or hairpiece is allowable in uniform only when it is used to cover natural baldness or physical disfiguration.

Male soldiers must also pay close attention to the sideburn and mustache regulations. Sideburns must be neatly trimmed, cut straight across in a horizontal line, and no longer than the lowest part of the exterior ear opening. A mustache may be worn if neatly trimmed and tapered; it may not have a chopped-off appearance. The hair from the mustache may not cover the top lip or extend sideways beyond an imaginary line drawn vertically from the corners of the mouth. Soldiers who choose to wear mustaches are advised to stay well within the regulation.

Other than sideburns and mustaches as described above, the face must be clean shaven. Exceptions can sometimes be granted for medical reasons when an authorized medical authority (usually a doctor) prescribes beard growth as a means of treating a medical ailment, such as a skin rash caused by shaving. When prescribed for medical treatment, specific details must be provided, such as the length of the treatment and the necessary length that the beard may grow, normally one-quarter of an inch.

Female soldiers are allowed to wear cosmetics provided they are applied conservatively and in good taste. No exaggerated makeup, extreme shades, or faddish styles are permitted. Lipstick and nail polish colors must also be conservative; colors such as purple, gold, blue, or white cannot be worn.

All soldiers, male and female, must keep their fingernails clean and neatly trimmed. Nails should not detract from a military appearance and should not interfere with the normal performance of duty.

Appearance and Fit of the Uniform

Each soldier is given a basic issue of uniforms and accessories, or "clothing bag," when he or she enlists in the Army. You are required to have a complete inventory of serviceable clothing bag items in your possession at all times; your initial and annual clothing allowances are designed to pay for replacement of uniforms as they wear out. The accompanying tables list the items contained in a 1992 clothing bag.

The appearance of the uniform is crucial to the overall soldierly appearance. The uniform should be properly fitted, in good repair, and cleaned and pressed. Today's uniforms often have blouses or shirts labeled "permanent press," which should mean that no pressing is needed. If the uniform piece does not *look* pressed, however, it needs a touch-up. The soldier's appearance should leave no doubts as to the degree of self-discipline and pride he or she possesses.

Some general rules apply:

- Articles carried in pockets must not protrude from the pocket.
- Pockets must not be filled so full they appear bulky.
- Keys or key chains may not be attached to the belt, unless required for special duty (such as charge of quarters).
- Buttons must be buttoned; snaps, snapped; and zippers, zipped.
- All brass parts of the uniform (such as belt buckles and belt tips) must be shined, scratch-free, and not corroded.
- Medals and ribbons must look clean and must not be frayed; they must be replaced when they look tattered or dirty.
- Shoes and boots must be shined to a high luster.
- When sleeves of jackets and coats are pressed, no crease is to be made.
- Trousers, slacks, shirts, and blouses will be creased during pressing.

Clothing Bag Items for Men, 1992

Bag, Duffel, Nylon, OG-106	1
Belt, Cotton, Web, Black	2
Boots, Combat, Leather, Black (Pair)	2
Buckle, Belt, Brass	1
Buckle, Belt, Trouser, Black	1
Cap, Camo Pattern (BDU)	2
Cap, Garrison, Wool Serge, AG-344	2
Coat, All Weather, Black	1
Coat, Camo (TBDU)	2
Coat, Cold Weather, Camo	2
Coat, Camo (HWBDU)	2
Coat, Men's, Wool Serge, AG-344	1
Drawers, Men's Boxer/Briefs, Brown	7
Gloves, Leather, Black, Dress	1
Glove Inserts, Wool	1
Gloves, Shell, Cold Weather	1
Handkerchiefs, Cotton, OG-107	6
Necktie, Men's, Wool, Black	1
PFU Sweatshirt	1
PFU Sweatpants	1
PFU Trunks	2
PFU T-shirt	2
Shirt, Men's, Long-sleeved, AG-415	1
Shirt, Men's, Short-sleeved, AG-415	2
Shoes, Men's, Dress, Black	1
Socks, Men's, Black	3
Socks, Men's, Wool, OG-408	7
Towel, Bath, Brown	4
Trousers, Men's, Serge, AG-344	2
Trousers, Camo (TBDU)	2
Trousers, Camo (HWBDU)	2
Undershirt, Men's, Cotton, White	2
Undershirt, Men's, Brown 436	7

The uniform must fit properly in order to look good. In addition, the Army has established definitive guidelines as to what "proper fit" means. The soldier should abide by those rules.

The black all-weather coat should have a sleeve length ½ inch longer than the service coat worn under the all-weather coat; this means the

Clothing Bag Items for Women, 1992

Bag, Duffel, Nylon, OG-106	1
Belt, Cotton, Web, Black	1
Boots, Combat, Leather, Black (Pair)	2
Buckle, Belt, Trouser, Black	1
Cap, Camo Pattern (BDU)	2
Cap, Garrison, Wool Serge, AG-344	2
Coat, All Weather, Black	1
Coat, Camo Pattern (TBDU)	2
Coat, Cold Weather, Camo Pattern (BDU)	2
Coat, Hot Weather Camo (HWBDU)	2
Coat, Poly/Wool Serge, AG-344	1
Gloves, Leather, Black, Dress	1
Gloves, Inserts, Wool, OG-208	2
Gloves, Shell, Cold Weather	1
Handbag, Synthetic, Black	1
Handkerchiefs, Cotton, OG-107	6
Necktab, Short-sleeved, AG-415	1
Necktab, Long-sleeved, AG-415	1
PFU Sweatshirt	1
PFU Sweatpants	1
PFU Trunks	2
PFU T-shirt	2
Shirt, Female, Short-sleeved, AG-415	2
Shirt, Female, Long-sleeved, AG-415	1
Shoes, Dress, Oxford Black	1
Skirt, Poly/Wool Serge, AG-344	2
Slacks, Poly/Serge, AG-344	2
Socks, Wool, OG-408	7
Towel, Bath, Brown 436	4
Trousers, Camo Pattern (TBDU)	2
Trousers, Hot Weather Camo (HWBDU)	2
Undershirt, Hot Weather Camo (HWBDU), Brown 436	7

sleeve length should be 1½ inches below the wristbone. For the male soldier, the bottom of the all-weather coat should be 1½ inches below the midpoint of the knee. For the female soldier, it should be 1 inch below the skirt length but not less than 1½ inches below the crease at the back of the knee.

Uniform coats and jackets should have a sleeve length of 1 inch below the wristbone, for any soldier.

Trousers, for all soldiers, should be fitted with the lower edge of the waistband at the top of the hipbone. A ½-inch leeway, either higher or lower, is allowed. Trousers are allowed to have a slight break in the crease across the front, where the hem rests slightly on the shoe. This avoids the "high-water" look, in which the socks show below the trouser hem. The front crease of the trousers must reach the top of the instep; the trouser leg is then cut diagonally so that the length in the back reaches a midpoint between the top of the heel and the top of the standard shoe.

Slacks, for female soldiers, follow the same basic fitting rules as those for trousers. One exception is the waistband, which is to be worn at the soldier's natural waistline.

Knee-length skirts have a 3-inch range in length. The shortest is to be not more than 1 inch above the crease at the back of the knee; the longest, not more than 2 inches below the crease at the back of the knee. (Note that the correct length of the all-weather black coat can be affected by the selected length of the skirt or dress.)

Appropriate undergarments are to be worn at all times with the military uniform.

Authorized Wear of the Uniform

Just as there are many rules on *how* to wear the uniform, there are also rules on *when* to wear it.

Generally, the Army uniform is worn while on duty. Exceptions can be made by the commander of a major command, by the Office of the Secretary of the Army, by HQDA, and by a few other high-ranking officials, but civilian clothes are authorized by these officials only when the requirements of the mission demand them. For the most part, soldiers will be in uniform while on duty.

Combining civilian clothing with the Army uniform is strictly prohibited. This ruling also specifically excludes wearing a commercial rucksack or backpack while in uniform, unless the soldier is riding a bicycle or motorcycle at the time. Otherwise, the rucksack can only be carried in the hand.

Civilian outdoor activities, such as volksmarches or orienteering, might seem suitable times for wearing the utility or field uniform (fatigues). Army regulations generally prohibit wearing the uniform, however, while participating in or observing such activities. The one exception is that a local commander may volunteer support personnel for such activities to serve as medical help or traffic control. The field uniform may then be the appropriate attire, at the discretion of the local commander.

Other times when the uniform may *not* be worn include when the soldier is participating in political activities, commercial interests, off-duty civilian employment, public speeches or unofficial interviews, picket lines, marches, rallies, public demonstrations, or any activity that may bring discredit on the Army. Recognized authorities can make exceptions to the wearing of the uniform during some of these activities if such actions are deemed appropriate. For details, see AR 600-50, *Standards of Conduct.*

Just as military regulations prohibit the wearing of the uniform during some activities, there are situations in which the wearing of the uniform is required. These include the requirement to wear either the Class A or Class B uniform while on a military airlift or a DOD contract flight. Wearing civilian clothing while traveling by commercial or private aircraft is allowed only when authorized by the commander. Otherwise the Class A or B uniform must be worn then as well. For overseas travel, the soldier should plan on wearing a uniform, unless he or she is instructed on travel orders that civilian clothing is mandatory.

Headgear must be worn with the uniform when the soldier is outdoors. Often the soldier has choices of which hat or headgear he or she wishes to wear with a particular uniform. Headgear is not required when the soldier is indoors, in a privately owned or commercial vehicle, or in a public conveyance (such as a subway, bus, train, or plane). When the soldier is in a military vehicle, the headgear is to be worn, unless wearing the headgear interferes with safe operation of the vehicle.

Female soldiers may choose not to wear headgear when attending evening social events in any of the following uniforms: the Army blue, white, or green dress uniform; or the green maternity uniform.

Mixing uniform pieces in manners not specifically authorized in the regulations is prohibited. All service uniform combinations are authorized for year-round wear. Weather conditions and assigned duties should be considered, however, when the choice of uniform is made.

Selected individual uniforms are discussed later in this chapter. For further information, consult AR 670-1, *Wear and Appearance of Army Uniforms and Insignia.*

Jewelry and Eyeglasses

Jewelry and eyeglasses must be conservative in order to be worn with the uniform. Faddish or exceptionally ornamental pieces are inappropriate. For instance, eyeglasses with initials or other adornments on the lens or the frame are not authorized.

A wristwatch, an ID bracelet, and two rings may be worn while in uniform. Wedding sets are considered as one ring. Even if the jewelry is conservative and in good taste, the soldier may be prohibited from wearing it, for health or safety reasons, by the local commander. A male soldier may also wear a conservative tie tack or tie clasp with the black four-in-hand necktie. A female soldier may wear a single set of small, conservative earrings that are spherical and unadorned; are gold, silver, or white pearl; fit snugly against the ear; do not extend below the earlobe (except that nonpierced earrings may have a band extending slightly below the lobe to the back of the ear); and do not exceed ¼ inch in diameter. Earrings are not authorized with field or utility uniforms, physical fitness uniforms, or organizational uniforms such as hospital, food, or service. When earrings are worn, a matched pair is required and only one earring may be worn on each earlobe. Male soldiers may never wear earrings while in uniform.

No jewelry, watch chains, pens or pencils, or similar items can be exposed on the uniform. Exceptions: the tie tack or clasp, and exposed pens or pencils while in the hospital duty, food service, or flight uniforms.

The Army permits certain exceptions to standard uniform wear based on religious practices and beliefs. Any granted exceptions can be temporarily revoked at the discretion of the commander because of health or safety requirements, or if mission requirements so dictate. Exceptions for religious practices allow the following:

- Visible religious articles and jewelry that comply with standards for authorized nonreligious articles and jewelry.
- Religious articles and jewelry that are not visible or apparent when the soldier is in uniform.
- Religious skullcaps of plain design and standard color, provided they do not exceed six inches in diameter (wearing of skullcaps is restricted to living quarters, indoor dining facilities, and worship service locations).

Soldiers desiring other deviations from standard military uniform appearance must request exceptions from HQDA, following guidelines provided in AR 600-20, chapter 5, *Army Command Policy.* Once approval from HQDA has been received, the local commander can approve the exception, retaining the right to temporarily revoke the exception, based on health, safety, or mission requirements.

Selected Individual Uniforms

To discuss fully each possible military uniform would require a book twice this size. Uniforms included in this section are those used most frequently.

Army Green Service Uniform (Male)

The Army green service uniform is a versatile ensemble of uniform components that can be worn in various combinations to make a Class A uniform, a Class B uniform, or a green dress uniform. While the dress uniform is for limited occasions, the Class A and Class B uniforms can be worn year-round for a wide variety of occasions: on- or off-duty, during travel, or at private or official informal social gatherings. A number of uniform accessories may be purchased at the discretion of the soldier. Soldiers may also decide to purchase Army green service uniforms from commercial sources; it is still the responsibility of the soldier, however, to ensure that the uniform he or she buys complies with all Army regulations.

The Class A uniform consists of the Army green coat and trousers, worn with either a long- or short-sleeved green shade 415 shirt and a black four-in-hand necktie. The Class B uniform omits the coat; the tie can also be omitted if the short-sleeved shirt is worn. The Army green dress uniform consists of the Army green coat and trousers, with a commercially purchased long-sleeved white shirt and a black bow tie. Boots, berets, or organizational items such as brassards or MP accessories are not authorized with the dress uniform. The dress uniform cannot be worn for duty or travel. It is restricted to formal social functions, private or official, and transit to and from such functions.

The Army green coat is a single-breasted, peaked-lapel coat with four buttons. The fit should provide a slight drape in both the front and the back, but it should be fitted slightly at the waist. No pronounced tightness at the waist or flare below the waist is authorized. The enlisted sleeve is plain. The length of the coat will extend below the crotch.

Matching Army green trousers are straight-legged, without cuffs. Trousers have side and hip pockets, and the left hip pocket has a buttonhole tab and button (which should always be buttoned). The enlisted trouser leg is also plain. A belt must always be worn with the trousers.

Uniform shirts bear the designation AG 415, whether long- or short-sleeved. Both are dress shirts, and both have shoulder loops, seven buttons, and two pockets with button-down flaps. Soldiers frequently have the flaps sewn closed to add to the military appearance of the shirt; a tailor can carefully sew the flap along the existing seam so that the extra stitching is not apparent.

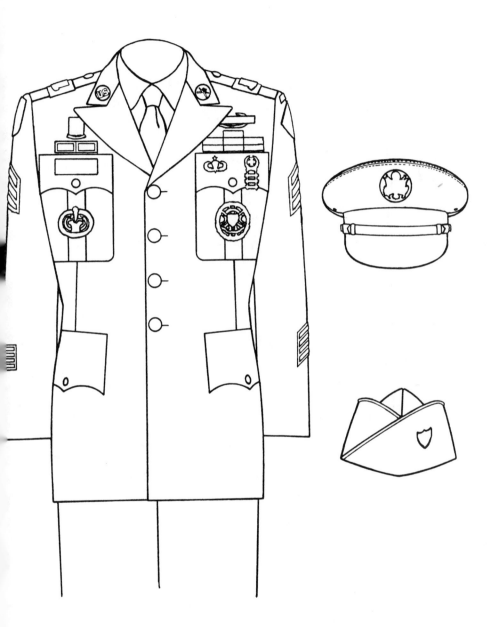

Army Green Uniform, Service Cap (top), and Garrison Cap

Class B Army Green Uniform, Short Sleeve Shirt, with and without Tie

The collar of the short-sleeved shirt is a "convertible collar" that can be worn with or without a tie. If the optional pullover or cardigan sweater is worn with the short-sleeved shirt, and the tie is not worn, the shirt collar should be worn outside the sweater. The optional windbreaker can also be worn with the AG 415 sweater as the Class B uniform.

Soldiers may choose to purchase and wear an optional wool shirt, AG 428. The AG 428 is styled like the AG 415 and is available with long or short sleeves.

Both long- and short-sleeved shirts must be tucked into the trousers, whether or not the coat is worn. The edge of the shirt opening should form a straight line with the front fly opening on the trousers and the outside edge of the belt buckle. (See illustration.)

For headgear, soldiers may (depending on the unit to which they are assigned) choose the Army green garrison cap or Army green service cap. The garrison cap should be worn so that the front vertical crease is centered on the forehead, although the cap should have a slight tilt to the right. This tilt should not be exaggerated, nor may the cap touch the top of the right ear. In addition, the crown of the cap should form a straight line. Reshaping the crown so that it peaks in the front and back and sways in the middle is not authorized.

If the soldier wears the Army green service cap, the ornamental chin strap is to remain across the visor. The service cap can be worn with either the Class A or Class B uniform. It should sit straight on the soldier's head, forming a line around the head parallel with the ground; it is not to be tilted to either side or to the front or back. The shape of the service cap should not be altered in any way.

Organizational berets and drill sergeant hats are also authorized headgear, except with the green dress uniform.

Accessories for Army green uniforms include:

- Black web belt, with a brass tip.
- Black bow tie (with dress uniform only).
- Buttons.
- Solid brass belt buckle.
- Cold weather service cap (only when wearing the black all-weather coat).
- Black all-weather coat.
- Black leather unisex dress gloves (required when wearing the Class A or dress uniform, the black all-weather coat, or the windbreaker).
- Military Police accessories.
- Black four-in-hand necktie.
- Black scarf (with black all-weather coat or windbreaker).

- White shirt (with green dress uniform only).
- Black oxford shoes.
- Black socks.
- Black leather combat boots (not with dress uniform).
- Olive green socks when wearing combat boots.
- Black cardigan sweater.
- Black pullover sweater (with Class B uniform only).
- White undershirt.
- Black windbreaker (with Class B uniform only).

Insignia, awards, badges, and accouterments differ for wear with the Class B uniform. For the Class A and dress uniforms, the following are authorized:

- Brassards (with Class A only).
- Branch of service scarves (with Class A only).
- Fourragère/lanyard.
- Distinctive items for infantry personnel.
- Branch insignia.
- U.S. insignia.
- Insignia of grade.
- Headgear insignia.
- Distinctive unit insignia.
- Regimental affiliation crest (required wear with the black pullover sweater).
- Combat leader's identification tab.
- OCS insignia.
- Full-color shoulder sleeve insignia for the current assignment.
- Full-color shoulder sleeve insignia for a former wartime unit.
- Nameplate.
- Organizational flash (worn only on organizational berets).
- Background trimming.
- Airborne, Ranger, Special Forces tabs.
- Overseas service bars.
- Service stripes.
- Decoration and service medal ribbons.
- Full-size medals (dress uniform only).
- Unit awards.
- U.S. badges (full-size or miniature, for identification, marksmanship, combat, or special skills; also special skill or marksmanship tabs).
- Foreign badges.

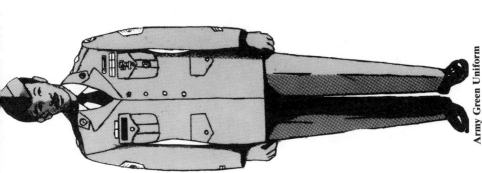

Army Green Uniform

A SOLDIER'S HAIR, SIDEBURNS, AND MUSTACHE ARE TO BE KEPT IN A NEAT MANNER AT ALL TIMES. (see AR 670-1 for guidelines.)

INSIGNIA OF BRANCH—Approximately 1" above notch and centered on collar with the center-line of the insignia bisecting the notch and parallel to the inside edge of the collar.

DISTINCTIVE UNIT INSIGNIA (crest)—Centered between outside edge of button and shoulder seam.

SPECIAL SKILL BADGE—¼" above ribbons.

SHOULDER SLEEVE INSIGNIA (Current Organization Patch)—½" down from shoulder seam and centered.

SERVICE RIBBONS—⅛" above pocket with or without ⅛" space between rows and will be worn from wearer's right to left in order of precedence.

INSIGNIA OF GRADE (Stripes)—centered halfway between shoulder seam and elbow and centered on sleeve.

MARKSMANSHIP BADGE—centered between top of button hole and top of pocket.

IDENTIFICATION BADGE—centered on pocket between bottom of flap and bottom of pocket.

SERVICE STRIPES (Hash Marks)—4" above bottom of sleeve and centered on sleeve (stripes run diagonally).

TROUSERS—will reach top of instep (may have a slight break in front), and cut diagonally to midpoint between top of heel and top of shoe at the rear.

GARRISON CAP—Worn with front vertical crease of cap centered on forehead in a straight line with nose. Cap will be slightly tilted to the right, but will not touch ear.

BLACK FOUR-IN-HAND TIE

US INSIGNIA—Approximately 1" above notch and centered on collar with centerline of insignia bisecting the notch and parallel to the inside edge of the lapel.

SHOULDER SLEEVE INSIGNIA/FORMER WARTIME ORGANIZATION—½" down from shoulder seam and centered.

UNIT AWARD EMBLEM—centered ⅛" above pocket.

NAMEPLATE—on flap of pocket centered between top of button and top of pocket.

INSIGNIA OF GRADE—same as other side.

OVERSEA BARS (Hershey Bars)—4" above and parallel to the bottom of the sleeve and centered.

IDENTIFICATION TAGS (Dog Tags)—Worn when engaged in field training, when traveling in aircraft, and when outside CONUS.

BELT—1¼" black web or woven elastic web with a black or brass tip. The tip will pass through the buckle to the wearer's left; the brass tip only will extend beyond the buckle.

BUCKLE—1¾" x 2¼" oval shaped, plain-faced, solid brass.

Authorized insignia for the Class B uniform include:

* Nameplate.
* Headgear insignia.
* Insignia of grade.
* Distinctive unit insignia (worn only on the black pullover sweater).
* Decorations and awards.

Green Classic Service Uniform (Female)

The Army green classic service uniform is the servicewoman's counterpart to the male soldier's Army green service uniform. The classic service uniform is also a versatile ensemble of components that can be arranged to form a Class A, Class B, and green dress uniform. All three uniforms can be worn year-round for a wide variety of occasions, including on- and off-duty, during travel, and for official and unofficial social occasions. The dress uniform should be worn for formal social occasions, but all three are acceptable for informal social occasions. It should be noted that the servicewoman has greater flexibility in the use of the green dress uniform than the serviceman is afforded.

The Class A uniform consists of the Army green classic coat and either the Army green classic skirt or slacks, an AG 415 short- or long-sleeved shirt, and a black neck tab. For the Army green classic dress uniform, a white shirt is substituted for the green 415 shirt. Combat boots, organizational berets, and items such as brassards and MP accessories, which can be worn with the Class A or Class B uniforms, are prohibited with the classic dress uniform.

The Class B uniform omits the coat. In addition, the black neck tab can be omitted if the short-sleeved 415 shirt is worn. The white shirt is not authorized for wear with the Class B uniform.

The Army green classic coat is a hip-length, single-breasted coat with four buttons and button-down shoulder loops. Two slanted flap pockets complement the front of the coat. The collar is notched and the sleeves are plain for the enlisted servicewoman.

Matching green classic slacks are straight-legged with a slight flare at the bottom. A zipper closure is located in the center front. The newer classic slacks have two side pockets, but older classic slacks with no pockets are still authorized for wear. Pant legs are plain for enlisted soldiers.

A green classic skirt can also be worn with the uniform coat. It is a knee-length skirt, slightly flared at the hem, with a waistband and side zipper closure (left side).

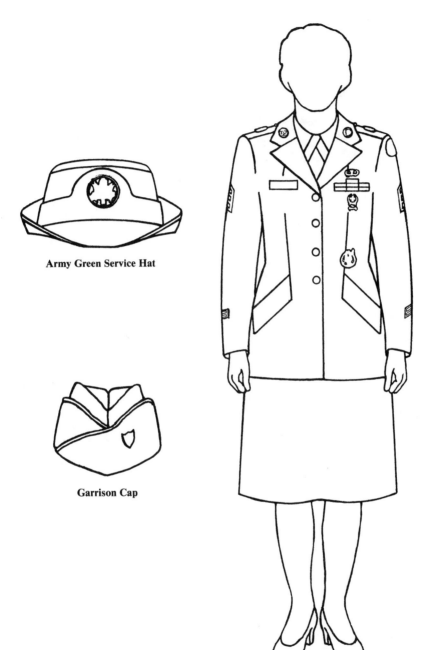

Army Green Service Hat

Garrison Cap

Army Green Classic Ensemble with Skirt

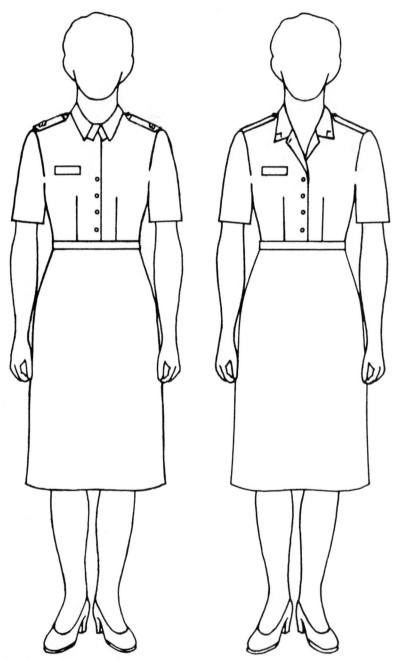

Class B Army Green Classic Ensemble, Short Sleeve Shirt, Skirt, with and without Neck Tab

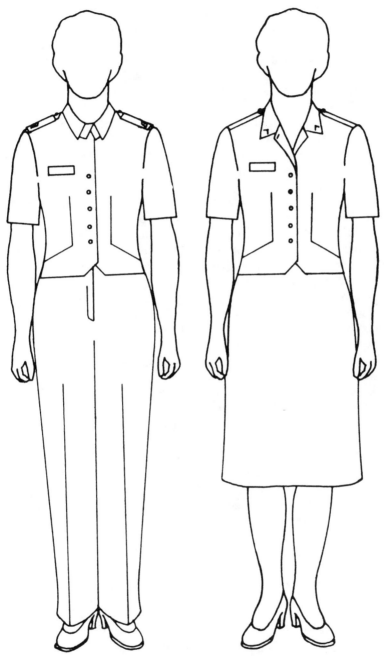

Class B Army Green Classic Ensemble, Short Sleeve Shirt and Neck Tab with Slacks, and Short Sleeve Shirt with Skirt

The green AG 415 shirt is available in short- or long-sleeved styles. Both have a cutaway design so that they can be worn on the outside of the skirt or pants; at the soldier's option, the shirt can also be tucked into the skirt or pants. The collar on the short-sleeved shirt has been designed so that it can be worn with or without the black neck tab.

Soldiers may choose to purchase optional wool shirts, AG 428, available in both long- and short-sleeved styles. Styling on the AG 428 shirts matches that of the AG 415 shirts in all aspects except for the fabric used.

Servicewomen may (depending on the unit to which they are assigned) choose either the garrison cap or the green service hat for headgear. Garrison caps can be worn with the Class A, Class B, or dress uniform. The cap should be worn with the front vertical crease centered on the forehead. No hair should show on the forehead below the front bottom edge of the cap, which should be situated approximately one inch above the eyebrows. (That normally corresponds to about two finger-widths above the eyebrows.) The cap will be opened on the head, so that the crown of the head is covered. The back vertical crease should fit snugly to the back of the head.

The other alternative for headgear is the green service hat. Hat insignia is to be worn centered on the hatband. This hat is an optional item, permissible for wear with the Class A, Class B, or dress uniform. It should be worn straight on the head so that the hatband would form a line parallel with the ground. Hair should not be visible on the forehead below the front brim of the hat. The brim should be ½ to 1 inch above the eyebrows (between one and two finger-widths).

Organizational berets and drill sergeant hats are also authorized for wear with the servicewoman's green classic uniform. When the classic dress uniform is worn for duty or for daytime social occasions, headgear is required; it can be worn without headgear to formal evening social events.

Most of the accessories available to servicemen for wear with the green service uniform are applicable (in female styles) for the servicewomen for wear with the green classic uniform. The exceptions are as follows. Servicewomen do not wear belts or buckles with the classic uniform, nor do they wear the necktie or bow tie. Their only color option for socks is black, and these can be worn only when slacks are worn. When specifically authorized, black combat boots can be worn, bloused, with slacks. Additional accessories available for the classic uniform are as follows:

- Black neck tab.
- Handbags, either black service handbag or optional black clutch, carried only with the Class A or Class B uniform.

INSIGNIA OF BRANCH – Same as US Insignia.

DISTINCTIVE UNIT INSIGNIA (Crest) – Centered between outside of button and shoulder seam.

SPECIAL SKILL BADGE – ¼" above ribbons.

SHOULDER SLEEVE INSIGNIA (current organization) – ½" down from shoulder seam and centered.

SERVICE RIBBONS – Centered with bottom line positioned parallel to bottom edge of nameplate.

MARKSMANSHIP BADGE – Centered parallel to top edge of top button ¼" below service ribbons. (Slight adjustment to conform to individual figure differences authorized.)

IDENTIFICATION BADGE – Centered with top edge of badge parallel to top edge of third button from top.

SERVICE STRIPES (Hash marks) – 4" above bottom of sleeve and centered (stripes run diagonally).

SOCKS – Optional plain black cotton or cotton nylon may be worn with black oxford shoes or Jodhpur boots, when worn with slacks.

SHOES – Black Oxford leather (nonpatent) with maximum of 3 eyelets, closed toe and heel (heel no higher than 2").

JEWELRY: EARRINGS – Screw-on or post-type on optional basis with service, dress, and mess uniforms only.
NECKLACE: A purely religious medal on a chain is authorized as long as neither is exposed.
A WRIST WATCH AND NOT MORE THAN TWO RINGS ARE AUTHORIZED.

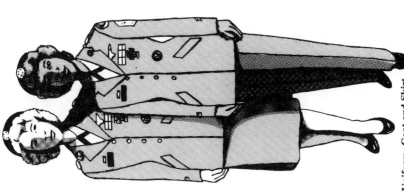

Classic Uniform, Coat and Skirt

Classic Uniform, Coat and Slacks

BERET – Worn tilted slightly to back of head with insignia centered on the forehead and not forward of forehead hairline (insignia will be placed ¾" from bottom edge of Beret front, parallel to floor and centered on eyelet).

US INSIGNIA – Bottom of disk centered approximately ⅝" up from notch with center line of insignia parallel to inside edge of lapel.

SHOULDER SLEEVE INSIGNIA – FORMER WARTIME ORGANIZATION – ½" down from shoulder seam and centered.

UNIT AWARD EMBLEM – Centered with bottom edge ⅛" above top of nameplate.

INSIGNIA OF GRADE (STRIPES) – Centered halfway between shoulder seam and elbow and centered on sleeve.

NAMEPLATE – Centered 1-2" above top edge of top button.

OVERSEA SERVICE BARS (Hershey Bars) – 4" above and parallel to bottom of sleeve and centered.

SKIRT – Not more than 1" above or 2" below crease in back of knee.

STOCKINGS – Unpatterned/non-pastel materials of sheer or semi-sheer, with or without seams.

PUMPS – Black Service, untrimmed, closed toe heel, heel 1" to 3" and sole thickness ½" max.

IDENTIFICATION TAGS (Dog Tags) – Worn when engaged in field training, when traveling in aircraft, and when outside CONUS.

- Black pumps.
- Sheer stockings.
- Black umbrella.

The insignia, awards, badges, and accouterments for the servicewomen's Class A and dress uniforms are the same as those allowed for the servicemen's Class A and dress uniforms, with the exceptions that servicewomen, because of MOS limitations, would not be authorized to wear distinctive items for infantry personnel or combat leader's identification tabs. Likewise, the authorized insignia for the Class B uniform is the same as for servicemen.

Green Maternity Service Uniform

The pregnant soldier has been provided a special uniform with considerable flexibility. The ensemble of components can be combined to form all three classes of uniforms, much like the green classic service uniform. The Class A uniform is composed of a green maternity tunic, matching maternity slacks or skirt, a long- or short-sleeved AG 415 maternity shirt, and a black neck tab. No maternity jacket is provided. For the Class B uniform, the tunic is omitted, and the neck tab may also be omitted if the short-sleeved shirt is worn. The Army green maternity dress uniform is identical to the Class A uniform except that slacks are not authorized as a maternity dress uniform component. No white maternity shirt is available for the dress uniform. At the commander's discretion, civilian clothes may be worn for formal functions by the pregnant soldier.

Headgear rules follow the standard servicewoman's uniform regulations. No headgear is required with the dress uniform for evening social functions.

The tunic is hip length, sleeveless, and scoop-necked. It has a front inverted pleat and adjustment tabs at the waist.

Both the skirt and slacks have a nylon knitted stretch-front panel and elastic waistbands.

Maternity AG 415 shirts are hip length, with a straight-cut bottom, since they are to be worn on the outside of the skirt or slacks. The short-sleeved shirt has a convertible collar that can be worn as a turn-down collar or closed with the neck tab. Maternity shirts have shoulder loops, standard with the nonmaternity servicewomen's shirts. Since the tunic has no shoulder loops, when it is worn over the shirt, the loops of the shirt are buttoned over the tunic so the shoulder marks are on top.

Accessories, insignia, awards, badges, and accouterments for the maternity uniforms follow the same regulations as those for the servicewomen's Class A, Class B, and dress uniforms.

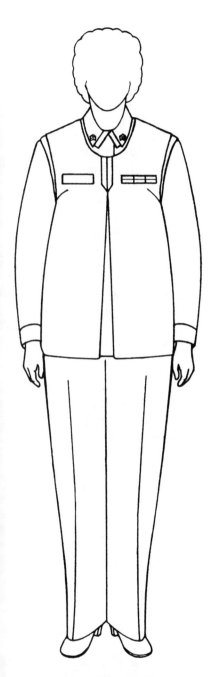

**Army Green Maternity Class A
Uniform with Pin-on Insignia**

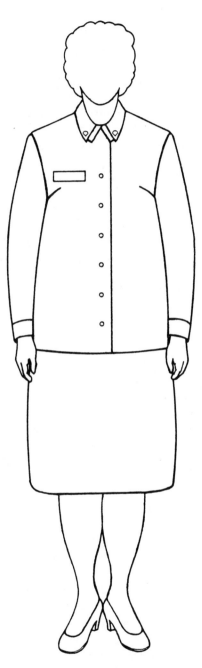

**Army Green Maternity Class B
Uniform with Pin-on Insignia**

Army Blue Uniform

The Army Blue (Dress) Uniform is an optional purchase item for enlisted soldiers. When specialized units use this uniform as an organizational uniform, it will be provided to the enlisted soldier at no cost.

Normally the Army blues cannot be worn as a duty uniform (except when it is required as an organizational uniform in units such as the 3rd U.S. Infantry, "The Old Guard"). Its use is reserved for formal social functions, official or private, and for other appropriate occasions as desired by the individual soldier. Weddings, for example, can be an appropriate occasion for the dress blues.

The styling and fit for the jacket, trousers, and skirt are the same for the blues as they are for the Army green service uniform (for males) and the Army green classic uniform (for females). No slacks are authorized for servicewomen with the Army blue uniform. Gold ornamental braiding is included on the jacket sleeve and shoulder loops, as well as on the outside seam of the trouser legs. The trousers come in both low-waisted and high-waisted styles. Servicemen use a commercially purchased long-sleeved white shirt with the dress blue uniform, while servicewomen use the military-issue short-sleeved white shirt.

The accessories, insignia, awards, badges, and accouterments follow most of the same regulations governing the wearing of the Army green dress uniforms, with a few differences. Gloves can be either white or black dress gloves. For servicemen, gold cuff links and studs are allowed, and a choice is permitted between the black four-in-hand necktie and the black bow tie. For servicewomen, in addition to the two types of handbags that can be carried with the green dress uniform, a black fabric handbag is available.

Clearly, the purchase of the dress blue uniform is a costly decision for a junior enlisted man or woman. The cost of the uniform items as of September 1992 were as follows: jacket, $105; pants, $38; and hat, $22 — at least $165, not counting the cost of service stripes, rank, and related sewing. Add a commercial white dress shirt (males), authorized awards and decorations, and other accessories, and the total can exceed $250.

Is the uniform's relatively lofty price significantly offset by its value? Consider its social worth to the soldier who understands the importance of appearing totally professional when attending Army formal or social functions. Also consider how a junior enlisted soldier properly wearing the dress blue uniform is viewed by senior NCOs and officers. In the Army, appearance does matter.

Selected outstanding soldiers may receive a complimentary set of

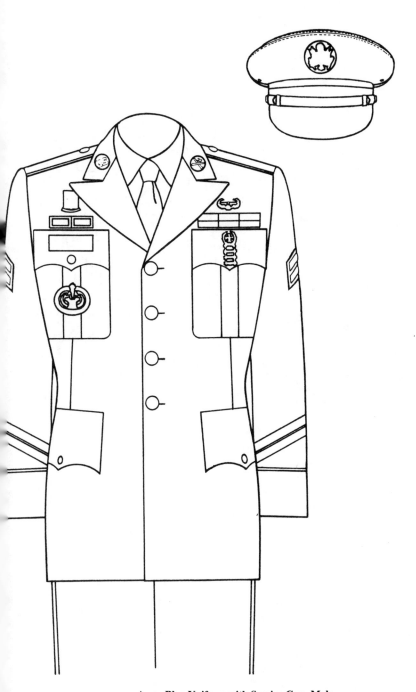

Army Blue Uniform with Service Cap, Male

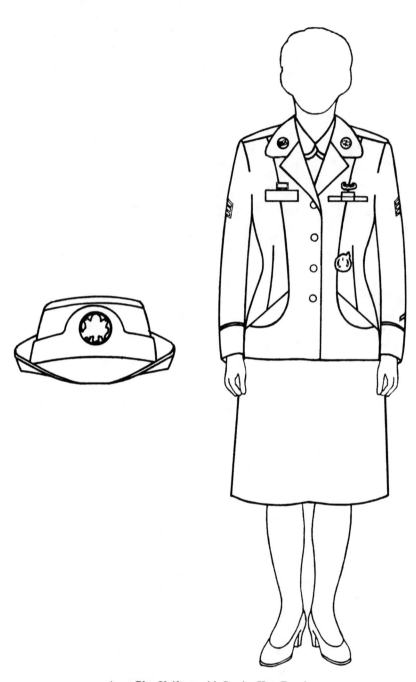

Army Blue Uniform with Service Hat, Female

dress blues as a result of their performance at annual soldier boards. During fall 1992, for example, the Indiana Chapter of the Association of the United States Army presented complimentary dress blues to the Fort Benjamin Harrison, Indiana, NCO of the Year and the Soldier of the Year—an approximate $500 value for outstanding achievement. Most soldiers, however, must make a purchase decision based on career goals or other factors.

Battle Dress Uniform

The temperate and hot weather battle dress uniforms (BDU) can be worn by all soldiers year-round, when authorized by the local commander. Even when authorized, however, they are for duty only and cannot be worn for travel or off the military installation, other than between the soldier's living quarters and duty station. BDUs are considered combat, field, training, or utility uniforms, not all-purpose uniforms. No components of the BDU are to be intermixed with other uniforms.

BDUs are functional, loose-fitting uniforms; alterations may not be made so that the fit is tight. A tight fit reduces air flow, which is needed for ventilation. A belt is required with the trousers, even though the coat is worn outside the trousers. A newly styled coat is authorized in addition to the older design. The new coat has a narrower collar, narrower waist take-up tabs, and a side flare on the breast bellow pockets. Coat sleeves can be rolled, if desired; if rolled, the camouflage pattern must remain exposed and the sleeve must be above, but not more than three inches above, the elbow.

The trousers are to be bloused at the top of the boots. A draw cord or blousing rubbers are provided for this purpose.

BDUs may not be starched and, by regulation, do not require pressing unless ordered by the commander for special occasions such as parades, reviews, inspections, or ceremonies. Pressing is generally authorized and encouraged, however.

For most soldiers, the BDU cap is the only permissible headgear. It is to be worn straight on the head, with no hair showing under the cap on the forehead. The cap should make a line around the head that is parallel with the ground; it should be tilted neither up nor down in front. During cold weather, earflaps on the cap may be worn down, including when the wearer is in formation, if the commander has prescribed a "uniformity" wear policy to cover such times. Subdued insignia of grade will be worn on the cap at all times. Soldiers authorized to wear berets or other organizational headgear may wear that headgear instead of the BDU cap.

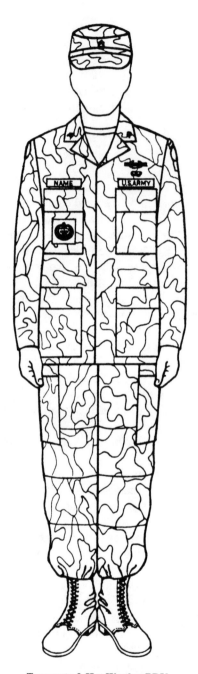

Temperate & Hot Weather BDU

Camouflage Cap

Camouflage Field Jacket

CAMOUFLAGE CAP—Straight on head so that cap band creates a straight line around the head parallel to the ground. (subdued insignia of grade ONLY and centered from top to bottom, right to left)

UNDERSHIRT—Army Brown or Green is authorized.

SHOULDER SLEEVE INSIGNIA—Current Organization—½" down from shoulder seam and centered. (subdued only)

'US ARMY' DISTINGUISHING INSIGNIA—Centered immediately above and parallel to top edge of pocket.

BLACK BOOTS—Clean and shined at all times (no patent leather).

SOCKS—ONLY Olive Green, shade 408, is authorized for wear with combat or organizational boots.

BLACK BUCKLE & BLACK TIPPED BELT ONLY COMBINATION AUTHORIZED.

Battle Dress Uniform (BDU)

HAIR—Neatly groomed and will not present an extreme, ragged, or unkempt appearance. Hair will not extend below bottom edge of collar, nor be cut to appear unfeminine. Styles will not interfere with the proper wearing of military headgear.

INSIGNIA OF GRADE—Subdued pin-on, or sew-on, will be centered on each collar bisecting the collar 1" from the point.

SHOULDER SLEEVE INSIGNIA—FORMER WARTIME ORGANIZATION—½" down from shoulder seam and centered (subdued only).

INSIGNIA NAMETAPE—Centered, immediately above and parallel to top of pocket.

If no other rain gear has been issued to the soldier, the black all-weather coat may be worn as a raincoat with the BDU, but only in the garrison (on the installation). When the cold weather camouflage coat (field jacket) is worn over the BDU, it must be buttoned and zipped. The shirt collar must be worn inside either coat. If the field jacket is worn, the Army-issue olive green scarf and black leather shell gloves may be worn, as well. In addition, female soldiers may carry a handbag when wearing BDUs, provided the handbag is not carried outside of the garrison environment, except between living quarters and duty station.

Insignia and accouterments authorized for wear with BDUs include:

- Subdued combat and special skill badges.
- Subdued special skill and marksmanship tabs.
- Subdued identification badges.
- Brassards.
- Branch insignia.
- Combat leader's identification tab.
- Grade insignia.
- Headgear insignia.
- Subdued shoulder sleeve insignia.
- Name tape and U.S. Army tapes.

No foreign badges, distinctive unit insignia, or regimental affiliation crests may be worn with the BDU.

Maternity Work Uniform

The maternity counterpart to the BDU, the maternity work uniform, follows the same basic regulations as those for the standard BDU, except that no belt is required for the trousers. In addition, since a separate field jacket is not issued for the pregnant soldier along with her maternity work uniform, she may wear her previously issued field jacket, unbuttoned and unzipped if necessary.

Desert Battle Dress Uniform

The Desert Battle Dress Uniform (DBDU) is issued as organizational clothing as prescribed by the commander—as it was to units that took part in the Persian Gulf War—and is considered year-round wear. Like the BDU, it is considered a field, training, or combat uniform and should not be worn when other uniforms are more appropriate; its components are

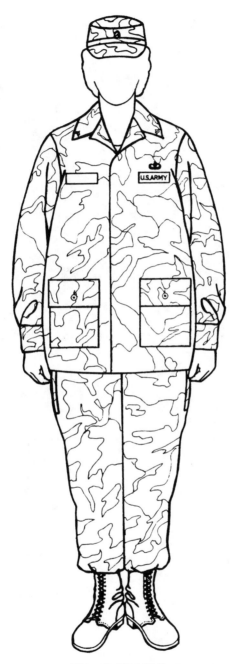

Maternity Work Uniform

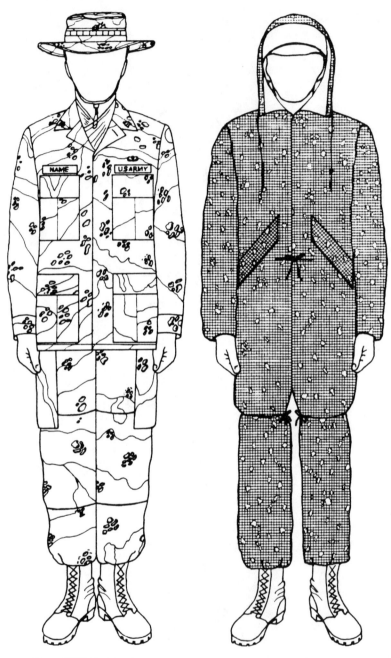

Desert BDU, Daytime Pattern   **Desert BDU, Nighttime Pattern**

not to be intermixed with other uniforms; and it cannot be worn for travel, except between the soldier's living quarters and duty station.

Much like BDUs, DBDUs are loose-fitting, and alterations to tighten the fit are not authorized. The rules for blousing trousers and rolling sleeves are the same as for BDUs. Normally the shirt and trousers are required, but local commanders can vary this policy if appropriate for health, comfort, or efficiency in certain climatic conditions. Undershirts worn with the DBDUs must be brown.

The DBDU hat is the only choice of headgear unless special organizational headgear has been authorized. The DBDU hat is to be worn with no hair showing on the forehead, and with the chin strap pulled up under the chin.

When the parka is worn, it must be buttoned, with the shirt collar inside. The olive green scarf and black leather shell gloves may be worn with the parka.

DBDUs have distinctive daytime and nighttime patterns (See illustration).

Insignia and accouterments authorized for wear with DBDUs include:

- Subdued combat and special skill badges (pin-on only).
- Brassards.
- Branch insignia (pin-on only).
- Grade insignia.
- Headgear insignia.
- Subdued shoulder sleeve insignia.
- Name and U.S. Army tapes.

No foreign badges, distinctive unit insignia, or regimental affiliation crests may be worn with the DBDU.

Cold Weather Uniform

The wool OG 108 cold weather uniform is another organizational clothing uniform issued by local commanders when appropriate. It too can be considered a year-round utility uniform. Because it is a utility or field uniform, it is not to be worn for travel or when other uniforms are more appropriate. Distinctive from rules governing BDUs and DBDUs, components of the cold weather uniform may be worn with other utility or organizational uniforms as a cold weather ensemble when such wear is prescribed by the commander.

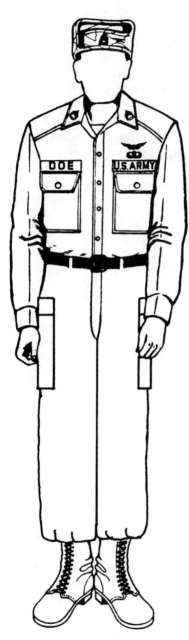

Cold Weather Uniform

Wool Serge Shirt, Female

This uniform is also designed to be loose-fitting, and no alterations to that fit are authorized. When the OG 108 shirt is worn as an outergarment, it must be tucked inside the trousers and worn with a belt. Trousers worn as an outergarment are to be bloused. Sleeves for the cold weather uniform may not be rolled.

Female soldiers may wear either the female OG 108 shirt or the male OG 108 shirt, depending on which is issued.

Either the BDU cap or the cold weather cap may be worn with the cold weather uniform. Organizational berets and headgear are also authorized. Wearing of the BDU cap follows the same regulations as described with the BDU uniform. Rules for wearing the cold weather cap are similar. No hair should show below the hat on the forehead. Earflaps should always be fastened—they are to be fastened beneath the chin when worn down, and against the cap when worn up.

The olive green scarf and black leather shell gloves may be worn with any outergarments authorized for the cold weather uniform. Coats must always be buttoned or zipped, and shirt collars must be inside the coat.

Insignia and accouterments authorized for wear with the cold weather uniform include:

- Subdued combat and special skill badges (pin-on only).
- Brassards.
- Subdued branch insignia (pin-on only).
- Combat leader's identification tab (on field jackets).
- Headgear insignia.
- Name and U.S. Army tapes.

Shoulder sleeve insignia are not authorized with the OG 108 shirt. Collar insignia, and name and U.S. Army distinguishing tapes are also not to be worn on the shirt if the shirt is authorized only as an undergarment. The name tape should not be worn on the cold weather parka (OG 107). Foreign badges, distinctive unit insignia, regimental affiliation crests, and sew-on badges and insignia of grade are not to be used with this uniform.

Food Service Uniform

The food service uniform is authorized for year-round wear by all soldiers in Career Management Field 94 when prescribed by the local commander and authorized under the provisions of CTA 50-900.

For men, the uniform consists of the white medical assistant's smock and trousers and black oxford shoes or combat boots, as prescribed by the

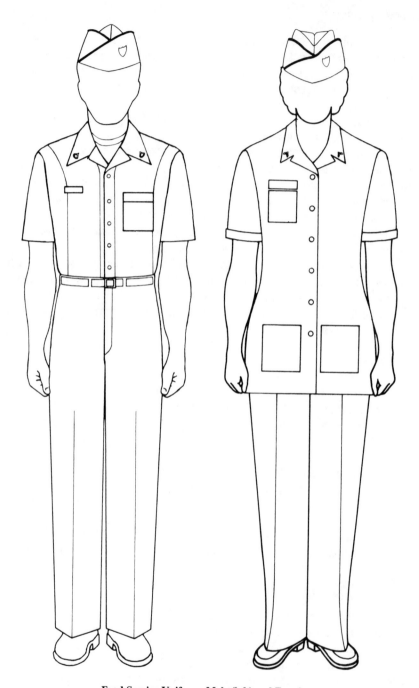

Food Service Uniform, Male (left) and Female

local commander. Women may wear the white hospital dress, white maternity dress, white maternity slacks and tunic, or white pantsuit. The following accessories are also authorized:

- Coat, black, all weather.
- BDU field jacket.
- Black gloves (dress, if worn with the black coat; black leather shell with insert if worn with the BDU field jacket).
- White undershirt.
- Black or olive green scarf, as authorized.
- Windbreaker.

The food service supervisor is authorized to wear a locally procured white shirt and black trousers in lieu of the medical assistant's smock and trousers. Women are additionally authorized to wear a black skirt.

This uniform is to be worn only while on duty or while in transit to or from the place of duty. The uniform is not authorized for field wear, but local commanders may allow the uniform to be worn when supporting civilian activities such as parades or ceremonies.

The standard headgear for this uniform is the green garrison cap, but it may not be worn while in the dining facility. Only the food handler's cap may be worn in the dining facility.

Insignia of grade, headgear insignia, and the nameplate are also required for this uniform.

Hospital Duty Uniform (Male)

The male hospital duty uniform may be worn year-round by soldiers in medical, dental, or veterinary specialties. The basic uniform consists of the white medical assistant's smock or the white physician's smock with white medical assistant's trousers.

Standard accessories include the web belt, the black all-weather coat or BDU field jacket with appropriate gloves, the garrison cap or organizational beret (the service cold-weather cap, OD 344 may be worn only when the black all-weather coat is worn), white undershirts, the black windbreaker, and the appropriate scarf, if desired. Shoes may be either white or black, with socks of the same color. The pullover sweater is not to be worn with this uniform, but the black cardigan sweater may be worn within a medical facility while on duty.

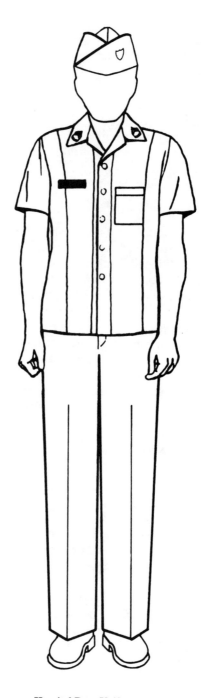

Hospital Duty Uniform, Male

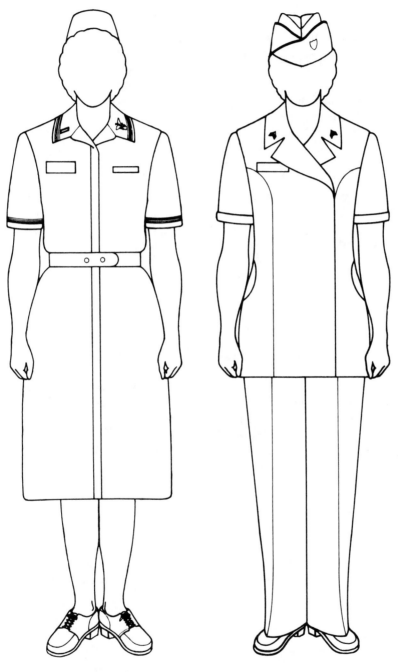

Hospital Duty Dress   **Hospital Duty Pantsuit**

Hospital Duty and Maternity Uniform (Female)

Female enlisted soldiers in a medical, dental, or veterinary MOS are authorized to wear one of the following five uniform combinations:

- Dress, women's. (A white, knee-length dress with short sleeves, buttoned down the front and belted.)
- White physician's smock.
- Women's hospital duty tunic and pants.
- White maternity dress.
- White maternity slacks and tunic.

Either the garrison cap or the black beret must be worn with all of these uniforms.

The two maternity combinations are of commercial design and manufacture but must be plain and unadorned, with collars suitable for wear of rank insignia.

The accessories authorized for the men's hospital uniform are also authorized for this uniform.

Physical Fitness Uniform

All soldiers are required to own the gray Army Physical Fitness Uniform (PFU). The uniform consists of the long-sleeved, zippered sweatshirt, sweatpants, gray T-shirt, and gray trunks. Commercial shoes and plain white, calf-length socks or black combat boots and green wool socks may be worn, as authorized by the local commander.

The only award authorized for wear on the PFU is the cloth, sew-on Physical Fitness Badge, which is worn centered on the left side of the T-shirt or sweatshirt, above the breast.

Awards and Decorations

Awards and decorations add the final polish to the soldier's professional appearance. You should feel proud of the accomplishments the decorations represent. Consequently, it is imperative that ribbons and medals be kept in impeccable condition. If they become soiled, they should be replaced.

Placement

All individual U.S. decorations and service medals (full-size medals, miniature medals, and ribbons) are worn above the left breast pocket or centered on the left side of the coat or jacket of the prescribed uniform (with the exception of the Medal of Honor, which is worn suspended around the neck). Decorations are worn with the one with the highest precedence displayed above and to the wearer's right of the others.

Full-size decorations and service medals are worn on the Army blue, white, and green dress uniforms when worn for social functions. They are worn in order of precedence (see lists below) from the wearer's right to left, in one or more lines, without overlapping within a line and with one-eighth-inch space between lines. No line may contain fewer medals than the one above it.

Service ribbons also are worn in the order of precedence from the wearer's right to left. Up to four ribbons may be worn in a single row; a second row cannot be started until the soldier has earned the fourth ribbon. The first two rows are block-style with either three or four ribbons in each, but subsequent rows can be stair-stepped to the right (flush left) if the soldier chooses. This is frequently done so that the coat collar does not cover any of the awards. The top row of ribbons can either be flush left (with the stair-step pattern) or centered over the row below it (with the block-style pattern). Ribbons are worn on the green shirt or with the Army green service uniforms and the Army blues.

Full-size decorations and service medals are presented to the soldier in addition to the ribbon that represents the decoration or medal. Often the full-size honors end up in a display case hung on the wall, but they can be worn on the dress blue or dress green uniform at social functions. Miniature decorations, replicas made to a one-half scale, are optional purchase items; miniatures can be worn only on dress blues or on formal civilian attire, if such attire is appropriate for the social function. No miniature exists for the Medal of Honor. Marksmanship badges or Driver and Mechanic badges are not worn with either full-size or miniature decorations. Any other special skill badges must be in miniature size if miniature decorations are used.

Order of Precedence

There is a definite ranking among categories of decorations and awards, and within each category there is an order of precedence for the individual medals. When awards of two or more categories are worn simultaneously, the following order of precedence should be observed: U.S. military decorations, U.S. unit awards, U.S. nonmilitary awards, Prisoner of War Medal, Good Conduct Medal, Army Reserve Components Achievement Medal, U.S. service and training ribbons, U.S. Merchant Marine awards, foreign military decorations, foreign unit awards, and non–U.S. service awards. Lists follow for major categories, showing order of precedence for individual awards within each group.

U.S. Military Decorations

Medal of Honor
Distinguished Service Cross
Navy Cross
Air Force Cross
Defense Distinguished Service Medal
Distinguished Service Medal
Silver Star
Defense Superior Service Medal
Legion of Merit
Distinguished Flying Cross
Soldier's Medal
Navy and Marine Corps Medal
Airman's Medal
Coast Guard Medal
Bronze Star Medal
Purple Heart
Defense Meritorious Service Medal
Meritorious Service Medal
Air Medal
Joint Service Commendation Medal
Army Commendation Medal
Navy Commendation Medal
Air Force Commendation Medal
Coast Guard Commendation Medal
Joint Service Achievement Medal
Army Achievement Medal
Navy Achievement Medal
Air Force Achievement Medal
Coast Guard Achievement Medal
Combat Action Ribbon

U.S. Unit Awards

Presidential Unit Citation (Army and Air Force)
Presidential Unit Citation (Navy)
Joint Meritorious Unit Award
Valorous Unit Award

Meritorious Unit Commendation (Army)
Navy Unit Commendation
Air Force Outstanding Unit Award
Coast Guard Unit Commendation
Army Superior Unit Award
Meritorious Unit Commendation (Navy)
Air Force Organizational Excellence Award
Coast Guard Meritorious Unit Commendation

U.S. Service Medals

Army of Occupation Medal
National Defense Service Medal
Antarctica Service Medal
Armed Forces Expeditionary Medal
Vietnam Service Medal
Southwest Asia Service Medal
Humanitarian Service Medal
Armed Forces Reserve Medal
NCO Professional Development Ribbon
Army Service Ribbon
Overseas Service Ribbon
Army Reserve Components Overseas Training Ribbon

Non–U.S. Service Medals

United Nations Service Medal
Inter-American Defense Board Medal
United Nations Medal
Multinational Force and Observers Medal
Republic of Vietnam Campaign Medal

Finishing Touches

The uniform isn't complete without the finishing touches added by uniform accessories, insignia, badges, awards and decorations, and accouterments. Space limitations make a full discussion of all possible uniform pieces impractical; the most common are included here.

Uniform Accessories

Uniform accessories include organizational berets, combat boots, buttons, scarves, rain cap covers, sweaters, and windbreakers, all of which have regulations governing their use.

Organizational berets come in three colors: black, green, and maroon. Black berets are worn by soldiers assigned to Ranger units or to the Ranger Department of the U.S. Army Infantry School. Green berets signify operational Special Forces Group personnel or soldiers who are Special Forces qualified or assigned to the U.S. Army First Special Operations Command, the U.S. Army John F. Kennedy Special Warfare Center, or the Special Operations Command for the Atlantic, Pacific, Europe, Central, or South regions. The maroon beret is for all personnel on jump status, whether assigned to airborne or non-airborne units.

The beret should be worn so that the headband is straight across the forehead, one inch above the eyebrow. The stiffener is positioned over the left eye; the beret is then draped over the right ear. An adjustment ribbon is provided for correcting the size; once adjusted, however, the ribbon should be knotted and cut, with the knot secured inside the edge binding at the back of the beret.

When organizational berets are authorized for wear, uniform trousers or slacks may be bloused if boots are also worn.

Black leather combat boots have a deep lug tread sole, a replaceable heel, a closed loop speed-lacing system, and a padded collar. Black laces are to be diagonally laced in the boots, with excess laces tucked into the top of the boot or under bloused trousers or slacks. Metal cleats and side tabs are authorized only for honor guards and ceremonial units.

Buttons are covered by regulations as well. Standard Army-issue buttons are gold-colored aluminum; yellow gold buttons are optional purchase items. White gold, or aluminum, buttons cannot be worn.

Rain cap covers protect service caps from damage due to inclement weather. The transparent plastic covers can be worn with either the green or blue service caps. No covers are available for the servicewoman's green service hat.

Scarves are handy in cold weather. The black wool scarf is worn with the black all-weather coat or the windbreaker. The olive green scarf is used with cold weather utility coats (either field jackets or parkas). Both are to be folded in half lengthwise, crossed left over right at the neck, and tucked neatly into the neckline of the outergarment.

Sweaters are optional purchase items, available in cardigan or pullover styles. The cardigan can be worn as an outergarment only in the immediate work area. It cannot be worn off-post or when traveling to and from living quarters unless it is worn under a service jacket or windbreaker and is not visible. The pullover style can be worn as an outergarment with the Class B uniform. When used as an outergarment, the sweater must be worn with shoulder marks indicating rank (if corporal or higher), name-

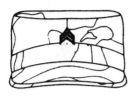

BDU Cap

Drill Sergeant Hat, Male

Helmet Cover

Drill Sergeant Hat, Female

Organizational Beret

Cardigan Sweater, Male

Cardigan Sweater, Female

Windbreaker

Pullover Sweater

plate (centered above the patch), and unit crest if one is authorized. Sleeves on uniform sweaters are never to be worn rolled or pushed up.

Windbreakers are another optional purchase item. They can be used as an outergarment with Class B uniforms in addition to the hospital duty and food service uniforms. The zipper is to be worn zipped at least three-fourths of the way up. Nonsubdued pin-on rank insignia is used with the windbreaker. With the rank insignia removed, the windbreaker may be worn with civilian clothing.

Insignia

Insignia worn by military personnel designate grade, branch of service, organization, duty assignments, and prior Army service.

Insignia of grade are required for all soldiers (except privates, E-1). Although the symbols of grade are always the same, the insignia themselves come in a variety of styles. Embroidered sew-on insignia are used on each sleeve of the Army green coat and the dress blue coat. Centered between the shoulder seam and the elbow of the sleeve, the insignia should have a background color that matches the coat to which it is sewn. Nonsubdued (shiny) pin-on insignia are required on the collars of the black all-weather coat, the windbreaker, and the hospital duty and food service uniforms. Enlisted personnel who are specialists and below wear the nonsubdued insignia on the collar of the AG 415 shirt as well. In each case the insignia are worn on both collars, one inch up from the collar point, with the center line of the insignia bisecting the points of the collar. Subdued pin-on insignia, used for utility uniform shirts and cold weather coats, are positioned in the same manner.

Shoulder marks are used with the AG 415 shirt for enlisted personnel grade corporal and above. When wearing the black pullover sweater, all personnel use shoulder marks to identify their grade. Shoulder marks are slipped over the shoulder loops so that the bottom of the insignia is closest to the shoulder. Soldiers can choose between two sizes so that the fit is appropriate to the shoulder width.

Branch insignia are required for MOS-qualified enlisted personnel. The branch-identifying symbol is placed over a plain disk. To maintain a soldierly appearance, branch insignia should be cleaned and shined frequently. Separating the insignia from the disk before cleaning ensures that no cleaning materials are left embedded in the crevices. Branch insignia should be worn on the left collar of the green or blue uniform coat. It should be placed one inch above the notch, and the center line of the insignia should be parallel to the inside edge of the collar. A plain disk with the initials "U.S." is worn in a similar manner on the right collar.

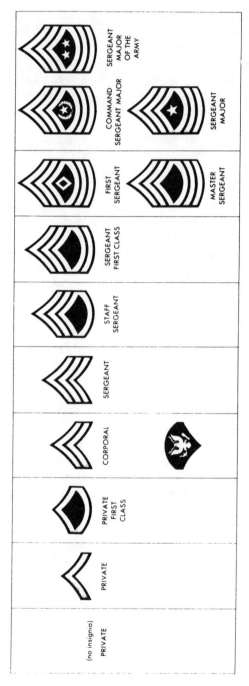

Army Ranks

Distinctive Items Authorized for Infantry Personnel

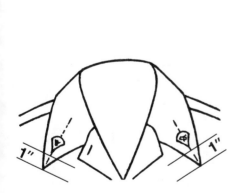

Polished Pin-on Insignia of Grade on Collars

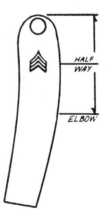

Sew-on Insignia of Grade

Insignia of Branch and U.S. on Army Green and Blue Uniforms

Insignia of Branch and U.S. on Army Green Classic Ensemble

Adjutant General's Corps

Air Defense Artillery

Armor

Branch Immaterial

Aviation

Cavalry

Chaplain Assistant

Chemical Corps

Civil Affairs

Corps of Engineers

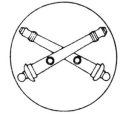

Field Artillery
Branch Insignia

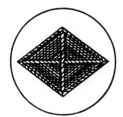

Finance

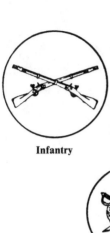

Infantry

Inspector General

Public Affairs

**Judge
Advocate General**

Medical Corps

Military Intelligence

Military Police Corps

Ordnance Corps

Quartermaster Corps

Signal Corps

Special Forces

**Transportation Corps
Branch Insignia**

**The Sergeant Major
of the Army**

Shoulder sleeve insignia (SSI) come in two authorized forms. The nonsubdued insignia for the soldier's current organization should be worn on the left sleeve of the Army green or dress blue coat, one-half inch below the top shoulder seam. If a special identifying tab for Ranger, Special Forces, or President's Hundred is worn, it is placed in the normal position for the SSI; the SSI is then positioned one-quarter inch below the tab. Subdued insignia is worn in the same position, but on utility uniforms.

Shoulder sleeve insignia for former wartime service is worn on the right shoulder of the same coats, if appropriate. Soldiers should follow details in AR 670-1 to determine which unit insignia to wear. Nonsubdued and subdued insignia are used in the same manner as the current organization insignia.

Certain combat arms soldiers are authorized to wear the combat leader's identification tab, but only during those times when they are actually filling the command position. At the unit level, the first sergeant, platoon sergeant, section leader, squad leader, tank commander, and rifle squad fire team leader can all wear the green cloth loop. Centered on both shoulder loops, the tab is worn with the Army green coat and the cold weather coat (field jacket).

Distinctive unit insignia (DUI) are used to promote esprit de corps among brigades, divisions, regiments, battalions, schools, or major commands. This insignia is worn in several locations on the uniform. It is to be centered above the nameplate when the black pullover sweater is worn; centered on the "left curtain" on the garrison cap, one inch from the crease; centered on the organizational flash of the organizational beret; and centered on the shoulder loops of the service uniforms. If shoulder marks (rank) are worn on the loops, the DUI is to be centered between the bottom of the rank insignia and the shoulder seam. The DUI can be centered on the combat leader's identification tab as well.

Nameplates, either glossy or nonglossy, are required with most uniforms; name tapes are used when nameplates are not.

Other common uniform items are service stripes, one authorized on the left sleeve for each three years of service, and overseas service bars, one authorized on the right sleeve for each six months of overseas service during war.

7

Pay and Entitlements

Any soldier who enlists in the Army for the money is in the wrong business, but you should be aware that your total earnings encompass more than just basic pay. Soldiers are afforded a number of benefits unavailable to their civilian counterparts. In addition to basic pay, allowances, leave, and other entitlements, soldiers enjoy many extras that do not show up on the LES, such as health care, travel opportunities, and PX and commissary privileges.

Knowing how the system of pay and entitlements works can be invaluable to the soldier. This chapter offers general guidelines on how to verify the accuracy of your Leave and Earnings Statement (LES); what types of pay, allowances, and leave are available to you; and the various deductions that will be taken from your paycheck. Specific details on the entitlements you have earned and instructions for completing necessary forms should be obtained from your Finance and Accounting Office (FAO).*

---

*Another helpful resource is *Armed Forces Guide to Personal Financial Planning*, 2nd edition, by Professor Michael E. Edleson and COL Hobart B. Pillsbury, USA. (Harrisburg, Pa.: Stackpole Books, 1992.)

ARMY/AIR FORCE LEAVE AND EARNINGS STATEMENT (ACTIVE AND RESERVE FORCES)

NAME (LAST, FIRST, MI)	SOC. SEC. NO.	GRADE	PAY DATE	YRS SVC	ETS	BRANCH	ADSN DSSN	PERIOD COVERED
SIMPSON EDWARD C	303857978	E6	820129	09	960111	ARMY	5056	1-30 APR 91

ENTITLEMENTS		DEDUCTIONS		ALLOTMENTS		SUMMARY	
TYPE	AMOUNT	TYPE	AMOUNT	TYPE	AMOUNT	+AMT FWD	.00
BASE PAY	1448.70	FED TAXES	68.23	AFAF	2.00	+TOT ENT	2,301.53
BAQ	418.50	FICA	110.83	BANK	241.00	-TOT DED	1,111.29
BAS	184.50	SGLI	8.00			-TOT ALMT	243.00
PRO PAY	198.00	USSH	.50			=NET AMT	947.24
VHA	51.79	EVEN $	.00			-CR FWD	.00
EVEN $	.04	MID-MONTH-PAY	923.73				
						=EOM PAY	
							947.24
TOTAL	2301.53		1111.29		243.00		

	BF BAL	ERND	USED	CRBAL	ETSBAL	LOST	PAID	USE LOSE	FED TAXES	WAGE PERIOD	WAGE YTD	MS	EX	ADD'L TAX	TAX YTD
LEAVE	60.0	17.5	28	49.5	190.5	.5	.0	2.0		1646.70	7159.35	M	5	.00	392.38

	WAGE PERIOD	WAGE YTD	TAX YTD	STATE TAXES	CODE	WAGE PERIOD	WAGE YTD	M S N	EX	ADD'L TAX	TAX YTD
ICA TAXES	1448.70	5794.80	443.31		WA	.00	.00	M	05	.00	.00

	BAQ TYPE	BAQ DEPN	VHA ZIP	RENT AMT	SHARE	STAT	JFTR	DEPNS	2D JFTR	BAS TYPE	CHARITY	TPC	PACIDN
PAY DATA	W/DEP	SPOUSE	29207	420.00	1	R				REGULAR	8.00		EBCOGR81

REMARKS: 5 2 0034003

RATE CHG BASIC PAY   910401(091)
CHANGE SDAP   910413(104)
VHA BASED ON W/DEP, ZIP 29207

STOP   EVEN $ PAYMENT 910401(091)
RATE CHG SGLI   910401(113)
BANK   1ST UN NATL BANK
ACCT# 3468222975

Leave and Earnings Statement

Pay

Military pay consists of basic pay, special and incentive pay, and allowances. Pay is computed on the basis of a 30-day month, and soldiers may elect to be paid once a month (at the end of the month) or twice a month (on the 15th and 30th of each month), as indicated on DA Form 3685, *Joint Uniform Military Pay System (JUMPS)-Army Pay Elections.* All information pertaining to a soldier's pay and entitlements is recorded each month on *JUMPS-Active Component/Joint Service Software (JSS) Leave and Earnings Statement (LES)* and *Net Pay Advice* (NPA) forms.

The Leave and Earnings Statement

The LES is a computerized monthly statement of account for each soldier paid under the system. The LES shows all entitlements earned, collections affected, and payments made during the period covered by the statement. In addition, the LES records all transactions that affect your leave account for the period of the statement. It also serves as the official leave record.

Usually payday means long check-cashing lines in the post exchange, long checkout lines in the commissary, and large crowds at the clubs. What it should involve, but frequently doesn't, is a few moments to review the LES for accuracy.

Ultimately, you are responsible for your own financial affairs. The computerized Army/Air Force JSS pay system is generally very accurate. But with the diversified pay allowances and changing duty status among the many soldiers handled by each FAO, mistakes can occur. The sooner an error is spotted and reported, the easier it is to correct — whether the error is an overpayment or an underpayment.

A regular review of the information provided on the LES should include checking of all credits and debits, including calculations of leave. Each month the LES shows how many days of leave were used and the balance remaining. Also, when you are promoted, you should take care in checking your monthly LES to ensure the appropriate raise is credited on the correct date. Any discrepancies should be brought immediately to the attention of the FAO through your chain of command.

Net Pay Advice

The NPA form is issued at mid-month to all soldiers in the active Army, even if they have not elected the mid-month pay option. The form provides mid-month pay data and administrative remarks for those sol-

ARMY/AIR FORCE NET PAY ADVICE (ACTIVE)

The amount in block 6 is your net pay for the payday indicated in block 4 and was sent to the financial organization in block 7 for credit to your account. When cashing a personal check at your financial organization on payday, advise your teller you are a participant in the Direct Deposit Program. It will help you with better service. If you are paid once a month or you do not have your pay sent to a financial organization for direct deposit, information in block 5 through 7 will not be present and this form is intended to provide you with the remarks information only.

1. MEMBER'S NAME AND ADDRESS	2. SSN 303-85-7978	3. ADSN/DSSN 5056	4. PAY DATE 15 APR 91
SIMPSON EDWARD C EBCOGR81	5. ACCOUNT NUMBER 3468222975		6. NET PAY AMOUNT $923.73
	7. YOUR NET PAY WAS FORWARDED TO: 1ST UN NATL BANK 1628 BROWNING RD ROOM 200 COLUMBIA SC 29227-0002		

8. REMARKS

INVEST IN THE FUTURE - BUY US SAVINGS BONDS!

Net Pay Advice

diers who have elected the mid-month option, and it provides administrative remarks to those soldiers who have not elected the mid-month option.

Basic Pay

Basic pay is established by law and is determined by your rank and the amount of time you have served on active duty. A basic pay table for 1993 is included, but as with any salary information, it will become quickly outdated. Current pay schedules are frequently available through military-oriented magazines and through insurance firms. Post newspapers and *Army Times* publish updated versions as well. Or you can check with your FAO for the current rate.

Monthly Basic Pay

Grade		*Years of Service*			
	Under 2	*2*	*3*	*4*	*6*
E-6	$1230.60	$1341.30	$1397.10	$1456.50	$1511.10
E-5	1079.70	1175.40	1232.70	1286.10	1370.70
E-4	1007.10	1063.80	1126.20	1213.20	1261.20
E-3	948.90	1001.10	1041.00	1082.10	1082.10
E-2	913.20	913.20	913.20	913.20	913.20
E-1	814.80	814.80	814.80	814.80	814.80
E-1 with less than 4 months — 753.60.					

You have a choice of how your pay is disbursed. Cash payments are authorized only for trainees; all other soldiers must elect sure-pay or check-to-unit options. Sure-pay allows the government to deposit your net pay directly into your checking or savings account at the financial institution of your choice. Once initiated, sure-pay is the simplest way of ensuring that your pay is deposited regularly. Choosing this option will help you avoid long waits in teller lines, late deposits while on TDY or on leave, and the risk of losing your paycheck or having it stolen. With the check-to-unit option, your check will be delivered to you at your unit. In addition, checks can be made payable to another individual (a dependent) or financial institution (through allotments), at an address other than your unit. If you choose, you may combine two of the payment methods in any designated dollar amounts.

Reserve Drill Pay

Reserve drill pay is established by law. It is pay a Reserve Component soldier receives based on grade and length of service. Unlike basic pay,

A private in the Army Signal Corps trains on fixed-station communications equipment at Fort Gordon, Georgia

Reserve drill pay is computed and paid for the number of days of service rendered. It is comparable to basic pay. For example, a Reserve private first class with two years of service receives $33.37 a day. Multiplied by 30, the amount equals the monthly basic pay ($1001.10) received by a Regular Army private first class with two years of service. Weekend drills are worth four one-day drills, so a Reserve private first class with two years of service would receive $133.48 for a weekend drill.

Special and Incentive Pay

The Army offers a number of special monthly pay entitlements to compensate you for special skills, for enduring hardships, for exposure to danger, to serve as an incentive for reenlistment in critical MOSs, or for performance of hazardous duties. Compensation may be granted based on rank and time in service or on time spent performing special skills or enduring hardships; or it may be standard for all individuals serving in that particular capacity. The FAO can advise you on the current compensation for each entitlement that you should receive. You should ensure that your LES reflects all appropriate entitlements.

Special Duty Assignment Pay: $110–$275

Recruiters, drill sergeants, and career counselors receive special duty assignment pay for the service they render to the Army. If the soldier does not spend the full month in a designated special duty position, the pay is prorated for the percentage of the month actually spent performing the special duty. While these MOSs require some special qualifications, they are volunteer duties, for which the Army awards extra compensation. (See the section on reenlistment bonuses in chapter 9.)

Foreign Duty Pay (FDP): $8–$22.50

When enlisted soldiers are assigned to arduous duty stations OCONUS, they receive extra compensation in the form of FDP. Arduous duty stations have been defined as those areas where:

- Dependents are not authorized. (A soldier with no dependents serving in such an area is still entitled to FDP.)
- Dependents are authorized but the accompanied tour length is less than 36 months. (The qualifying factor is the duty assignment, not dependent status.)
- The climate is extreme. (Specific guidelines include assignments located at or above a latitude of 58° north, at or below a latitude of 58° south, and between latitudes 15° north and 15° south—in other words, extremely cold climates near the polar regions or extremely hot climates near the equator.)
- The country is Communist-controlled.

Soldiers cannot receive both FDP and Sea Duty Pay, nor can they receive FDP if they are assigned to a qualifying duty station that is also their home of record.

Sea Duty Pay (SDP): $50–$520

Soldiers, in addition to sailors, can go to sea. While these assignments do not abound in the Army, when a soldier is assigned to a ship and is in a sea duty status, he is entitled to extra pay. The soldier, together with the unit commander (skipper), provides documentation to the Sea Service Office (SSO), Fort Eustis, Virginia. SDP is prorated, based on the number of days of creditable sea duty and the number of consecutive months of sea duty the soldier has currently completed. A Sea Pay premium of $100 per month is paid to soldiers who have spent more than 36 months of consecutive duty at sea.

Overseas Extension Pay: $80/month or 30 days' leave

Qualified enlisted soldiers serving in designated locations overseas can extend their tours overseas for either additional special pay or for extra leave. The minimum length of the extension is usually 12 months. Not all soldiers qualify for this benefit. For information on the MOSs currently included under this regulation, check with the FAO of an overseas unit.

Foreign Language Proficiency Pay: $25–$100

Soldiers who hold an MOS requiring proficiency in a foreign language are entitled to this additional pay to enhance their proficiency in that language.

Hostile Fire Pay (HFP): $110

National defense, the true "business" of the Army, sometimes means that soldiers are subjected to hostile fire or are stationed permanently or temporarily in an area designated as a hostile fire area. As a partial compensation for the danger the soldier is exposed to, he or she receives HFP, also called imminent danger pay, for any month in which at least part of the time was served in a hostile fire area. Soldiers who participated in Operation Desert Storm and previous conflicts were eligible for HFP. A soldier on TDY orders for less than 30 days in a hostile fire area must submit a letter requesting the credit for HFP to his commander for approval. The letter should provide the soldier's Social Security number, TDY Special Order number, and a description of the tactical or strategic combat organization in which the soldier participated, or the circumstances under which he or she was subjected to hostile fire.

Diving Pay: $110–$300

To qualify for diving pay, a soldier must be a rated diver serving in an assignment designated on the manpower documents as a diving position of MOS 00B or 7242. If the duty has not been designated as a diving position, approval for that designation can be routed through HQDA (DAFD-ZA), Washington, DC 20310.

Flight Pay: $110–$200

Enlisted soldiers serving either as crewmembers with flying status or non-crewmembers with flying status are eligible for flight pay, considered a form of Hazardous Duty Incentive Pay (HDIP). Both crewmembers and non-crewmembers must be performing duties essential to the mission of the aircraft and duties that can be performed only during flight. Non-crewmembers must be performing duties that cannot be performed by regular crewmembers in order to qualify for the special pay.

Parachute Duty Pay: $110

Another form of HDIP, parachute duty pay, is authorized for soldiers who are students at a parachute or airborne school or at the John F. Kennedy Center for Military Assistance (if performing parachute duty) and for soldiers performing the duties of a parachutist at either an airborne unit, a non-airborne unit with a designated parachutist position, a school, or a service test section. Parachutists also receive the pay when they serve in a designated position at an approved quartermaster airborne facility concerned with maintenance, testing, and/or parachute packing and rigging, or when they serve with a pararescue team. If the position involves high-altitude, low-opening (HALO) jumps, the pay level is $165.

Demolition Pay: $110

Soldiers whose primary duty assignments involve the demolition of explosives are eligible for demolition pay. This HDIP is reserved for students or instructors in specific schools who have the Special Skill Identifier (SSI) 75D or who have the MOS 55D; or for soldiers with either the SSI or MOS assigned to manpower positions in units or sections approved or designated as Explosive Ordnance Disposal Activities. Soldiers holding the SSI 75D or MOS 55D who work temporarily in the demolition of explosives, or who perform the work as an additional duty, also are eligible for the pay. Qualifying schools are the U.S. Naval School Explosive Ordnance Disposal; the U.S. Naval Ordnance Station, Indian Head,

Maryland; or the U.S. Army Missile and Munitions Center and School, Redstone Arsenal, Alabama. Soldiers do not have to work in explosive demolition for a full month to receive the incentive pay for that month.

Experimental Stress Pay: $110

When soldiers are assigned to experimental stress duty where they are involved with thermal stress experiments or pressure chamber experiments, they receive special pay. They do not have to be involved with the experimentation for a full month to receive incentive pay for that month. Laboratories authorized to perform thermal stress experiments with human subjects are the U.S. Army Natick Laboratory, Natick, Massachusetts; the U.S. Army Chemical Research and Development Laboratory, Edgewood Arsenal, Maryland; and the U.S. Medical Research Laboratory, Fort Knox, Kentucky. The Natick Laboratory is also designated as a site for experimental pressure chamber work with human test subjects, in addition to the Armed Forces Institute of Pathology, Washington, DC.

Toxic Fuels (or Propellants) Pay: $110

Duty involving toxic fuels or propellants also results in HDIP, but as with other HDIPs, the duty must be designated by official manpower documents.

Dual Incentive Pay

The Army recognizes that a soldier may be serving simultaneously in more than one form of hazardous duty. In such cases, dual incentive pay may be applicable, but the dual pay can be authorized only by HQDA (DAPC-ZA), Washington, DC. Soldiers serving in two forms of hazardous duty should request that their FAO submit the necessary forms to receive authorization.

Selective Reenlistment Bonus

The Selective Reenlistment Bonus (SRB) is a retention incentive paid to soldiers in selected MOSs who reenlist or voluntarily extend their enlistment for additional obligated service. The objective of the SRB is to increase the number of reenlistments or extensions in critical MOSs that do not have adequate retention levels to man the career force. For more information on reenlistment bonuses, see chapter 9 and check with your career counselor.

Advance Pay

Under certain circumstances, you may be able to draw advance pay. Up to three months of your basic pay is authorized as advance pay when you make a PCS move, as discussed in chapter 5. Only one month's pay can be granted at the old duty station or en route to the new duty station if the money was not anticipated and requested from the old duty station. Two additional months' pay can be granted by the FAO at the new duty station, if the advance pay is approved by your new commander. A DA Form 2142, *Pay Inquiry*, is used to request the advance.

Since advance pay is a debt that must be repaid, you must have adequate time remaining before your ETS to reimburse the Army. The debt will be repaid over a maximum of one year and will be automatically deducted from your pay. The LES will document the payments.

Advance pay is not your right for each PCS. It is granted on a case-by-case basis, and you must explain the specific need for the extra funds. Such funds are in addition to the dislocation allowance, the temporary lodging allowance, or the advance station housing allowance.

Other circumstances can occur in which you are caught short of funds that are essential to the proper performance of your duty. For instance, if a uniform is damaged and must be replaced, you are expected to pay for the replacement based on the clothing allowance you have been receiving. Under emergency conditions, if you are without funds to purchase the needed clothing items, you can charge them. This debt must also be repaid, and generally it is deducted in full from your next month's pay. If a one-time collection would cause you undue financial hardship, however, you may request a monthly collection plan with payments at least as large as the monthly clothing allowance.

Allowances

Allowances are entitlements given to cover specific needs such as food, clothing expenses, and housing. When the government fulfills the need for you, you will not receive an allowance. For instance, soldiers living in the barracks are provided their housing. Consequently, they are not eligible for a housing allowance.

Allowances differ from other types of pay in one significant way — they are not taxable. Various types of allowances and qualifications for receiving them are specified in this section.

Basic Allowance for Subsistence

Commonly called "separate rations," the Basic Allowance for Subsistence (BAS) is restricted to cases when a government mess hall is not available and when no rations are provided to the soldier. When a soldier is authorized to live off-post, he or she will usually be awarded BAS as well. BAS is normally awarded during the time in which the soldier is on leave and during authorized travel time for PCS moves. The per diem (economic area allowance) rate is normally reduced, however, by the daily BAS rate. After a PCS, the soldier should verify with his new FAO whether BAS will be awarded at the new assignment. Authorization forms must be completed with each new unit.

BAS will not allow the soldier to eat gourmet meals. Actually, the daily rates were based on cost to the government to provide meals for the soldier through quantity purchasing and preparation. Rates in effect as of January 1993: *This is paid on the month following leave taken automatically*

	E-1 (less than 4 months)	All Other Enlisted
When on leave or authorized to mess separately	$6.14/day	$6.65/day
When rations in-kind are not available	$6.93/day	$7.50/day
When assigned to duty under emergency conditions where no government messing facilities are available	$9.19/day	$9.94/day

Basic Allowance for Quarters

Commonly called the "housing allowance," Basic Allowance for Quarters (BAQ) is intended to compensate soldiers who do not have housing provided by the government. Three categories have been established:

- Soldiers with dependents. (If government housing is not provided for the soldier and dependents, BAQ is awarded to help offset the cost of renting in the civilian community.)
- Soldiers without dependents living in government barracks or quarters. (A partial BAQ is provided to compensate for the inconveniences of living in a barracks situation. This token BAQ is called a partial rate.)
- Soldiers without dependents living off post. (BAQ is less than the rate for soldiers of the same rank who have dependents; it is considerably more, however, than the partial rate.)

For Army couples, when both are servicemembers, the guidelines change somewhat. If the couple has children, the soldier with the higher rank will receive BAQ at the "with dependents" rate; the spouse will receive BAQ at the "without dependents" rate. In addition, if the couple has no children, each spouse will receive the BAQ without dependents rate.

When government quarters on post are provided to families, the soldier forfeits his BAQ. Since BAQ covers only part of housing costs, using government quarters can be a significant savings. Some government quarters are not up to par, however, and have been rated substandard by the government. In these cases, the soldier forfeits only a percentage of the BAQ and in essence pays a reduced rent for the substandard housing.

BAQ Rates (January 1993)

Pay Grade	Without Dependents		With Dependents
	Full Rate	*Partial Rate*	
E-6	$307.80	$9.90	$452.40
E-5	283.80	8.70	406.50
E-4	246.90	8.10	353.70
E-3	242.40	7.80	329.10
E-2	197.10	7.20	313.20
E-1	175.20	6.90	313.20

Special Allowances

BAQ and BAS are monthly allowances provided for subsistence, or food and housing. The Army also provides a number of special allowances that are not necessarily paid on a monthly basis.

Family Separation Allowances (FSA) cover two specific situations that increase the cost of housing for the soldier with dependents. First, if a soldier is assigned overseas to an area where dependents are not authorized, and if no government quarters are available to that soldier, he or she will receive an FSA equivalent to the BAQ of a soldier without dependents. This FSA is in addition to the soldier's standard BAQ to provide housing for dependents. FSA is also awarded when the soldier with dependents is either overseas, in a dependent-restricted area, where quarters are provided, or when he is on temporary duty away from the family for 30 days or more. In both cases the FSA is $60 per month. This allowance is not payable during times of declared war.

Variable Housing Allowances (VHA) help offset the cost of housing in areas where rent is higher than the national average. Many areas provide no VHA. This monthly allowance is still provided to soldiers stationed overseas when their families are living in a high-cost area in the United States. VHA rates are constantly revised. You can obtain a current list from your FAO.

Station Housing Allowances (SHA) are similar to VHAs except that they are awarded for overseas areas. In addition, Advance Station Housing Allowance (ASHA) is paid to help the soldier with the high costs of securing housing overseas, covering such costs as paying advanced rent and security deposits. The ASHA must be repaid, but it can be spread out over a 12-month period.

Rent-Plus is another method of easing housing expenses overseas. Under this program the actual expenses of the soldier are considered, including rent, average utility costs, and additional costs associated with an overseas lease. Not all overseas areas have the Rent-Plus allowance.

Cost-of-Living Allowances (COLA) are yet another allowance for soldiers stationed outside of the United States. COLA is meant as a means of repaying the soldier for the excess costs of living in the overseas area. It does not relate solely to housing. Therefore, soldiers living in the barracks overseas are still awarded COLA but at a reduced rate of 47 percent of the daily COLA rate for a soldier without dependents.

Dislocation Allowances are one-time payments, equal to two months' BAQ, to help defray the costs of moving. Soldiers with dependents always receive the allowance with a PCS; soldiers without dependents receive the allowance only if they were entitled to BAQ at both the previous and the new duty assignment. Dislocation allowances are taxable, however.

Temporary Lodging Allowances (TLA) are also used for soldiers moving from one duty assignment to another. The TLA is determined for each area, based on cost of living. Its purpose is to partially reimburse the soldier for extra expenses incurred through the necessity of using temporary quarters that do not provide facilities for preparing meals. The daily rate, usually not authorized for more than 60 days, is determined in part by the number of dependents. Single soldiers usually receive one-half of the local per diem rate.

Per Diem is a daily allowance provided for soldiers working on temporary duty away from their normal duty station, and soldiers and dependents while in transit during a PCS move. It covers both housing and meals, although realistically it is often insufficient to fully cover the costs of motels and restaurant dining. Check with your FAO for the per diem rate.

The Clothing Maintenance Allowance (CMA) is provided for the general upkeep and maintenance of the service uniform. This payment carries with it an unspoken obligation—to keep the uniform in good condition. As of 1992, for soldiers with three or less years' service, the rate is $180.00 for men and $205.20 for women. Soldiers who have more than three years' service receive $259.20 (men) or $291.60 (women). The allowance is paid annually on the soldier's Basic Active Service Date (BASD) month.

Other clothing allowances are also possible. If the soldier is required to work in civilian clothes — in investigative work, for instance — or in some designated overseas areas, he or she is provided a one-time Special Clothing Allowance (SCA), from $644 to $1,087, which is intended for the purchase of new civilian clothing. While on temporary duty to an area where civilian clothes are required, soldiers are also eligible to receive the SCA — up to $401 if the TDY is more than 30 days.

Leave and Passes

Even before entering the Army, the prospective soldier learns about the vacation benefits the military offers. Called "leave" in military jargon, the soldier knows his benefit — 30 days a year, far more than most civilians enjoy. That is not, however, the full picture. Many soldiers are not aware of the full range of leaves and passes through which they can be excused from their normal duty and still receive their full pay. There are two basic types of leave: chargeable leave, which is deducted from the soldier's leave account; and non-chargeable leave, which is granted in addition to a soldier's normal allowable leave.

Chargeable Leave

Thirty days of annual leave are earned at a rate of 2.5 days per month, whether the soldier is on active duty or is a member of the Army Reserve or National Guard who is serving full-time on active duty during a given 30-day period. You draw against your earned, or accrued, leave much in the same way you would draw against a balance in a banking account. The "bank statement" for annual leave is shown on the LES. You are not allowed to accrue more than 60 days of leave, unless in a combat zone, where the ceiling is 90 days.

Misconduct or disciplinary action can prevent a soldier from earning the designated 2.5 days a month. If you are AWOL, confined by military or civilian authorities, or away from duty and in excess leave, you do not earn further leave during that period.

Before annual leave commences, DA Form 31, *Request and Authority for Leave,* must be filled out and signed by your commander authorizing the absence from work. Travel in conjunction with a PCS is rarely disapproved. (Travel time granted to make a PCS move does not count against your accrued leave.) Soldiers often request annual leave when they are already going to be away from the duty station for temporary duty. Generally, commanders try to approve any leave requests that do not present a conflict with the needs of the Army.

Advance leave is like a loan—the soldier is requesting to take more from his or her account than is currently there. Commanders can approve advance leave when the soldier has enough time remaining before ETS to reasonably repay the advance.

Emergency leave is charged against your accrued leave or is granted as advance leave if an adequate amount of accrued leave is not available. When an emergency situation arises, such as the death of an immediate family member, a dying family member, an illness in an immediate family member where the presence of the servicemember is deemed essential, or under circumstances where the absence of the soldier causes severe or unusual hardship on the family, the emergency must be verified by the American Red Cross. The commander is then authorized to approve emergency leave.

If you are overseas and must travel back to the United States to handle the emergency situation, the first part of the trip (to an international airport within the United States) is government-paid transportation. If you must travel from the United States to an overseas location, travel from the international airport is at government expense. Soldiers traveling from one overseas location to another overseas location take the full trip at government expense, even if part of the trip must be in the United States. For instance, if the soldier is in Europe and must travel to the Pacific, travel from Europe to the U.S. East Coast, then from the East Coast to the West Coast, and finally from the West Coast to the Pacific location will all be government-paid transportation.

These same travel benefits apply to dependents as well, whether or not they are traveling with the servicemember. No travel benefits are available for soldiers stationed in the United States who must travel to another U.S. location on emergency leave.

Rest and Recuperation Leave (R&R) is available to soldiers serving in areas authorized to award hostile fire pay. R&R is also chargeable leave, but the leave offers a rest period for the soldier serving in a difficult situation.

Non-Chargeable Leave

Convalescent leave is not charged against your accrued leave, nor is it considered an advance leave. This leave is granted by hospital commanders to patients who need the extra time for rehabilitation or recuperation. Basically, they are well enough to be discharged from the hospital but not yet ready to resume duty.

Graduation leave is available at the discretion of the commander for graduates of the U.S. Military Academy upon their commissioning. It is not charged against accrued leave. (See chapter 9 for details on the possibility of attending the Military Academy.)

Special leave is granted to some soldiers who extend their overseas assignments. Not all overseas locations qualify, and soldiers must have certain MOS ratings. The first sergeant or the FAO overseas can provide current information. Generally this non-chargeable 30-day leave is reserved for combat arms MOSs. The special leave is a matter of choice for the soldier. Granting special leave negates eligibility for overseas extension pay.

Another limited overseas program is the Environmental and Morale Leave (EML) Program, applicable to designated underdeveloped (Third World) or Communist-controlled (Second World) countries. Although leave is chargeable under the EML Program, transportation costs for the soldier and dependents to a designated "relief destination" are paid by the government; and travel time is not chargeable as leave. Areas chosen for this program by the Department of Defense are selected because of the unusually difficult living conditions, which cause excessive physical and mental discomfort. The program is designed to provide temporary relief to avoid a "deleterious effect" on the soldier.

Soldiers and their families stationed in the Latin American countries of Belize, Bolivia, Colombia, El Salvador, Guatemala, Honduras, Paraguay, or Peru can travel to Miami; those in Burma, Indonesia, Malaysia, Nepal, Sri Lanka, or Thailand can travel to Hong Kong; if stationed in the People's Republic of China, soldiers and dependents can travel to Malaysia; and military families in Argentina or Canada can receive government-paid transportation to New York City.

Passes

Passes differ from leave in two respects. First, they are not chargeable against your accrued leave or as advance leave. In addition, they are granted only for short periods of time.

The regular pass is limited to a maximum of three days (72 hours). Basically, it covers your normal off-duty time on weekends and holidays. Under certain circumstances, the regular pass can be rescinded.

Special passes, limited to a maximum of four days (96 hours) are rewards given to deserving soldiers for exceptional service. Frequently they are granted to the Soldier of the Month or the Soldier of the Quarter, for example. In addition, they can be used to allow a soldier to participate in religious retreats or events, to handle personal problems, or to compensate for required duty that has extended over an unusually long period of time. Passes may not be used in conjunction with leave.

Deductions from Your Pay

Each month, your LES will reflect both involuntary and voluntary deductions from your pay. Involuntary deductions include taxes, repayment of debt, and punitive action. Voluntary deductions are options you authorize for life insurance, savings, education, and a variety of other purposes.

Taxes

Military pay in general is subject to income and Social Security taxes. You do not pay tax on subsistence, quarters, and uniform allowances. Dislocation allowance and reenlistment bonuses, however, are taxable.

Any nonmilitary earnings, including pay received while employed during off-duty hours (including proceeds from gambling), and the income of any of your dependents are taxable.

Your military pay is excluded from federal income tax for service in any area that the president of the United States designates by Executive Order to be a combat zone. Whenever this exclusion applies, all military pay received by enlisted personnel while on active duty in such a zone is not taxed.

Soldiers who claim legal residence in states that have a personal income tax must pay their state taxes. Deductions from military pay for state taxes are made automatically, just as they are for federal income taxes. The Soldier's and Sailor's Civil Relief Act, however, ensures that if you are stationed in a state that is not your legal residence, that state cannot tax your service pay. Legal residence is established when a soldier executes DD Form 2058, *State of Legal Residence Certificate.*

The following states do not withhold income tax from the pay of military personnel: Alaska, Florida, Illinois, Michigan, Montana, Nevada, New Hampshire, South Dakota, Tennessee, Texas, Vermont, Washington, and Wyoming. Soldiers claiming legal residence in foreign countries or U.S. territories are also exempt from paying state income taxes.

A number of states do not require military personnel claiming them as their legal residence to pay income taxes unless they are stationed there. These states are California, Idaho, Missouri, New Jersey, New York, Oregon, Pennsylvania, and West Virginia.

Servicemembers who are legal residents of all other states must pay state income taxes regardless of where they are stationed.

Other Involuntary Deductions

All soldiers are required to contribute to the United States Soldier's Home (USSH). Fifty cents is deducted from the paycheck each month to fulfill this obligation.

Involuntary deductions from your pay can also be made for the following reasons: as a result of court-martial sentencing or nonjudicial (Article 15, UCMJ) punishment; to repay indebtedness to the Army; to collect back taxes; to collect overpayment due to administrative error; to enforce child support or alimony obligations when ordered by civilian courts; or to collect for dishonored checks written to the commissary or other military store, if the check has not been honored within seven days after you are notified of the returned check.

Under special circumstances, your indebtedness to the Army can be cancelled or remitted. Handled on a case-by-case basis through your commander, cancellation or remission of indebtedness is not commonplace, but it is possible under extreme circumstances.

Voluntary Deductions

Voluntary deductions from your pay include a wide variety of options, from life insurance to educational opportunities.

Servicemen's Group Life Insurance (SGLI) is an option, and most soldiers elect to take this inexpensive term life insurance policy. The maximum allowable coverage is $200,000. Unless you specifically request no coverage or reduced coverage, the premium is automatically deducted from your paycheck. The rate for the insurance is 8 cents per month per $1,000 coverage; this means the maximum coverage of $200,000 costs $16 per month.

Another voluntary deduction is made when you elect to use government laundry and drycleaning services (Quartermaster Laundry) through your unit. The charges for these services will be deducted automatically each month until you request termination of the service or upon PCS.

Allotments are another form of voluntary deductions. Many different kinds of allotments are recognized; most can be initiated by using DA Form 3684.

Two types of Army Emergency Relief (AER) allotments are authorized. AER allotments are used to repay AER loans. The allotment must be for a minimum of $5 per month and must be established for at least three months. AER-C allotments are for voluntary AER contributions to the AER fund. The allotment is established for a minimum of 3 but not more than 12 months' duration.

CFC allotments, similar to AER-C allotments, are voluntary contributions for the purpose of paying pledges to the Combined Federal Campaign fund. CFC allotments are always 12 months long, January to December, for not less than $2 per month.

FED allotments are used to repay delinquent taxes or other debts to federal, state, or local agencies. Indebtedness to the Army may not be repaid through an FED allotment.

SPT-V allotments allow you to make voluntary contributions to your family, divorced spouse, or dependent relative, through a bank, building and loan association, or credit union, to the individual's account. Such allotments can also be made directly to the allotee. Although you can have multiple SPT-V allotments, no more than one can be made to any single allotee. If the allotment is made to an institution, you are responsible for arranging proper crediting.

SPT-I allotments are a result of court-ordered garnishment of wages for dependent support. These allotments cannot be changed at the soldier's request, since they are the result of legal action.

FININ allotments are made to financial institutions for credit to your savings, checking, or trust accounts for any purpose you direct, except repayment of loans on time payments. You may have only two such allotments.

HOME allotments are made for the purpose of paying a mortgage on a home, mobile home, or house trailer that you use as a residence. Only one such allotment is authorized.

INS allotments are used to pay premiums on commercial life insurance policies. Such allotments cannot be used for premiums on policies covering your spouse or children, or for health, accident, or hospitalization insurance. Multiple INS allotments are authorized.

Two types of bond allotments are authorized: BOND and MBOND. BOND allotments allow you to purchase U.S. Savings Bonds through payroll deductions. The BOND allotment covers the full charge for the bond. MBOND allotments allow you more flexibility in purchasing U.S. Savings Bonds because the purchase can cover a period of two to four months. In both cases, multiple allotments are allowed, and the bonds can be mailed to you, the owner, the co-owner, or the beneficiary, or can be retained at the Defense Finance and Accounting Service at Fort Benjamin Harrison, Indiana, for safekeeping.

REDCR allotments are used to repay loans made from the American Red Cross. Multiple allotments are allowed but must extend for at least three months. The minimum REDCR allotment is $5 per month.

GIBIL allotments are used to enroll soldiers for benefits under the Montgomery GI Bill. Unless you specifically decline enrollment, you are automatically enrolled in the program, which deducts $100 from the monthly basic pay for one year. Participants may not elect to disenroll from the program after having chosen to participate, nor are contributions refundable. However, participation is the only way for first-term soldiers to establish eligibility for GI Bill benefits.

8

Benefits and Services

Every soldier who has ever served in the Army is aware that the military lifestyle differs from life in the civilian community. The esprit de corps, the team effort, and the shared hardships combine to mold a unique community.

The Army community offers you and your family a number of benefits and services that a first-termer could miss if someone didn't point them out. Some benefits are not hidden. What soldier could miss the post exchange or the movie theater? The post gymnasium is another popular attraction on Army posts throughout the world. The bowling alleys and clubs boast a busy nightlife. Military families learn quickly where the commissary and child care facilities are on post.

Other benefits deserve a bit of highlighting. Even the obvious services may have subtle benefits you have not considered. For instance, soldiers living in the barracks frequently avoid shopping at the commissary because they are only picking up a few things. With savings ranging from 20 to 35 percent over civilian grocery stores, however, even a short list would produce a sizable savings. In addition, commissaries provide quick check-out service for people purchasing 10 or fewer items. Most commissaries also give priority to soldiers in uniform during the lunch hour.

Active Army soldiers, both in uniform and in civilian clothing, and their family members must present a military or family member ID card to enter the commissary. Since 1 January 1990, National Guard and Reserve soldiers and their families have been required to present their Armed Forces Commissary Privilege cards and military or family member ID cards to enter and shop in commissaries.

Many PXs offer catalog shopping in addition to the department-store exchange. They also accept major credit cards and offer deferred payment plans. In addition, for large purchases, the PX offers a liberal layaway plan that allows you to spread the payments over three to six months for a nominal fee.

Medical and Dental Benefits

Quality health and dental insurance is as much a necessity as auto or home insurance—and more vital! Without health or dental insurance, even a minor accident may devastate your budget. Military couples and single parents can attest to the potential for accidents and trips to an emergency room.

Bumps, bruises, cuts, scrapes, colds, broken bones, pulled muscles, chipped or broken teeth—all can happen at the worst time financially. Fortunately, soldiers in active federal service are completely covered free of charge by the Army's direct medical and dental care programs. And military family members, once enrolled in the Defense Enrollment Eligibility Reporting System (DEERS) through the local military personnel office (MILPO), may receive either direct care when available or covered care from civilian doctors and dentists.

There are exceptions, of course, and include soldiers assigned to remote duty stations and those (Army recruiters, for example) stationed in the United States but far from military medical and dental facilities. In these cases, the Army fully covers the cost of care provided by civilian providers. Also, soldiers who get medical or dental care for an illness or an injury that resulted through misconduct or an action beyond the bounds of military regulations may not be covered. In this exception, a "line of duty" investigation will determine whether the Army or the soldier must pay for the care.

Single soldiers, it can be argued, realize the greatest benefit because their care is free—line-of-duty investigation notwithstanding—and they escape the civilian-military medical red tape.

If you are a military spouse or parent, you must become familiar with the direct military health and dental care programs where you work. You also need to contact the health benefits advisor at your local hospital or clinic about the Civilian Health and Medical Program of the Uniformed Services (CHAMPUS) and the Uniformed Services Active Duty Dependents Dental Plan (commonly called the Delta Dental Plan). The more you know about CHAMPUS and DDP, the more you will realize how valuable they are.

CHAMPUS

CHAMPUS shares most of the cost of care from civilian hospitals and doctors when you can't get care through a military hospital or clinic. The program is intended to supplement your benefits from a military hospital or clinic. CHAMPUS is not free; you must pay part (a "co-share" amount) of the costs, as well as for care that is not covered by CHAMPUS. There are rules or limits on certain care, and some is not covered at all. See your local health benefits advisor for a copy of the *CHAMPUS Handbook*; pages 22–52 show what is and is not covered.

CHAMPUS pays for only medically necessary care and services that are provided at an "appropriate level." Claims for services that do not meet this definition may be denied. For example, using emergency room services for the patient's convenience, rather than for a genuine emergency, would not be covered.

You or your care provider (hospital, doctor) must file claims before CHAMPUS will pay its share of the bills. Pages 77–89 of the *CHAMPUS Handbook* explain how to fill out a claim. As stated above, all CHAMPUS-eligible persons must be enrolled in DEERS before CHAMPUS claims can be paid, so make sure your family members are enrolled through your local MILPO. Family members must have a Social Security number to be enrolled.

The most important advice about CHAMPUS is this: Get to know your health benefits advisor. It is the advisor's job to explain your benefits, help you understand the cost-sharing system and annual deductible requirement, and help get the care you need—at the best price and in the most convenient manner. There is an advisor at all military hospitals and most clinics.

Expanded Dependent Dental Plan

In FY93, DDP benefits were expanded and the cost increased. Monthly rates now are $9.65 ($115.80 per year) for single coverage and $19.30 ($231.60 a year) for family coverage.

This voluntary program is a super deal for soldiers with families. The DDP covers 100 percent of the cost of diagnostic and preventive care. Enrolled members cost-share on other services, with the plan covering 80 percent for restorative work and sealants and 50 percent for oral surgery, endodontics, periodontics, crowns and casts, prosthetics, and orthodontics.

The expanded plan, which became effective 1 April 1993, covers both active Army and Reserve Component personnel. Reserve and National Guard personnel must have orders assigning them to active duty for a period of 24 months or more in order to qualify.

Full-time active duty (Regular Army) soldiers must be aware of several enrollment conditions. Currently enrolled soldiers were automatically enrolled in the expanded plan in March 1993, as were nonenrolled servicemembers who had 24 months remaining on active duty. To be eligible for enrollment, soldiers must have one or more CHAMPUS-eligible family members, be on a CONUS assignment (including Guam and Puerto Rico), and have 24 months remaining on active duty. Family members residing overseas with their military sponsors receive dental care through the Army's direct-care system, not through DDP.

If not disenrolled within the four-month period that began in March 1993, soldiers are obligated to remain enrolled for the full 24-month period. Soldiers who have requested retirement or have fewer than 24 months remaining on active duty were not automatically enrolled in the plan. Soldiers who are eligible for reenlistment and intend to remain on active duty for at least 24 months may voluntarily enroll. Voluntarily enrolled soldiers must remain enrolled for the minimum period of 24 months.

More than 100,000 dental offices across the nation participate in the plan. Participants take care of submitting claim forms and are paid directly by DDP. Most dental professionals will not require you pay up front for fully covered services. Your family can go to any licensed dentist you choose, but the fees of nonparticipating dentists may not be fully covered, and you could be required to pay up front and file your own claims. Using a DDP-participating dentist can save you time, money, and paperwork. The health benefits advisor at your installation can tell you more about the DDP and has a current list of participating dental offices.

Relief Agencies

The expression "the Army takes care of its own" has special meaning when its members face financial crises, family emergencies, and other problems. A number of relief agencies, among them Army Emergency Relief, the American Red Cross, and Army Community Services, exist to help soldiers handle these situations.

Army Emergency Relief

Through Army Emergency Relief (AER) assistance, Army personnel and their families, reservists on active duty, and needy widows and orphans of Army members can receive help during financial emergencies.

Conducted in coordination with the American Red Cross, AER is a private nonprofit corporation that serves as the Army's emergency financial assistance organization. It provides emergency loans to eligible recipients who are faced with unforeseen situations requiring immediate financial attention. Under special circumstances, grants (requiring no repayment) may also be provided. Most assistance, however, must be repaid.

Any soldier facing a valid emergency should be provided AER assistance, but assistance is not provided when the request is based on convenience or comfort instead of valid need. Examples of authorized emergencies are as follows:

- Nonreceipt of pay, allowances, or allotments.
- Loss of funds by theft.
- Authorized medical care under CHAMPUS (Civilian Health and Medical Program of the Uniformed Services) that requires a down payment.
- Funeral expenses incurred for a dependent or parent.
- Travel expenses needed for emergency leave.
- Payment of initial rent and deposit.
- Payment of rent to avoid eviction.
- Payment of utility bills to avoid termination of services.
- Cost of vehicle insurance premiums.
- Costs incurred for a privately owned vehicle deemed essential because transportation is needed for an ill dependent or pregnant wife.

Under a new program, AER assistance is now available to fund a soldier's college education. To take advantage of the program, you must be attending school at least half-time (generally two three-semester-hour courses) and be working toward an undergraduate degree. The AER also sponsors loans to soldiers to help pay for their children's college education.

Except for unusual circumstances, AER assistance is not authorized for divorces, marriages, ordinary leave or vacations, consolidation of debts, business ventures or investments, legal fees, income taxes, continuing assistance, gambling debts, or funds to replace those overdrawn from bank accounts.

Loan repayments generally begin on the first day of the second month after the assistance is provided. For example, for a loan made in the middle of January the first payment would be due 1 March, and would be made by allotment from the February paycheck. Loan payments can be spread out over a 12-month period or until the individual's expiration of term of service (ETS)—whichever period is shorter. Payment plans are generally constructed to take advantage of the AER pay allotment option.

The American Red Cross

The American Red Cross provides another form of help—that of verifying the emergency so that the commander can act more swiftly to help the soldier. This is especially the case when the soldier is assigned overseas and an emergency occurs elsewhere, often literally halfway around the world. The first details of a family emergency are frequently sketchy at best, and confusing at their worst. The Red Cross works on behalf of the soldier to gather the facts and provide him or her with clear information so an appropriate decision or action can be made. The role of the Red Cross is intricately involved with command decisions on emergency leave and compassionate reassignments, deferments, and hardship discharges.

Emergency Leave Procedures

To avoid potentially tragic delays or related problems, you need to make sure family members residing at your home of record are aware of American Red Cross procedures. First, your next of kin should maintain the telephone number of the local Red Cross office, and he or she should call if a family emergency arises. Your family should be prepared to supply your rank, your job and where you work, your Social Security number, your complete military unit address and phone number, and your complete residential address and phone number.

If you are informed of an emergency, either by next of kin over the phone or directly through your command, ask your supervisor (during duty hours) or the charge of quarters or staff duty officer (after duty hours) to call the local Red Cross to verify it. Emergency leave and emergency funds cannot be authorized until the emergency is verified. While officials verify the emergency, pack and arrange necessary departure details such as getting airline tickets, transportation to the airport, and perhaps renting a car.

Remain calm. Worrying won't help; it will wear you down and make the trip home exhausting. Remember, you are going home for your family members, to be there for them. They will need your strength and support during a crisis.

If while you are home on an emergency leave you find that you need a leave extension, it will help if you know how to call your unit supervisor or first sergeant, especially if you are stationed overseas. Make sure you know how to call your unit from the United States. You will need to know your unit's phone number, the local area code, and the country code. For assistance in the United States, dial 00 to reach the international operator.

One more point: Share information in this section with your fellow soldiers and be prepared to assist if one of them gets an unfortunate phone call or visit in the middle of the night.

The Army Community Services Center

The Army Community Services (ACS) Center provides a different but vital type of assistance. Counselors there provide referral services to the military family and to the soldier, as well as in-house counseling on such matters as budgeting, personal or family problems, services available in the civilian community (libraries, parks and recreation programs, and so on), special educational needs for gifted or handicapped children (including information about the Exceptional Family Member Program), and assistance for the military spouse seeking employment in a new community. In addition, almost all ACS centers maintain a lending closet with items such as bedding, dishes, and other household goods that may be needed before PCS shipment arrives. Larger installations often have 24-hour hotlines through ACS to help with late-night emergencies.

Morale Support and Recreation

The Army community offers a variety of facilities and opportunities that will help you make the most of your leisure time. For instance, you can enjoy a show at the USO, work out at the gym, or take advantage of military travel benefits. Services are also available to help ease the transition of moving to a new duty station.

The USO

The United Services Organization (USO) is a private, nonprofit organization that was founded in 1941 as a "home away from home" for members of the armed forces. Today it operates 160 stations all over the world, which are manned by both paid staff members and volunteers.

PCS moves are an accepted part of military life. The USO provides a haven for the newcomer—a place to have a cup of coffee, meet new people, relax, and enjoy a small slice of America no matter where you are assigned. USOs are available in large metropolitan areas in CONUS, as well as overseas. Many large airports, such as O'Hare International in Chicago, have a small USO facility for military travelers.

USOs are famous for featuring name entertainers, but they also offer information about the post and local civilian community, cultural exchanges, local tours, socials, dances, recreation halls, free movies, and a relaxing atmosphere where you can just "get away from it all" for a while.

The Armed Services YMCA

Since 1861, the Armed Services Young Men's Christian Association (YMCA) has been serving the special needs of military personnel. The "Y" attempts to bridge the gap between soldiers and the community in which they are stationed by providing wholesome recreational activities and social services. The Y focuses its efforts on the needs of young enlisted soldiers, particularly those whose families have yet to develop the skills needed to handle the challenges of military life. The Y's employees and volunteers help soldiers and their families deal with such situations as family separations and domestic violence and help foreign-born spouses to adjust. They also offer counseling and referral services for those with special needs.

Funded through voluntary contributions, community fund-raisers, the United Way, and the Combined Federal Campaign, Armed Services YMCAs or affiliated YMCAs are located near many major military installations.

Special Services

Most soldiers are familiar with the gymnasium, one of the many facilities run by Special Services (or Morale, Welfare, and Recreation). But on many posts much, much more is available. Special Services frequently rents camping gear, tents, trailers, boats and trailers, and other items at affordable prices. Some installations charge by rank—the more you have, the more you pay.

Tours are another benefit offered by Special Services. Group travel can bring costs into a more manageable range, and Special Services provides guides for all group tours it sponsors. At many posts, tickets to local attractions (and concerts) may be purchased at a reduced rate. Contact your post's Information, Tickets, and Tours (ITT) office for more details.

Travel Benefits

Space-available travel, often called "Space-A," is a means by which you (and your family) can catch a free ride on a government plane that happens to be going in the right direction. No travel agents help out here, though, and reservations are not allowed. In fact, as the name implies, soldiers fly for free if there is extra room not needed by cargo or by personnel traveling on government business.

The process is not complicated. You sign in on a register and then wait. Priorities are established through a full set of regulations. Top priority goes to soldiers on emergency leave.

Servicemembers must be on leave to use Space-A flights. Soldiers cannot get around the waiting period—which can be extensive—by signing up for a flight and then reporting back to duty for the interim wait. Attempting such a trick usually means the soldier is charged for annual leave even though he or she returned to duty for several days.

To use the free service, you simply must be prepared to "wait it out." A one-time-per-trip administration fee of $10 is charged. Luggage is strictly limited to two bags and a total maximum weight of 66 pounds.

Legal Assistance

The Legal Office at your post exists to provide soldiers with a variety of significant services. The Legal Officer can help you understand the military justice system and assist you with routine legal matters such as powers of attorney and wills.*

Many types of assistance are routinely provided through the JAG Office. Documents such as powers of attorney and wills can be handled through a military lawyer. In addition, advice on the legal aspects of marriage, divorce, debts, adoption, child support, taxes, claims against the government, motor vehicle registration, or change of name can be attained through the military legal system. Appeals of an NCOER can also be initiated through the JAG Office.

The Soldiers' and Sailors' Civil Relief Act (SSCRA) is a federal law that helps soldiers who have difficulty meeting their legal obligations because they are in the military service. Under the act, a soldier who incurred debts before joining the Army may be able to reduce the amount of his or her monthly payments, but the debts themselves will not be forgiven. In addition, the act can protect a soldier who is sued through a court located far from where the soldier is stationed. The legal suit is not dismissed, but it is postponed until the soldier can attend the court. The act does not protect a soldier from honoring a lease he or she signs after joining the Army. Military transfer does not automatically cancel a lease.

---

*Another helpful resource is *The Servicemember's Legal Guide*, 2nd edition, by LTC Jonathan P. Tomes, USA. (Harrisburg, Pa.: Stackpole Books, 1992.)

Complaints can also be handled through the Legal Office when the soldier feels his complaint should be handled by someone other than the first sergeant or commanding officer. The Inspector General (IG) receives complaints, investigates the facts, and turns the case over to the official who can best correct the situation if indeed the complaint is justified. If the IG finds that the soldier registering the complaint did not have all the facts, the IG will try to explain the reasons for the situation to the soldier.

If a complaint cannot be solved at the local level, it is referred to the next higher command and ultimately can be referred to the Inspector General of the Army. Soldiers may make complaints when they feel they have been wronged by a commanding officer, when they feel a civilian business has discriminated against them, or when they feel a situation needs correcting. Many complaints, however, can be handled at the company level.

Legal restrictions exist for every soldier. Soldiers may not accept gifts or solicit contributions for gifts from other soldiers who are junior in grade or rank. In addition, a soldier may not sell goods or services to another soldier junior in grade or rank. Exceptions are made when a soldier sells personal property or a home on a one-time basis to another soldier. A soldier's freedom of expression also is more restricted than that of a civilian. For example, a soldier cannot speak out in public against civilian leaders, campaign for a political candidate, or attend a demonstration while wearing a military uniform. In addition, soldiers should not use military rank or title when writing a letter to an editor that is intended for publication.

Your Legal Rights

You have certain well-defined rights under the military system of law. Among these, the most basic are the right to due process of law, the right to a defense lawyer, the right to remain silent, and certain rights under search and seizure regulations.

Due process of law has the same meaning in the military as it does in the civilian legal system: a person must be considered innocent until proven guilty. Guilt can be determined only through a trial in which evidence is presented. The defendant cannot be found guilty unless the government proves beyond a reasonable doubt that he or she did indeed commit the offense. The soldier has the right to be present to hear and cross-examine all witnesses. He or she can also call witnesses for the defense and present evidence. Often these functions are performed on behalf of the soldier by a defense lawyer, assigned free of charge, from the Judge Advocate General's (JAG) Corps.

JAG lawyers are fully qualified attorneys who have the same obligations to their clients as civilian attorneys. The lawyer acts in the best interest of the client — and cannot reveal anything the soldier says under the attorney-client relationship. Soldiers always have the right to free counsel when facing a special court-martial or a general court-martial; government counsel may represent the soldier at a summary court-martial, but this is not required under the UCMJ. Under any circumstances, the soldier has the right to acquire a civilian lawyer of his choosing, but the cost of such services must be paid by the defendant.

Whatever the legal proceedings, the soldier has the right to remain silent, as provided in the Fifth Amendment of the Constitution; no soldier is required to provide information that may be self-incriminating. As in the civilian community, the accused must be advised of his or her right to remain silent before being questioned. If the soldier was not so advised, any testimony obtained through that questioning cannot be used in a court-martial against the accused.

Rights of protection from search and seizure are quite different for the soldier and the civilian. While still protected by the Fourth Amendment to the Constitution, the soldier can have his or her person or property searched under certain circumstances. For instance, the commanding officer can order a search of the person or property of any soldier under his command. The order for a search must be based on probable cause.

When a soldier is arrested, he or she is subject to a legal search. Any personal property in the immediate possession of the soldier at the time of arrest can also be searched. If a soldier agrees to a search, the search is legal. Perhaps the most significant difference between the civilian's and soldier's search rights is that the soldier's person or property may be legally searched under an inspection to check unit readiness. Criminal evidence found during a unit "health and welfare" inspection is therefore admissible at a military trial.

For more information about your rights, visit your local MOS library and ask for AR 27-10, *Military Justice*; FM 27-14, *Legal Guide for Soldiers*; and FM 27-1, *Legal Guide for Commanders*.

The *Military Justice* regulation contains information about investigations and the prosecution of crimes, nonjudicial punishment and procedures for courts-martial, the military judiciary and magistrate programs, courts of inquiry (including soldiers rights), the appeals process, victim/witness assistance, and much more. (For even more detailed information about military law, ask the librarian for the thick Uniform Code of Military Justice.)

Besides being a good read, *Legal Guide for Soldiers* is very educational. It highlights your personal rights and legal responsibilities; it covers administrative law (including nonpunitive disciplinary measures), investigations, and the complaint process; it offers a summarized official view of military justice; and states maximum punishments. Appendix B, Sources of Information and Assistance, is especially useful.

The *Legal Guide for Commanders* reads somewhat like its counterpart but is more detailed and serves as a desk reference for commanders (and first sergeants). Why, as you read *Enlisted Soldier's Guide*, are you being advised to read a guide for commanders? You should know about the legal authority commanders can wield and how they are guided to tackle legal problems in a unit. Commanders also use the guide to assist soldiers who are making a claim, who don't understand their rights, who are being investigated, who need legal assistance, who are receiving nonjudicial punishment, or who are being separated from service. Also included, in Section III, is information about civil rights associated with public accommodations, fair housing, and equal opportunity.

Article 15

Minor offenses are often handled by administrative measures through Article 15 of the Uniform Code of Military Justice (UCMJ). This is nonjudicial punishment. The soldier must be notified in writing that the commanding officer plans to impose an Article 15. If, however, the soldier requests an open hearing, he or she can choose trial by court-martial. Generally, the soldier has 72 hours to decide which type of hearing he or she prefers, and has the right to discuss such a decision with a lawyer. It should be noted that punishment under a court-martial is often more severe than that given under Article 15.

A commanding officer who imposes an Article 15 also has clemency powers — that is, the power to lessen a punishment, suspend punishment, or remit or cancel any parts of the punishment not yet served. Clemency is granted when the commander feels that the soldier is deserving due to past performance.

Every soldier has the right to appeal an Article 15. Reasons for appeal include nonguilt, unduly severe punishment, or failure by the commander to follow the rules for giving the Article 15. Such appeals are made to the commander immediately above the commander who gave the Article 15, and should be made within 15 days.

Substance Abuse

Of particular concern to the Army is alcoholism or the use of illegal drugs among servicemembers. Stated quite simply, the use of illegal drugs or the abuse of chemical substances is not tolerated in the military. One method by which the Army identifies drug abusers is through a program of urinalysis screening designed to detect the presence of a wide variety of substances, including cocaine, heroin, PCP, amphetamines, barbiturates, and marijuana. Recently, steroids were added to the list of testable substances.

If a soldier is identified by the command as a substance abuser, he or she may be subject to punishment under Article 15 of the UCMJ; formal court-martial proceedings could also be initiated. Other possible consequences include bars to reenlistment or separation proceedings. In addition, the commander will generally order that the soldier begin treatment with the Alcohol and Drug Abuse Prevention and Control Program (ADAPCP).

The situation is somewhat different for soldiers who recognize that they have a substance problem and seek help. Generally, if a soldier voluntarily enrolls himself in the ADAPCP, he may not be prosecuted on the basis of the information he discloses to assist in his treatment.

Substance abuse can wreck the careers and lives of the users and those around them. The ADAPCP program is designed to rehabilitate the soldier and make him or her a productive player on the Army team. The trained counselors in the program work with the command and the soldier to overcome his or her dependency and to ensure that he or she remains "clean" after completing the program. Soldiers who are designated as rehabilitation failures are separated from service. Further, all corporals and below identified as illegal drug users and having three or more years of service will be processed for separation. If you need more information on the ADAPCP program, contact the post ADAPCP counselor, an Army doctor, or your first sergeant.

Avoiding Sexual Harassment

All soldiers should understand that sexual harassment is counterproductive; it impairs Army members' ability to work professionally and contribute to the Army mission. Sexual harassment often is judged as criminal conduct. Offenders may be severely punished and see their Army careers ruined. To help you avoid offending or being victimized, here are some tips:

- Be wary of any person who offers something you want or need in exchange for sexual favors.
- Be a peer group leader; do not tolerate off-color comments about the opposite sex — especially in the presence of the opposite sex.

- Know that the senior Army leadership strictly enforces punishment for sexual harassment.
- Sexual harassment can result in formal counseling, an official reprimand, or court-martial. (In 1991, after an NCO was convicted of sexual harassment, he was hit with a Bad Conduct Discharge, reduced to private, and sentenced to three months' confinement.)

As stated in a 1992 issue of *Soldiers* magazine, "Sexual harassment is unacceptable behavior. . . . It's a violation of our professional ethic. Gender should not be an issue. A soldier is a soldier (an Army civilian is an Army civilian), and we expect peers, subordinates, and superiors to recognize the contributions of that soldier (or Army civilian) to the nation's defense and readiness."

Unwelcome comments, gestures, and physical contact are types of "socializing" that become sexual harassment when unwelcome, when repeated, when deliberate, and when considered offensive to the victim. A victim should first tell the person doing the harassing that the behavior is offensive and should not be repeated. If the behavior continues, the victim should report it.

Sexual harassment is not listed as an infraction in the UCMJ, but it is punishable as a violation of Article 92 of the code, "Personal Relations," and other articles. Article 92 is a general order prohibiting permanent party soldiers from nonprofessional social relationships with trainees. Other common UCMJ violations (and the penalties) associated with sexual harassment are indecent assault (five years, dishonorable discharge), indecent language (six months, BCD), and cruelty or maltreatment (one year, dishonorable discharge). If either party is married, tack on adultery (one year, dishonorable discharge).

A sexual harassment victim may go through his or her chain of command (or civilian supervisor or more senior supervisor), local equal opportunity advisor, the chaplain, provost marshal, judge advocate general, and the inspector general. Sexual harassment falls under the Army's equal opportunity program, outlined in AR 600-20, *Army Command Policy.*

9

Career Decisions

Just as one day you enlisted, some day you will face separation, unless you reenlist. So what you do in the meantime is vital to your future (and, if you are married, your family's future). Have you remained qualified to reenlist? What are your "re-up" options? Do you want to reenlist? What if you choose not to re-up?

If you separate, you will most certainly need to go to work unless a lottery jackpot or some other bonanza drops into your lap. If you choose not to re-up but have a remaining service obligation, you will still have military career decisions to make, about joining the Army Reserve or the Army National Guard. If, on the other hand, you choose to remain in service to the nation full time, do *you* have what it takes to become a professional NCO or warrant or commissioned officer?

If you were 18 or 19 years old when you enlisted and you continued your Army career, you would be only 38 or 39 when you would become eligible for retirement. Would you like to draw an Army retirement check before age 40, knowing that check would arrive monthly for the rest of your life?

Did you know that effective 1 October 1993, soldiers must make it to staff sergeant or higher to be eligible to serve beyond 15 years? Soldiers who do not make it past sergeant may serve only 13 years. And promotable corporals and specialists—those who do not get promoted before their separation dates—may serve no more than 8 years. As indicated solely by the enlisted retention control points stated in AR 601-208, it takes a lot of soldiering to remain competitive today.

The Separation Decision

The first career decision any soldier nearing the end of the first enlistment must make is whether to reenlist in the Army. Soldiers who decide to separate will seek transition assistance and an honorable discharge.

Career and Alumni Program

Soldiers who choose to separate and those being involuntarily separated should know about the Army Career and Alumni Program (ACAP), a transition and job assistance initiative located at 62 military sites worldwide. Each ACAP site includes a Transition Assistance Office (TAO) and a Job Assistance Center (JAC), which are available for all active and Reserve Component soldiers, Army civilians, and military and civilian family members. The TAO provides eligible clients with transition advice and serves as a focal point for problems. The JAC provides job search training, individual assistance and counseling, and a referral service.

Transition Assistance

The TAO helps personnel leaving the Army to make the transition to civilian life by providing the following:

- Individual transition plans.
- Information on available resources.
- Assistance with the Defense Outplacement Referral System.
- Federal and public sector job information.

The TAO staff likes to see personnel 180 days before separation, but separating servicemembers are eligible to be seen at the ACAP office until discharge.

Job Assistance

The JAC, which complements the TAO, conducts individual counseling and small- and large-group workshops to help separating personnel do the following:

- Establish goals.
- Target a second career.
- Develop a résumé.
- Prepare essential correspondence.
- Prepare for interviews.
- Find hidden markets for job skills. (Only about 20 percent of jobs available are advertised, according to one ACAP official.)
- Learn to dress for success.
- Track job leads.
- Evaluate employment agencies, job fairs, and automated résumé services.
- Build negotiating skills.
- Evaluate job offers.

Separating servicemembers are encouraged to start the ACAP process 180 days prior to discharge. Commanders at every echelon know the importance of allowing soldiers enough time to take advantage of the service. The Army leadership supports the JAC and will continue to ensure commanders support it, too. Ultimately, the JAC strives to provide eligible clients with the skills to pursue and secure employment, but it is up to the client to apply what is learned.

Employment Network

The Army Employment Network (AEN) is an ACAP database that contains information from employers who are committed to considering Army personnel for jobs. The AEN provides the company name, location of all branches of the company, total number of personnel hired annually, the types of positions for which a company hires, points of contact, and in some cases a listing of available positions. The AEN also contains information from employment-related service providers that may also have information about other organizations that can assist, such as the National Education Association, the Noncommissioned Officers Association, the National Association of Nurses, and others.

The ACAP is linked to regional Office of Personnel Management computers, which list federal jobs, and is also tied to the departments of Labor and Veterans Affairs, which with the ACAP conduct a three-day job-training seminar, three-hour training session, and six-hour training workshop. Clients choose the seminar, session, or workshop, depending on their needs and time.

Soldiers interested in what ACAP offers should visit their local office and pick up the brochure Client Bill of Rights. Clients should be told up front that they are presented to potential employers as "quality products who are leaders, drug-free, healthy, educated, and motivated." For more information about ACAP, call toll-free in CONUS (800) 445-2049. If you are stationed overseas, call DSN 221-0993. If you are a corporal or sergeant, you should visit your local ACAP office and learn more about the program, then relate it to every soldier you supervise.

Discharges

The most desirable (and most common) type of discharge is the honorable discharge. A soldier can be denied an honorable discharge only on the basis of a pattern of misbehavior, not because of an isolated occurrence — unless the occurrence is criminal. A general discharge is reserved for the soldier whose service to the Army has been satisfactory, but not meritorious. A discharge at the convenience of the Army can be either an honorable or general discharge, depending on the soldier's conduct while on active duty.

Dependency or hardship discharges are granted when a soldier's continued service would put his or her family in serious dependency or hardship. Some reasons for this type of discharge: a member of the soldier's family or of his or her spouse's family dies or is disabled; the soldier is the sole surviving son or daughter of a family; or the soldier is a single parent.

The Reenlistment Decision

If you decide that the Army is still right for you, you should consider all options before reenlisting. Begin early. Visit your unit retention office. Discuss your decision with your fellow soldiers. Seek counseling from your immediate supervisor and others in your direct chain of command. Talk to your family. Consider at least the following:

- Why you are reenlisting.
- How reenlisting can enhance your career.
- Whether you will receive a Regular or Selective Reenlistment Bonus.
- MOS training and schooling, or MOS reclassification options.
- Travel and assignment options.
- Your promotion potential.
- The needs of the Army and the nation.

Reenlistment Bonuses

The Army offers reenlistment bonuses as a means of encouraging soldiers in certain critical MOSs to reenlist or extend their current enlistments. Critical MOSs are determined by inadequate retention or reenlistment levels. The Army updates the list of critical MOSs regularly and publishes it through the DA Circular 611 series. Your unit's retention NCO should be able to provide you with the list.

The Selective Reenlistment Bonus (SRB) Program is available to all soldiers, regardless of rank, who hold a primary MOS designated as critical. Soldiers reenlisting through the SRB Program are eligible for reenlistment bonuses of up to $20,000 if they reenlist or extend for a minimum of 3 years. They may receive a maximum of three such SRBs during their military career, and only one in each established time zone. The zones, based on time of active military service, are Zone A, extending from 21 months to 6 years; Zone B, from 6 to 10 years; and Zone C, from 10 to 14 years of active military service.

The actual amount of the SRB is determined by a formula based on the soldier's monthly basic pay. The bonus cannot exceed six times the monthly pay, multiplied by the number of years of additional obligated service, nor can the bonus exceed $20,000. The SRB is based on the current needs of the Army and on current reenlistment trends in specific MOSs. The more critical the Army's need, the higher the SRB. Consequently, frequently no MOS qualifies for the maximum rate.

The following examples illustrate how the program operates. A soldier receiving basic pay of $800 a month reenlists under the SRB Program for four years; the bonus amount for his MOS is the maximum, six times the monthly basic pay. The SRB bonus would be [$800 × 6] × 4 = $19,200. If, however, the soldier was receiving a basic pay of $1,000 a month, the SRB bonus would not be [$1,000 × 6] × 4 = $24,000; instead, this soldier would receive the maximum allowable bonus — $20,000. Another soldier is receiving the basic pay of $800 a month, but is in an MOS for which the Army only pays two times the monthly pay. That soldier, reenlisting for four years, would receive [$800 × 2] × 4 = $6,400.

Since qualifying MOSs and their SRB rates fluctuate based on the needs of the Army, interested soldiers should contact their retention office to obtain current information.

The SRB bonus will be paid in addition to any other pay and allowance to which the soldier is already entitled.

Medical soldiers rappel during survival skills training at Camp Bullis, Texas

Training and Duty Station Options

If you decide to remain on active duty, you have a number of options. Upon reenlistment, you can elect additional training, a particular duty station elsewhere, or current duty station stabilization.

Options for the first-termer include airborne training, U.S. Army Intelligence and Security Command and Electronic Warfare training, U.S. Army Information Systems Command training, Language School training, and other MOSs that have openings for new soldiers who qualify. Other options include reenlisting for Special Forces, combat arms unit of choice, and the U.S. Army 3d Infantry (Old Guard).

Soldiers willing to extend their enlistment or reenlist can also apply for a number of interesting career development programs: explosive ordnance disposal, presidential support activities (working at the White House), technical escort (for chemical, ammunitions, and EOD specialists), Army Bands, instructors at service schools, drill sergeants, and recruiters. Selection of a new duty station may also be an option for your reenlistment. You may be eligible for the overseas area option, the CONUS-to-CONUS station option or, if overseas, the CONUS station of choice option.

Information and requirements for each career program are contained in AR 614-200; reenlistment NCOs and career counselors can also be of assistance to the soldier who wishes to explore some of the more unusual career options within the Army system.

Career Opportunities for Women

The Army continues to restrict women from MOSs that would intentionally place them in direct combat. This policy does not mean that women will not find themselves in combat situations; they have been there and are likely to continue to be. It does mean that certain high-risk MOSs, Skill Qualification Identifiers (SQI), and Additional Skill Identifiers (ASI) are closed to women, according to Update 2, AR 611-201, *Enlisted Career Management Fields and Military Occupational Specialties*.

The regulation states, "The Direct Combat Probability Coding Policy determines where women may serve. Women may not serve in units or in positions in units that would routinely require them to participate in direct combat."

Recognizing the high probability that soldiers classified in some MOSs, SQIs, and ASIs will routinely engage in direct combat, the Army keeps 47 such high-risk MOSs, two SQIs (Ranger and Ranger-Parachutist), and one ASI (NBC Reconnaissance) closed to women. A complete listing of closed MOSs is in AR 611-201, chapter 4.

According to the regulation, the MOSs closed to women represent about 14 percent of the total. In other words, 86 percent of the MOSs in the Army are open to women.

A Pregnant Soldier's Options

A pregnant soldier is faced with a number of choices, the most basic of which being whether to separate from the Army. This decision can be very difficult because of its far-reaching ramifications. Once the soldier has decided to be retained on active duty, she will be expected to complete her full enlistment before she is again given the choice of continuing in the military or returning to civilian life.

Staying in the military as a mother of a newborn child does not afford the soldier special privileges, but she normally will not receive PCS orders for an overseas assignment during the pregnancy. Such orders can often be deferred or deleted (for up to one year) if they should indeed be issued. (See *Overseas Assignments* in chapter 5 for more details.) After the child is born and the mother is released from normal postnatal care, however, the military mother is given no unique consideration for assignments. She is expected to fulfill the needs of the Army just like any other soldier. This means that she could receive orders for worldwide assignments, including to dependent-restricted overseas areas.

The Army is concerned for the welfare of the child, but it does not adjust the assignment process to accommodate the new mother. Instead, the Army requires each soldier with dependents unable to care for themselves to file an approved *Family Care Plan*. (See chapter 5 for details.) Failure to complete an adequate plan will result in a bar to reenlistment. The plan specifies what actions the soldier has taken to ensure care for her dependents in the event she is assigned to an area where dependents are not authorized. In addition, she is expected to make provisions for the care of her dependents while she is away for military duty (on a daily basis and in the event of a necessary TDY).

One other consequence of the pregnant soldier's decision to continue in the military is the possibility of involuntary separation. If the soldier cannot handle her normal duties during the pregnancy or once she is a new mother, she may be separated from the service involuntarily. Such decisions are made on the grounds of unsatisfactory performance of duty or misconduct, whichever is appropriate. Involuntary separation is covered by AR 635-200, paragraphs 5-8 and 13-2, in addition to chapter 14. If a soldier in an entry-level status becomes pregnant, she will be evaluated by a medical officer to determine if she can fully participate in the training required for the MOS. If it is determined that she cannot participate in the training, she will be involuntarily discharged. Otherwise, the soldier will be retained unless she specifically requests discharge under AR 635-200, chapter 8.

The soldier will be provided medical care during and after the pregnancy. Again, she has a choice. She may remain at her present duty assignment and receive care through a military facility within 30 miles of that location; or if such care is not available, she will be treated through a civilian doctor and civilian facilities. On the other hand, she may choose to take ordinary leave, advance leave, and excess leave so that she may return to her home or other appropriate and desired location for her maternity care and the birth of her child.

Once labor begins, her leave status will change to convalescent leave for the period of labor, hospitalization, and postpartum care. Convalescent leave for postpartum care is limited to the amount of time the doctor specifies as essential for the medical needs of the mother. Generally, postpartum convalescent leave does not exceed 42 days. Leave status and the pregnant soldier are covered in AR 630-5, chapter 9, section II.

If the soldier decides to return home to deliver the baby, it is her responsibility to first ensure that military facilities near her home have obstetrical care available; many do not provide such care. The soldier cannot choose to return home for maternity care and have the government pay for that care at a civilian facility. This is prohibited in AR 40-3, except for bona fide medical emergencies that justify the use of a civilian facility. Using civilian facilities away from the duty location means that the soldier, not the government, is normally responsible for the medical bills. The Health Benefits (CHAMPUS) Advisor at the nearest military medical facility is the best source for further information on this matter.

The Army provides maternity uniforms at no cost to the soldier who decides to continue her military career after she is pregnant. In addition, BAQ or government quarters will be provided under standard military guidelines, depending on the availability of quarters at the installation where the soldier is assigned. The Post Housing Office at each installation and the first sergeant at each unit are good sources for more details.

If the pregnant soldier chooses to separate from the Army, she receives an honorable discharge and any benefits applicable to soldiers with the amount of time in service she has at the time of separation. Separation due to pregnancy is authorized under chapter 8 of AR 600-200.

Unit commanders must counsel women who are eligible for pregnancy separation. The Chaplain's Service and the American Red Cross also offer counseling, and the JAG office can instruct the soldier in legal matters regarding the birth and care of her child. The soldier will have at least a week to consider her options but must indicate her choice of either separating or remaining on active duty in writing.

Whether the soldier is allowed to reconsider her choice depends on the choice she initially made. If she originally chose to stay on active duty but then decides to separate, the Army must separate her. On the other hand, if she originally elected to separate and then decides she wants to remain in the Army, the case will be reviewed and a decision whether to retain her will be based on the best interests of the Army.

An abnormal pregnancy places a difficult burden on the woman involved. The Army allows a woman the option of seeking a discharge in the event of a miscarriage, abortion, or premature delivery, if she had been pregnant for at least 16 weeks at the time the pregnancy terminates.

Medical treatment for obstetrical and postpartum care is provided at government expense through a military medical facility. The separating soldier may not use CHAMPUS or civilian medical facilities at government expense. In fact, the pregnant soldier is required to sign a statement before she decides to separate from the military, clearly stating that she understands that under no circumstance can CHAMPUS, any military department, or the Department of Veterans Affairs reimburse her civilian maternity care expenses; the statement further clarifies that she understands that any costs for civilian care will be her personal financial responsibility. Therefore, careful planning must be made to ensure that she settles in an area where military medical facilities provide maternity care. The separating pregnant soldier will be authorized postpartum care for up to six weeks after the birth of the child.

Other Military Opportunities

Your career choices at the end of your first term are not limited to just whether to reenlist in the Army or return to civilian life. You may elect to serve in the Army Reserve or Army National Guard while pursuing a civilian career. Or you may decide to seek a commission or a warrant through Officer Candidate School, Warrant Officer Entry Courses, the United States Military Academy, or a Reserve Officer Training Corps (ROTC) program.

All Army installations have reenlistment NCOs and in-service recruiters who can provide more detailed information about these options.

The Army Reserve

The Army Reserve is a federal military force composed of the Ready Reserve and the Standby Reserve. The Ready Reserve is made up of combat support and combat service support units, available for quick mobilization in times of national emergency or war. The Standby Reserve, on the other hand, is a pool of soldiers who have a remaining military obligation and are eligible for recall to active duty.

Through the Ready Reserve, the former soldier can supplement his or her civilian income while taking full advantage of the leadership training he or she received while on active duty. Reservists receive four days' pay for each weekend of Reserve training, usually held monthly. An additional requirement is a two-week annual training session. Salary ranges depend on time in service and pay grade. For instance, a sergeant with four years' time in service would receive $2,658 annually.

Each soldier leaving active duty who enlists in the Ready Reserve within 60 days of discharge from the Army retains his or her active rank, pay grade, and time-in-grade status. Privileges include the $200,000 SGLI, space-available dental care, and commissary and post exchange privileges (12 visits per year).

The Army National Guard

The Army National Guard is a federal-state military force. Its primary mission is to maintain combat divisions and support units available for active duty in time of national emergency or war. Under its state mission, the Guard protects life and property and preserves state internal security.

Pay and benefits are essentially the same for the Guard as for the Reserve. One unique feature about the Guard is its Officer Candidate School (OCS) program. The one-year program provides all training on weekends through the state OCS; Guard members can also attend the active Army OCS and earn a commission in 14 weeks.

Officer Candidate School

Enlisted personnel who elect to remain on active duty may be eligible to apply for Officer Candidate School (OCS) training.* Applicants must:

- Be between 19.5 and 29 years of age upon enrollment.
- Not be assigned to a COHORT unit.
- Have completed at least 2 years (60 semester hours) of college.
- Achieve a minimum score of 90 on the Officer Selection Battery (OSB).

---

*For more information on life as an Army officer, see *Army Officer's Guide, 46th edition* by LTC Lawrence P. Crocker, USA (Ret.). (Harrisburg, Pa.: Stackpole Books, 1993.)

During their assignment at OCS, candidates are paid at the E-5 level unless they held higher rank prior to their assignment.

The 14-week program is rigorous and requires a high level of physical fitness, mental fortitude, and dedication to succeed. Upon completion of the course, graduates who choose to accept a commission are commissioned as second lieutenants.

Warrant Officer Entry Course

Warrant officers are highly specialized experts and trainers who operate, maintain, administer, and manage the Army's equipment, support activities, and technical and tactical systems for their entire careers. The career progression of warrant officers is designed to encourage them to seek in-depth knowledge of particular systems and activities and maintain proficiency in their particular skills.

The Warrant Officer Entry Course, located at Fort Rucker, Alabama, trains selected enlisted personnel in the fundamentals of leadership, ethics, personnel management, and tactics. Following completion of the rigorous six-week course, the warrant officers go on to additional specialized training in their particular MOSs.

To qualify for entry to the Warrant Officer Entry Course, a soldier must:

- Be a sergeant or higher rank.
- Have earned a high school diploma or GED equivalency.
- Have served three years' active enlisted service prior to appointment.

Warrant officers may serve in a variety of MOSs, but there is an emphasis on maintenance and aviation specialties.

For additional information, consult DA Pam 350-1 or contact your unit reenlistment officer.

The U.S. Military Academy

Soldiers who wish to attend the U.S. Military Academy at West Point may seek direct nomination under the provisions of AR 351-12 if they meet the entrance requirements without further study. For additional information on direct nomination, write the Admissions Office, U.S. Military Academy, West Point, NY 10966.

An alternative for soldiers who need additional academic preparation to compete for an appointment is provided through the U.S. Military

Academy Preparatory School (USMAPS). The sole function of USMAPS is to mold its students into qualified West Point cadets. Its success rate is impressive — approximately 95 percent of its graduates gain admission to West Point.

With so much to gain through the program, the soldier might expect to pay a high price for the opportunity, but his or her only cost is the dedication and perseverance expected of any serious student. The soldier continues to receive full pay and benefits, is provided housing and meals, and is still eligible for promotions under standard Department of the Army policies. The only expense a soldier incurs is about $300 worth of distinctive clothing and school supplies. The soldier incurs no additional service obligation by attending USMAPS.

Located at Fort Monmouth, New Jersey, USMAPS provides academic, military, and physical training. The 10-month school, divided into two semesters, emphasizes English and mathematics in the academic arena. The August-to-January term helps prepare students for the Scholastic Aptitude Test (SAT) and American College Test (ACT), which are required for admission to most colleges and universities. The small class size and individual attention aid students in mastering algebra, plane geometry, trigonometry, and introductory principles of analytic geometry and calculus. English courses emphasize grammar, usage, rhetoric, reading comprehension, vocabulary development, literature, and composition. Two daily required study sessions help students stay abreast of their studies.

Military training is part of the daily routine as well. No soldier retains his "official rank" while at the school. All are considered "cadet candidates" and are addressed as "Mister" or "Miss." Throughout the program, cadet candidates rotate among various leadership positions in the cadet battalion so that each has the opportunity to develop leadership potential.

Physical training is another highlight of USMAPS. In preparation for the rigors of cadet life at West Point, cadet candidates participate in physical education and intramural sports on a daily basis, developing their strength, coordination, and stamina. As an option, students may choose among a variety of school teams that compete with community colleges, other preparatory schools, and junior varsity college teams in the area. Teams include football, soccer, cross country, volleyball, men's and women's basketball, wrestling, indoor and outdoor track, baseball, lacrosse, tennis, swimming, softball, golf, and orienteering.

Dances, pep rallies, clubs, student government, and yearbook and newspaper staffs are but a few of the extracurricular and social functions that round out the collegiate atmosphere of the school. Leaves and passes are offered as privileges for weekends, holidays, and semester breaks.

Visits by friends or family during the school week are discouraged, however, due to the students' heavy school commitment.

To qualify for admission, a soldier must be:

- A United States citizen.
- At least 17 but not yet 21 years old on 1 July of the year entering the school.
- Not married and without dependents.
- Physically qualified (pregnancy is a disqualifying factor).
- A high school graduate (or the equivalent).
- Of high moral character.

To apply, soldiers must submit a complete application package no later than 15 March of the year in which they hope to enter the school. The packet consists of:

- A letter of application.
- A legible copy of the most recent Medical Examination (SF 88) and Report of Medical History (SF 93), neither more than one year old.
- A complete high school transcript, or a copy of the GED certificate with test scores.
- College transcripts for any college credit received.
- General Technical (GT) score from the Army Classification Battery of tests administered before induction into the Army.
- ETS date. (The soldier must have enough time in service remaining to complete the school; if not, he must extend or reenlist before arriving at the school.)
- Most recent Army Physical Fitness Test score, not more than one year old.
- Results of SAT.
- A recent photograph.
- An evaluation by his immediate commanding officer.
- A handwritten, one-page essay on the questions "Why I Wish to Attend USMAPS" and "What Are My Goals in Life?"

Further information can be obtained by writing Admissions, USMAPS, Fort Monmouth, NJ 07703-5509, or phoning (201) 532-1807 (civilian) or 992-1807 (DSN).

ROTC

One other option for the soldier is to separate from the service under a special ROTC scholarship program, earn a degree, be commissioned a second lieutenant, and return to active duty. The Army provides for 200 soldiers annually to be discharged from the service early to attend college full-time under the Army ROTC Program.

The Army Reserve Officers' Training Corps (ROTC) offers two- and three-year scholarships for active duty enlisted personnel. Through the "Green to Gold" program, these soldiers become civilians specifically to enter the ROTC program, complete a baccalaureate program, and then be commissioned as officers in the Regular Army or the Army Reserve. Once discharged, the soldier forfeits the pay and benefits of active duty, but he or she may still use any veterans educational benefits earned while on active duty. In addition a monthly stipend of $100 is provided, as well as full payment of college tuition, fees, and standard allowance for books and supplies.

The ROTC cadet is not a soldier in civilian clothes. The former soldier leads the life of a normal college student with very few additional responsibilities. Cadets must complete prescribed military science courses, a minimum of one semester of foreign language, an ROTC Advanced Camp (a paid six-week training program between the junior and senior years), and any other training required by the Secretary of the Army as a requirement for commissioning.

Returning to active duty as a Regular Army second lieutenant is not a guarantee. Based on the needs of the Army, some cadets are commissioned as second lieutenants in the U.S. Army Reserve instead. Cadets select the branch of service in which they would prefer to serve, but branch selection is also not guaranteed; again, the needs of the Army must take precedence. Active duty service can sometimes be delayed up to two years at the request of the individual in order to complete postgraduate studies; educational delays are also based on the needs of the Army at the time of commissioning.

To qualify for consideration for one of the 200 scholarships, a soldier must have completed at least one year but not more than two years of college; 125 soldiers will be selected for three-year scholarships and 75 others will be selected for two-year scholarships. Scholarships cover the *time remaining to finish the degree.* To be eligible, the soldier must:

- Be a citizen of the United States.
- Be on active duty at least until 1 June of the year in which he or she will begin full-time college study in September.
- Be less than 25 years of age on 30 June of the year in which he or she will receive a commission. (This requirement can be adjusted up to four years based on time spent on active duty. For instance, a soldier with two years' active duty service would have to be younger than 27 on 30 June of the year of commissioning.)

- Be medically qualified. (Medical qualifications for ROTC are more stringent than those for general active duty service.)
- Demonstrate strong leadership potential.
- Have a GT Aptitude Area score of at least 115.
- Have an accumulative grade point average of 2.0 on a 4.0 scale for all college work completed thus far.
- Have passed the Army Physical Fitness Test within the past year with a minimum score of 180 and a minimum of 60 points in each event.
- Be accepted as an academic junior for the two-year scholarship, or as an academic sophomore for the three-year scholarship, by an institution offering Army ROTC.

If a servicemember has a bar to reenlistment, plans on studying for the ministry, has completed one undergraduate degree and is working on a second, or is in the weight control program, he is ineligible for the scholarship program.

Soldiers may apply to the program between 15 December (of the preceding year) and 31 March of the year in which they wish to enroll in school. Applications, available as early as 15 October, should be submitted early in this period so that any missing information or documents can be supplied before the 1 April deadline. Incomplete packets, as of April, will not be considered. The application packet can be requested from U.S. Army ROTC Cadet Command, ATTN: ATCC-C, Fort Monroe, VA 23651-5000.

Packets consist of several forms:

- TRADOC Form 471-1-R, Application for Active Duty Enlisted Personnel 2- and 3-Year ROTC Scholarship (completed by the soldier).
- TRADOC Form 471-2-R, Active Duty Enlisted Personnel 2- and 3-Year ROTC Scholarship Application Data. (The soldier gives this form to his immediate supervisor, who evaluates the soldier's performance and potential. The form is then routed to the supervisor's commander, and higher up the chain of command if that individual is not a field grade officer.)
- TRADOC Form 113-R, ROTC Scholarship Applicant Snapshot (A full-length photo is preferred; one in military uniform is desirable.)
- Complete TRADOC Form 477-R-FL, Letter of Acceptance. (This form must be completed by the university or college the soldier wishes to attend. Soldiers must complete university enrollment application forms and be accepted by the university *before* school

officials can complete this form. Separate application forms may be required for the school's ROTC program; the professor of military science must also complete part of Form 477-R-FL.)

Transcripts from all colleges where the soldier has received academic credit must also be received before the 1 April deadline. Additionally, official test results must be furnished for any college credit obtained through CLEP or USAFI.

Soldiers accepted into the program will be assigned an early discharge date prior to the beginning of the school program. At their discharge, they will enlist for eight years in the U.S. Army Reserve. School time counts toward the Reserve obligation. Upon graduation from college, all scholarship recipients apply for an Army commission. Those receiving a Reserve commission finish their obligation in a local Reserve unit. Those receiving a Regular Army commission return to active duty. If they later terminate their Army career *before* the original eight-year obligation has expired, they must finish the remaining obligation with the Reserve.

Some limitations are placed on what a scholarship recipient may study. Fields of study are grouped into six categories: engineering, physical science, business, social sciences, nursing, and other (such as humanities, medical fields, and pre-law). The Army needs highly trained, technical officers, so the preponderance of scholarships go to enlisted soldiers planning on entering technical fields.

For the soldier interested in a possible career as an Army officer, or the soldier who simply wants to make the road toward the baccalaureate degree shorter than by attending college part-time, the ROTC Scholarship Program offers a viable alternative.

Code of Conduct

For Members of the U.S. Armed Forces

I   I am an American, fighting in the forces which guard my country and our way of life. I am prepared to give my life in their defense.

II   I will never surrender of my own free will. If in command, I will never surrender my men while they still have the means to resist.

III   If I am captured I will continue to resist by all means available. I will make every effort to escape and aid others to escape. I will accept neither parole nor special favors from the enemy.

IV   If I become a prisoner of war, I will keep faith with my fellow prisoners. I will give no information or take part in any action which might be harmful to my comrades. If I am senior, I will take command. If not, I will obey the lawful order of those appointed over me and will back them up in every way.

V   When questioned, should I become a prisoner of war, I am required to give name, rank, service number, and date of birth. I will evade answering further questions to the utmost of my ability. I will make no oral or written statements disloyal to my country and its allies or harmful to their cause.

VI   I will never forget that I am an American, fighting for freedom, responsible for my actions, and dedicated to the principles which made my country free. I will trust in my God and in the United States of America.

The Code of Conduct, passed as an executive order in 1955 and amended in 1988, was originally written to provide guidance to soldiers in the event that they were captured or became prisoners of war during hostilities. But the Code encompasses much more—it captures the spirit and pride that a soldier must have in order to be a part of the Army team.

The Code defines the exemplary conduct expected of members of the American armed forces. Only by knowing the Code and applying its principles can soldiers live up to the high standards required of men and women in military service.

Chain of Command

It is to your benefit to know your Chain of Command. Listed here are the personnel normally found in the formal Chain of Command within an Army unit. Check with your first sergeant to fill in the names. The number of personnel and the terminology for the positions within the chain vary in some Army units.

Chain of Command

Commander in Chief	President of the United States
Secretary of Defense	_____
Secretary of the Army	_____
Chairman of the Joint Chiefs of Staff	_____
Chief of Staff, Army	_____
MACOM Commander	_____
Corps Commander	_____
Post Commander/Division Commander	_____
Brigade Commander	_____

Battalion Commander   _____

Company Commander   _____

Platoon Leader   _____

Squad Leader   _____

The NCO Support Channel complements and parallels the Chain of Command and provides a structure for the day-to-day activities of the Army.

NCO Support Channel

Sergeant Major of the Army   _____

MACOM Command Sergeant Major   _____

Post Command Sergeant Major   _____

Brigade Command Sergeant Major   _____

Battalion Command Sergeant Major   _____

First Sergeant   _____

Platoon Sergeant   _____

Squad Leader   _____

Selected Acronyms

ABCMR	Army Board for the Correction of Military Records
ACES	Army Continuing Education System
ACS	Army Community Services
ADAPCP	Army Alcohol and Drug Abuse Prevention and Control Program
AEA	Assignment Eligibility and Availability
AER	Army Emergency Relief
AFQT	Armed Forces Qualification Test
AI	Assignment Instruction
AIT	Advanced Individual Training
AMOS	Additional Military Occupational Specialty
ANCOC	Advanced Noncommissioned Officer Course
APFT	Army Physical Fitness Test
APOD	Aerial Port of Debarkation
APOE	Aerial Port of Embarkation
AR	Army Regulation
ARC	American Red Cross
ASEP	Advanced Skills Education Program
ASI	Additional Skill Identifier
AWOL	Absent Without Leave
BAQ	Basic Allowance for Quarters
BASD	Basic Active Service Date
BDFS	Bachelor's Degree for Soldiers
BDU	Battle Dress Uniform
BESD	Basic Enlisted Service Date

BNCOC	Basic Noncommissioned Officer Course
BSEP	Basic Skills Education Program
BT	Basic Training
CAP III	Centralized Assignment Procedure III System
CE	Commander's Evaluation
CHAMPUS	Civilian Health and Medical Program of the Uniformed Services
CID	Criminal Investigation Division
CLEP	College Level Examination Program
CMF	Career Management Field
COHORT	Cohesion, Operational Readiness, and Training
CONAP	Continental United States Area of Preference
CONUS	Continental United States
CPMOS	Career Progression Military Occupational Specialty
CQ	Charge of Quarters
CSEP	Career Soldier's Education Program
CTT	Common Tasks Test
DA	Department of the Army
DANTES	Defense Activity for Non-traditional Education Support
DEERS	Defense Enrollment Eligibility Reporting System
DEROS	Date of Estimated Return from Overseas
DMOS	Duty Military Occupational Specialty
DOD	Department of Defense
DODDS	Department of Defense Dependents Schools
DOR	Date of Rank
DROS	Date Returned from Overseas
DVA	Department of Veterans Affairs
EAD	Entry on Active Duty
EDAS	Enlisted Distribution and Assignment System
EML	Environmental and Morale Leave
ENTNAC	Entrance National Agency Check
EOD	Explosive Ordnance Disposal
EPMS	Enlisted Personnel Management System
ETS	Expiration of Term of Service or Enlisted Training System
FAO	Finance and Accounting Office
FORSCOM	U.S. Army Forces Command
GCM	General Court Martial
GCMCA	General Court-Martial Convening Authority
GED	General Educational Development
HAAP	Homebase Advanced Assignment Program

HBA	Health Benefits Advisor
HOR	Home of Record
IET	Initial Entry Training
IG	Inspector General
ISR	Individual Soldier's Report
ITEP	Individual Training Program
ITT	Intertheater Transfer
JAG	Judge Advocate General
JSEP	Job Skills Education Program
JTR	Joint Travel Regulations
JUMPS	Joint Uniform Military Pay Schedule
LES	Leave and Earnings Statement
LOD	Line of Duty
MAC	Military Airlift Command
MACOM	Major Army Command
MEDDAC	Medical Department Activity
MPRJ	Military Personnel Records Jacket
MOS	Military Occupational Specialty
NAC	National Agency Check
NCOA	Noncommissioned Officer Academy
NCOER	Noncommissioned Officer Evaluation Report
NCOES	Noncommissioned Officer Education System
NMS	New Manning System
OCONUS	Outside Continental United States
OCS	Officer Candidate School
OJE	On-the-Job Experience
OJT	On-the-Job Training
OMPF	Official Military Personnel File
OP	Operating Procedures
OSUT	One-Station Unit Training
PCS	Permanent Change of Station
PERSCOM	U.S. Army Personnel Command
PLDC	Primary Leadership Development Course
PMOS	Primary Military Occupational Specialty
POR	Preparation of Replacements for Oversea Movement
POV	Privately Owned Vehicle
PSC	Personnel Support Center
PSNCO	Personnel Staff Noncommissioned Officer
PT	Physical Training
PTC	Primary Technical Course
PX	Post Exchange
RE code	Reenlistment Code

ROTC	Reserve Officers' Training Corps
R&R	Rest and Recuperation
SD	Special Duty
SDNCO	Staff Duty Noncommissioned Officer
SDT	Self-Development Test
SIDPERS	Standard Installation/Division Personnel Reporting System
SMOS	Secondary Military Occupational Specialty
SOC	Servicemen's Opportunity Colleges
SOCAD	Servicemen's Opportunity College Associate Degrees
SOP	Standard Operating Procedures
SQI	Skill Qualification Identifier
SRB	Selective Reenlistment Bonus
SSN	Social Security Number
TA	Tuition Assistance
TCO	Test Control Officer
TDA	Table of Distribution and Allowances
TDY	Temporary Duty
TE	Technical Escort
TIG	Time in Grade
TIS	Time in Service
TLA	Temporary Lodging Allowance
TLE	Temporary Lodging Entitlement
TOE	Table of Organization and Equipment
TRADOC	U.S. Army Training and Doctrine Command
TSO	Test Scoring Officer
UCMJ	Uniform Code of Military Justice
USAEREC	U.S. Army Enlisted Records and Evaluation Center
USAR	U.S. Army Reserve
USASSC	U.S. Army Soldier Support Center
USATC	U.S. Army Training Center
USMA	U.S. Military Academy
USMAPS	U.S. Military Academy Preparatory School
VHA	Variable Housing Allowance

Index

S-1

Go to PAC - Personal Action Center

DLA - Dislocation Allowance